Teaching Mathematics to English Language Learners

Today's mathematics classrooms increasingly include students for whom English is a second language. *Teaching Mathematics to English Language Learners* provides readers with a comprehensive understanding of both the challenges that face ELLs and ways in which educators might address them in the secondary mathematics classroom. Framed by a research perspective, this book presents practical instructional strategies for engaging learners that can be incorporated as a regular part of instruction. The authors offer context-specific strategies for everything from facilitating classroom discussions with all students, to reading and interpreting mathematics textbooks, to tackling word problems. A fully annotated list of mathematics web and print resources completes the volume, making this a valuable reference to help mathematics teachers meet the challenges of including all learners in effective instruction.

Special Features:

- Practical examples of mathematics problems and exercises make turning theory into practice easy when teaching ELLs
- Engaging vignettes vividly illustrate real-life interactions of veteran teachers and ELLs in the classroom
- Graphs, tables, and charts provide additional access points to the text in clear, meaningful ways

Gladis Kersaint is Associate Professor of Mathematics Education at the University of South Florida.

Denisse R. Thompson is Professor of Mathematics Education at the University of South Florida.

Mariana Petkova is a doctoral student in Mathematics Education at the University of South Florida, and a high school mathematics teacher in Hillsborough County.

Teaching English Language Learners Across the Curriculum
Series Editors: Tony Erben, Bárbara C. Cruz, Stephen J. Thornton

Teaching Mathematics to English Language Learners
Gladis Kersaint, Denisse R. Thompson, Mariana Petkova

Teaching English Language Learners in Career and Technical Education Programs
Victor M. Hernández-Gantes and William Blank

Teaching English Language Learners through Technology
Tony Erben, Ruth Ban, Martha Castañeda

Teaching Social Studies to English Language Learners
Bárbara C. Cruz and Stephen J. Thornton

Teaching Mathematics to English Language Learners

GLADIS KERSAINT, DENISSE R. THOMPSON,
MARIANA PETKOVA

Routledge
Taylor & Francis Group

NEW YORK AND LONDON

First published 2009
by Routledge
270 Madison Ave, New York, NY 10016

Simultaneously published in the UK
by Routledge
2 Park Square, Milton Park, Abingdon, Oxon OX14 4RN

Routledge is an imprint of the Taylor & Francis Group, an informa business

Typeset in Minion by Prepress Projects Ltd, Perth, UK
Printed and bound in the United States of America on acid-free paper by Edwards Brothers, Inc.

Library of Congress Cataloging in Publication Data
Kersaint, Gladis.
    Teaching mathematics to English language learners/Gladis Kersaint, Denisse R. Thompson, Mariana Petkova.
    p. cm.—(Teaching English language learners across the curriculum)
    Includes bibliographical references and index.
    1. Mathematics—Study and teaching—Curricula. 2. English language—Study and teaching—Foreign speakers. I. Thompson, Denisse Rubilee, 1954– II. Petkova, Mariana. III. Title.
    QA11.2.K47 2008
510.71—dc22
                    2008001565

ISBN 10: 0-415-95788-5 (hbk)
ISBN 10: 0-415-95789-3 (pbk)
ISBN 10: 0-203-89452-9 (ebk)

ISBN 13: 978-0-415-95788-5 (hbk)
ISBN 13: 978-0-415-95789-2 (pbk)
ISBN 13: 978-0-203-89452-1 (ebk)

Contents

Figures

Tables

Series Introduction

No educational issue has proven more controversial than how to teach linguistically diverse students. Intertwined issues of ethnic and cultural differences are often compounded. What is more, at the time of writing, December 2007, how immigrants and their heritages *ought* to fit with the dominant culture is the subject of rancorous debate in the United States and a number of other nations.

However thorny these issues may be to some, both legally and ethically, schools need to accommodate the millions of English language learners (ELLs) who need to be educated. Although the number of ELLs in the United States has burgeoned in recent decades, school programs generally remain organized via traditional subjects, which are delivered in English. Many ELLs are insufficiently fluent in academic English, however, to succeed in these programs. Since policymakers have increasingly insisted that ELLs, regardless of their fluency in English, be mainstreamed into standard courses with all other students, both classroom enactment of the curriculum and teacher education need considerable rethinking.

Language scholars have generally taken the lead in this rethinking. As is evident in Part 1 of the volumes in this series, language scholars have developed a substantial body of research to inform the mainstreaming of ELLs. The primary interest of these language scholars, however, is almost by definition the processes and principles of second language acquisition. Until recently, subject matter has typically been a secondary consideration, used to illustrate language concerns. Perhaps not surprisingly, content-area teachers sometimes have seen this as reducing their subjects to little more than isolated bits of information, such as a list of explorers and dates in history or sundry geological formations in science.

In contrast, secondary school teachers see their charge as effectively conveying a principled understanding of, and interest in, a subject. They look for relationships, seek to develop concepts, search for powerful examples and analogies, and try to explicate principles. By the same token, they strive to make meaningful connections among the subject matter, students' experience, and life outside of school. In our observations, teacher education programs bifurcate courses on content-area methods and (if there are any) courses designed to instill principles of teaching ELLs. One result of this bifurcation seems to be that prospective and in-service teachers are daunted by the challenge of using language principles to inform their teaching of subject matter.

For example, Gloria Ladson-Billings (2001) has experimented with how to prepare new teachers for diverse classrooms through a teacher education program focused on "diversity, equity, and social justice" (p. xiii). Teachers in her program are expected, for instance, to confront rather than become resigned to low academic expectations for children in urban schools. From Ladson-Billings's perspective, "no matter what else the schools find themselves doing, promoting students' academic achievement is among their primary functions" (p. 56).

The authors in this series extend this perspective to teaching ELLs in the content areas. For example, how might ELLs be included in a literature lesson on Hardy's use of landscape imagery in *The Mayor of Casterbridge*, or an economics lesson on the principle of comparative advantage, or a biology lesson on the ecosystem of a pond? Such topics, experienced educators quickly recognize, are often difficult for native speakers of English. How can teachers break down these subjects into topics in a way that is educationally significant for ELLs?

The purpose of this series is to assist current and prospective educators to plan and implement lessons that do justice to the goals of the curriculum and make sense to and interest ELLs. If the needs of diverse learners are to be met, Ladson-Billings (2001) underscores that innovation is demanded, not that teachers merely pine for how things once were. The most obvious innovation in this series is to bring language scholars and specialists in the methods of teaching particular school subjects together. Although this approach is scarcely unique, it remains relatively uncommon. Combining the two groups brings more to addressing the problems of instruction than could be obtained by the two groups working separately. Even so, these volumes hardly tell the reader "everything there is to know" about the problems addressed. But we do know that our teacher education students report that even modest training to teach ELLs can make a significant difference in the classroom. We hope this series extends those successes to all the content areas of the curriculum.

Preface

As mathematics educators in Florida, we have been accustomed to having English language learners (ELLs) in our classrooms for many years. In addition to a large Hispanic/Latino population, teachers in Florida encounter and teach ELLs from a broad range of backgrounds (e.g. Haitian, Bosnian, Brazilian, European, Asian, and Middle Eastern) and experiences, including some students who had never attended school. Although in past years, students at the earliest stages of English language proficiency might have been in special pull-out classes and taught by non-mathematics language specialists, since the early 1990s it has been more common for ELL students to be mainstreamed into mathematics classes at their level of mathematics proficiency, not their level of English proficiency.

Although educators in Florida, California, Texas, and states along the southern U.S. border have long addressed the challenges of ELLs in their classrooms, the situation is no longer confined to these border states. As we have communicated with other educators and visited classrooms from the East Coast to the West Coast and from the North to the South, it is clear that the teaching of ELLs is now an issue facing mathematics educators throughout the country, whether in rural or urban settings. Indeed, many states, such as Georgia, North Carolina, Kansas, and Minnesota, have experienced an influx of non-English speaking students since the mid-1990s. Finding ways to address the needs of such students is a challenge and a necessity for mathematics teachers.

In this book, we share information and strategies that we believe will be helpful to other educators working to meet the needs of their ELL students. Based on our research and experiences, we believe it is important to have communication-rich classrooms so that students explain their thinking with peers as they work to make sense of mathematics. It is through language that ELLs come to understand not only mathematics but English as well. Such classrooms are environments in which teachers and students have built a climate of trust and respect in which everyone's contributions are valued.

This book is a collaborative effort of three mathematics educators from different cultural backgrounds, including a classroom mathematics teacher who is herself an English language learner and teaches in a school setting in which she has numerous English language learners as students. Our experiences working with non-English speaking students from various ethnicities have occurred in urban areas, such as Miami, and in rural areas of Florida with many migrant workers.

We have structured this book in four parts, each with a different focus.

- Part 1, written by an expert in teaching English as a second language, provides an overview of theory and research on teaching ELLs across content disciplines. The information in Part 1 provides background on the stages of second language development, principles that guide instruction when ELLs are present in the classroom, different types of programs to meet the needs of ELLs, differences among ELLs from different cultures, and what teachers can expect from ELLs in the classroom. The chapters in Part 1 are designed to orient teachers to the broad perspectives on meeting the needs of English language learners.

- Part 2 focuses on issues related to ELLs that are mathematics-specific. In particular, it addresses the broad expectations for mathematics education for all students based on the standards movement since the late 1980s. Further, the chapters in Part 2 focus on challenges that ELLs might experience in the mathematics classroom, including the nature of mathematics language, learning environments that support ELLs, mathematics tasks designed to encourage thinking and discourse, cultural influences on mathematics learning and engagement, and the importance and necessity of providing assessment accommodations.

- Part 3 provides classroom practices that teachers can implement as they engage in mathematics instruction. Throughout the chapters in Part 3, we have offered suggestions that teachers can implement on a regular basis as a normal part of their instruction, rather than as special strategies for use with ELLs alone. We have attempted to be sensitive to the time pressures that teachers face and offer suggestions that will be beneficial for all students, and particularly for ELLs. Specifically, we offer strategies for engaging ELLs in classroom discourse and problem solving, helping ELLs learn essential mathematical vocabulary, and adjusting assessments to be fair and appropriate for ELLs. The final chapter in Part 3 raises issues that need to be addressed by teachers who are themselves English language learners, whether or not they have students who are English language learners. Collectively, these chapters encourage the use of strategies that provide ELLs with the access and opportunity to learn mathematics.

- The final sections of the book contain a glossary and an annotated list of internet and print resources that may be of interest to those interested in reading and researching more on the issues and strategies highlighted in this book.

We hope that readers of this book will find the suggestions and strategies helpful and that the research background will give them a better understanding of their English language learners. We look forward to hearing from readers as they implement these strategies with their students.

Part 1
Your English Language Learner

Tony Erben
University of Tampa

1.1
Orientation

English language learners (ELLs) represent the fastest growing group throughout all levels of schooling in the United States. For example, between the 1990–1991 school year and the 2000–2001 school year, the ELL population grew approximately 105 percent nationally, while the general school population grew only 12 percent (Kindler, 2002). In several states (including Texas, California, New Mexico, Florida, Arizona, North Carolina, and New York), the percentage of ELLs within school districts ranges anywhere between 10 and 50 percent of the school population. In sum, there are over 10 million ELLs in U.S. schools today. According to the U.S. Department of Education, one out of seven students in our nation's classrooms speaks a language other than English at home. Although many of these students are heritage language learners and are proficient in English, many others are recent immigrants with barely a working knowledge of the language let alone a command of academic English. Meeting the needs of such students can be particularly challenging for all teachers given the often text-dependent nature of content areas. The language of the curriculum is often abstract and includes complex concepts calling for higher-order thinking skills. Additionally, many ELLs do not have a working knowledge of American culture that can serve as a schema for new learning.

But let's now look at these English language learners. Who are they and how do they come to be in our classrooms?

ELL is the term used for any student in an American school setting whose native language is not English. Their English ability lies anywhere on a continuum from knowing only a few words to being able to get by using everyday English, but still in need of acquiring more English so that they can succeed educationally at school. All students enrolled in an American school, including ELLs, have the right to an equitable and quality education. Traditionally, many ELLs are placed in stand-alone English to speakers of other languages (ESOL) classes and learn English until they are deemed capable of following the regular curriculum in English. However, with the introduction of federal and state legislation such as *No Child Left Behind* (2002), Proposition 227 in California, and other English-only legislation in other states, many school systems now require ELLs to receive their English instruction not through stand-alone ESOL classes, but directly through their curriculum content classes.[1] Today "mainstreaming" is the most frequently used method of language instruction for ELL students in U.S. schools. Mainstreaming involves placing ELLs in content-area classrooms where the curriculum is delivered through English; curricula and instruction are typically not modified in these classrooms for non-native English speakers (Carrasquillo & Rodriguez, 2002). According to Meltzer and Hamann (2005), placement of ELLs in mainstream classes occurs for a number of reasons including assumptions by non-educators about what ELLs need, the scarcity of ESOL-trained teachers relative to demand, the growth of ELL populations, the dispersal of ELLs into more districts across the country, and restrictions in a growing number of states regarding the time ELLs can stay in ESOL programs. They predict that, unless these conditions change, ELLs will spend their time in school (1) with teachers not adequately trained to work with ELLs, (2) with teachers who do not see it as a priority to meet the needs of their ELLs, and (3) with curricula and classroom practices that are not designed to target ELL needs (Coady *et al.*, 2003). As we shall later see, of all possible instructional options to help ELLs learn English, placing an ELL in a mainstreamed English-medium classroom where no accommodations are made by the teacher is the least effective approach. It may even be detrimental to the educational progress of ELLs.

This then raises the question of whether or not the thousands of curriculum content teachers across the United States, who now have the collective lion's share of responsibility in providing English language instruction to ELLs, have had preservice or in-service education to modify, adapt, and make the appropriate pedagogical accommodations within their lessons for this special group of students. This is important: ELLs should remain included in the cycle of everyday learning and make academic progress commensurate with grade-level expectations. It is also important that teachers feel competent and effective in their professional duties.

The aim of Part 1 of this book is to provide you the reader with an overview of the linguistic mechanics of second language development. Specifically, as teachers you will learn what to expect in the language abilities of ELLs as their proficiency in English develops over time. Although the rate of language development among ELLs depends on the particular instructional and social circumstances of each ELL, general patterns and expectations will be discussed. We will also outline for teachers the learning outcomes that ELLs typically accomplish in differing ESOL programs and the importance of the maintenance of first language development. School systems differ across the United States in the ways in which they try to deal with ELL populations. Therefore, we describe the pedagogical pros and cons of an array of ESOL programs as well as clarify terminology used in the field. Part 1 will also profile various ELL populations that enter U.S. schools (e.g. refugees vs. migrants, special needs) and share how teachers can make their pedagogy more culturally responsive. Finally, we will also survey what teachers can expect from the cultural practices that ELLs may engage in in the classroom as well as present a myriad of ways in which both school systems and teachers can better foster home–school communication links.

1.2
The Process of English Language Learning and What to Expect

It is generally accepted that anybody who endeavors to learn a second language will go through specific stages of language development. According to some second language acquisition theorists (e.g. Pienemann, 2007), the way in which language is produced under natural time constraints is very regular and systematic. For example, just as a baby needs to learn how to crawl before it can walk, so too a second language learner will produce language structures only in a predetermined psychological order of complexity. What this means is that an ELL will utter "homework do" before being able to utter "tonight I homework do" before ultimately being able to produce a target-like structure such as "I will do my homework tonight." Of course, with regard to being communicatively effective, the first example is as successful as the last example. The main difference is that one is less English-like than the other. Pienemann's work has centered on one subsystem of language, namely morphosyntactic structures. It gives us an interesting glimpse into how an ELL's language may progress (see Table 1.1).

Researchers such as Pienemann (1989; 2007) and Krashen (1981) assert that there is an immutable language acquisition order and, regardless of what the teacher tries to teach to the ELL in terms of English skills, the learner will acquire new language structures only when (s)he is cognitively and psychologically ready to do so.

What can a teacher do if an ELL will only learn English in a set path? Much research has been conducted over the past 20 years on this very question and the upshot is that, although teachers cannot change the route of development for ELLs, they *can* very much affect the rate of development. The way in which teachers can stimulate the language development of ELLs is by providing what is known as an acquisition-rich classroom. Ellis (2005), among others, provides useful research generalizations that constitute a broad basis for "evidence-based practice." Rather

TABLE 1.1. Generalized patterns of ESOL development stages

Stage	Main features	Example
1	Single words; formulas	My name is_____. How are you
2	Subject–Verb object word order; plural marking	I see school I buy books
3	"Do"-fronting; adverb preposing; negation + verb	Do you understand me? Yesterday I go to school. She no coming today.
4	Pseudo-inversion; yes/no inversion; verb + to + verb	Where is my purse? Have you a car? I want to go.
5	3rd person –s; do-2nd position	He works in a factory. He did not understand.
6	Question-tag; adverb–verb phrase	He's Polish, isn't he? I can always go.

Source: Pienemann (1988).

than repeat them verbatim here, we have synthesized them into *five principles for creating effective second language learning environments*. They are presented and summarized below.

Principle 1: Give ELLs Many Opportunities to Read, to Write, to Listen to, and to Discuss Oral and Written English Texts Expressed in a Variety of Ways

> Camilla had only recently arrived at the school. She was a good student and was making steady progress. She had learned some English in Argentina and used every opportunity to learn new words at school. Just before Thanksgiving her science teacher commenced a new unit of work on the periodic table and elements. During the introductory lesson, the teacher projected a periodic table on the whiteboard. She began asking the students some probing questions about the table. One of her first questions was directed to Camilla. The teacher asked, "Camilla, tell me what you see on the right hand side of the table." Camilla answered, "I see books, Bunsen burner, also pencils."
>
> Of course the teacher was referring not to the table standing in front of the whiteboard, but to the table projected onto the whiteboard. Though a simple mistake, the example above is illustrative of the fact that Camilla has yet to develop academic literacy.

In 2001, Meltzer defined academic literacy as the ability of a person to "use reading, writing, speaking, listening and thinking to learn what they want/need to learn AND [to] communicate/demonstrate that learning to others who need/want to know" (p. 16). The definition is useful in that it rejects literacy as something static and implies agency on the part of a learner who develops an ability to successfully put her/his knowledge and skills to use in new situations. Being proficient in academic literacy requires knowledge of a type of language used predominantly in classrooms and tied very much to learning. However, even though it is extremely important for ELLs to master, not many content teachers take the time to provide explicit instruction in it. Moreover, many content teachers do not necessarily know the discipline-specific discourse features or text structures of their own subject areas.

Currently, there is much research to suggest that both the discussion of texts and the production of texts are important practices in the development of content-area literacy and learning. For ELLs this means that opportunities to create, discuss, share, revise, and edit a variety of texts will help them develop content-area understanding and also recognition and familiarity with the types of texts found in particular content areas (Boscolo & Mason, 2001). Classroom practices that are found to improve academic literacy development include teachers improving reading comprehension through modeling, explicit strategy instruction in context, spending more time giving reading and writing instruction as well as having students spend more time with reading and writing assignments, providing more time for ELLs to talk explicitly about texts as they are trying to process and/or create them, and helping to develop critical thinking skills as well as being responsive to individual learner needs (Meltzer & Hamann, 2005).

The importance of classroom talk in conjunction with learning from and creating texts cannot be underestimated in the development of academic literacy in ELLs. In the case above, rather than smiling at the error and moving on with the lesson, the teacher could have further developed Camilla's vocabulary knowledge by easily taking a two-minute digression from the lesson to brainstorm with the class all the ways the word *table* can be used at school—in math, social studies, language arts, etc.

Principle 2: Draw Attention to Patterns of English Language Structure

In order to ride a bike well, a child needs to actually practice riding the bike. Sometimes, training wheels are fitted to the back of the bike to help the younger child maintain his/her balance. In time, the training wheels are taken away as the child gains more confidence. As this process unfolds, parents also teach kids the rules of the road: how to read road signs, to be attentive to cars, to ride defensively, etc. Although knowing the rules of the road won't help a child learn to ride the bike better in a physical sense, it will help the child avoid being involved in a road accident. Knowing the rules of the road—when and where to ride a bike, etc.—will make the child a more accomplished bike rider. Why use this example? Well, it is a good metaphor to explain that language learning needs to unfold in the same way. An ELL, without much formal schooling, will develop the means to communicate in English. However, it will most likely be only very basic English. Unfortunately, tens of thousands of adult ELLs across this country never progress past this stage. School-age ELLs have an opportunity to move beyond a basic command of English—to become accomplished communicators in English. However, this won't happen on its own. To do so requires the ELL to get actively involved in classroom activities, ones in which an ELL is required to practice speaking.

As mentioned above, early research into naturalistic second language acquisition has evidenced that learners follow a "natural" order and sequence of acquisition. What this means is that grammatical structures emerge in the communicative utterances of second language learners in a relatively fixed, regular, systematic, and universal order. The ways in which teachers can take advantage of this "built-in syllabus" are to implement an activity-centered approach that sets out to provide ELLs with language-rich instructional opportunities and offer ELLs explicit exposure and instruction related to language structures that they are trying to utter but with which they still have trouble.

Principle 3: Give ELLs Classroom Time to Use their English Productively

A theoretical approach within the field of second language acquisition (SLA) called the interaction hypothesis and developed primarily by Long (1996; 2006) posits that acquisition is facilitated through interaction when second language learners are engaged in negotiating for meaning. What this means is that, when ELLs are engaged in talk, they make communication modifications that help language become more comprehensible, they more readily solicit corrective feedback, and they adjust their own use of English.

The discrepancy in the rate of acquisition shown by ELLs can be attributed to the amount and the quality of input they receive as well as the opportunities they have for output. Output means having opportunities to use language. Second language acquisition researchers agree that the opportunity for output plays an important part in facilitating second language development. Skehan (1998) drawing on Swain (1995) summarizes the contributions that output can make: (1) by using language with others, ELLs will obtain a richer language contribution from those around them, (2) ELLs will be forced to pay attention to the structure of language they listen to, (3) ELLs will be able to test out their language assumptions and confirm them through the types of language input they receive, (4) ELLs can better internalize their current language knowledge, (5) by engaging in interaction, ELLs can work towards better discourse fluency, and (6) ELLs will be able to find space to develop their own linguistic style and voice.

It behooves teachers to plan for and incorporate ELLs in all language activities in the classroom. Of course an ELL will engage with an activity based on the level of proficiency (s)he has at any given time and the teacher should take this into account when planning for instruction. Under no circumstances should ELLs be left at the "back of the classroom" to linguistically or pedagogically fend for themselves.

Principle 4: Give ELLs Opportunities to Notice their Errors and to Correct their English

Throughout the day, teachers prepare activities for students that have the sole intent of getting them to learn subject matter. Less often do teachers think about the language learning potential that the same activity may generate. This can be applied to ELLs: Teachers encourage them to notice their errors, to reflect on how they use English, and to think about how English works, which plays a very important role in their language development. In a series of seminal studies, Lyster and his colleagues (Lyster, 1998; 2001; 2004; 2007; Lyster & Ranta, 1997; Lyster & Mori, 2006) outline six feedback moves that teachers can use to direct ELLs' attention to their language output and in doing so help them correct their English.

Example 1

Student: "The heart hits blood to se body. . ."
Teacher: "The heart pumps blood to the body."

In the above example, an ELL's utterance is incorrect, and the teacher provides the correct form. Often teachers gloss over explicitly correcting an ELL's language for fear of singling out the student in class. However, *explicit correction* is a very easy way to help ELLs notice the way they use language.

Example 2

Student: "I can experimenting with Bunsen burner."
Teacher: "What? Can you say that again?"

By using phrases such as "Excuse me?", "I don't understand," or "Can you repeat that?", the teacher shows that the communication has not been understood or that the ELL's utterance contained some kind of error. *Requesting clarification* indicates to the ELL that a repetition or reformulation of the utterance is required.

Example 3

Student: "After today I go to sport."
Teacher: "So, tomorrow you are going to play sports?"
Student: "Yes, tomorrow I am going to play sport."

Without directly showing that the student's utterance was incorrect, the teacher implicitly *recasts* the ELL's error, or provides the correction.

Example 4

Teacher: "Is that how it is said?" or "Is that English?" or "Does that sound right to you?"

Without providing the correct form, the teacher provides a *metalinguistic clue*. This may take the form of asking a question or making a comment related to the formation of the ELL's utterance.

Example 5

Teacher: "So, then it will be a . . ." (with long stress on "a")

The teacher directly gets the correct form from the ELL by pausing to allow the student to complete the teacher's utterance. *Elicitation* questions differ from questions that are defined as metalinguistic clues in that they require more than a yes/no response.

Example 6

Student: The two boy go to town tomorrow."
Teacher: "The two boys go to town tomorrow." (with teacher making a prolonged stress on "boy"

Repetitions are probably one of the most frequent forms of error correction carried out by teachers. Here a teacher repeats the ELL's error and adjusts intonation to draw an ELL's attention to it.

Using these corrective feedback strategies helps to raise an ELL's awareness and understanding of language conventions used in and across content areas.

Principle 5: Construct Activities that Maximize Opportunities for ELLs to Interact with Others in English

One day, when we had visitors from up north, our daughter came home very excited and said that the teacher had announced that the class would be learning Spanish from the beginning of the month. Our friend, ever the pessimist, said, "I learned Spanish for four years at high school, and look at me now, I can't even string a sentence together in Spanish." What comes to mind is the old saying, "use it or lose it." Of course, my friend and I remember our foreign language learning days being spent listening to the teacher, usually in English. We were lucky if we even got the chance to say anything in Spanish. Since we never used Spanish in class, our hopes of retaining any Spanish diminished with each passing year since graduation. My daughter's 20-year-old brother, on the other hand, had the same Spanish teacher that my daughter will have. He remembers a lot of his Spanish, but also that his Spanish classes were very engaging. A lesson would never pass in which he didn't speak, listen to, read, and write in Spanish. He was always involved in some learning activity and he always expressed how great it was to converse during the class with his friends in Spanish by way of the activities that the teacher had planned.

I use this analogy as it applies to ELLs as well. In order for ELLs to progress with their English language development, a teacher needs to vary the types of instructional tasks that the ELL will engage in. Student involvement during instruction is the key to academic success whereas constant passive learning, mostly through lecture-driven lessons, will greatly impede any language learning efforts by an ELL.

Our five principles provide a framework with which to construct a curriculum that is sensitive to the language developmental needs of ELLs. However, to further solidify our understanding of an ELL's language progress, it is necessary to have a clear picture of what ELLs can do with their language at different levels of proficiency and what implications this has for instruction. Although many taxonomies exist that seek to categorize the developmental stages of second language learners, many education systems throughout the United States have adopted a four-tier description.

The four stages are called Preproduction, Early Production, Speech Emergence, and Intermediate Fluency (Krashen & Terrell, 1983).

The **preproduction stage** applies to ELLs who are unfamiliar with English. They may have had anything from one day to three months of exposure to English. ELLs at this level are trying to absorb the language, and they can find this process overwhelming. In a school context, they are often linguistically overloaded, and get tired quickly because of the need for constant and intense concentration. An ELL's language skills are at the receptive level, and they enter a "silent period" of listening. ELLs at this stage are able to comprehend more English than they can produce. Their attention is focused on developing everyday social English. At the preproduction stage, an ELL can engage in nonverbal responses; follow simple commands; point and respond with movement; and utter simple formulaic structures in English such as "yes," "no," "thank you," or use names. ELLs may develop a receptive vocabulary of up to 500 words.

By the time an ELL enters the **early production stage**, (s)he will have had many opportunities to encounter meaningful and comprehensible English. They will begin to respond with one- or two-word answers or short utterances. ELLs may now have internalized up to 1,000 words in their receptive vocabulary and anything from 100 to 500 words in their active vocabulary. In order for ELLs to begin to speak, teachers should create a low-anxiety environment in their classrooms.

At this stage, ELLs are experimenting and taking risks with English. Errors in grammar and pronunciation are to be expected. Pragmatic errors are also common. Teachers need to model/demonstrate with correct language responses in context. Redundancies, repetitions, circumlocutions, and language enhancement strategies are important for teachers to use when interacting with ELLs at this level.

At the **speech emergence stage**, an ELL will begin to use the language to interact more freely. At this stage, ELLs have a 7,000-word receptive vocabulary. They may have an active vocabulary of up to 2,000 words. By this time, ELLs may have had between one and three years' exposure to English. It is possible that they have a receptive understanding of academic English; however, in order to make content-area subject matter comprehensible, teachers are advised to make great use of advance organizers. Teachers should make explicit attempts to modify the delivery of subject matter, to model language use, and to teach metacognitive strategies in order to help ELLs predict, describe, demonstrate, and problem solve. Because awareness of English is growing, it is also important for teachers to provide ELLs at this stage with opportunities to work in structured small groups so that they can reflect and experiment with their language output.

At the stage of **intermediate fluency**, ELLs may demonstrate near-native or native-like fluency in everyday social English, but not in academic English. Often teachers become acutely aware that, even though an ELL can speak English fluently in social settings (the playground, at sport functions, etc.), they will experience difficulties in understanding and verbalizing cognitively demanding, abstract concepts taught and discussed in the classroom. At this stage ELLs may have developed up to a 12,000-word receptive vocabulary and a 4,000-word active vocabulary. Teachers of ELLs at the intermediate fluency level need to proactively provide relevant content-based literacy experiences such as brainstorming, clustering, synthesizing, categorizing, charting, evaluating, journaling, or log writing, including essay writing and peer critiquing, in order to foster academic proficiency in English.

At the University of South Florida, we have developed online ELL databases that have been created to provide pre- and in-service teachers with annotated audio and video samples of language use by ELLs who are at each of the four different levels of language proficiency. The video and audio files act as instructional tools that allow teachers to familiarize themselves with the language ability (speaking, reading, writing) of ELLs who are at different stages of development. For example, teachers may have ELLs in classes and not be sure of their level of English language development, nor be sure what to expect the ELL to be able to do with English in terms of production and comprehension. This naturally impacts how a teacher may plan for instruction. By looking through the databases, a teacher can listen to and watch representations of ELL language production abilities at all four levels (preproduction, early production, speech emergence, and intermediate fluency). In addition, the databases feature interviews with expert ESOL teachers, examples of tests used to evaluate the proficiency levels of ELLs, and selected readings and lesson plans written for ELLs at different levels of proficiency. Lastly, they provide case studies that troubleshoot pedagogical problem areas when teaching ELLs.

There are three databases: one that features ELLs at the elementary school level, one featuring ELLs at the middle school level, and one featuring ELLs at high school.

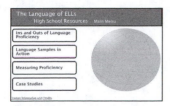
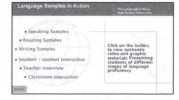

The three ELL databases can be found at:

- http://esol.coedu.usf.edu/elementary/index.htm (elementary school language samples);
- http://esol.coedu.usf.edu/middleschool/index.htm (middle school language samples);
- http://esol.coedu.usf.edu/highschool/index.htm (high school language samples).

It is important to remember that a lack of language ability does not mean a lack of concept development or a lack of ability to learn. Teachers should continue to ask inferential and higher-order questions (questions requiring reasoning ability, hypothesizing, inferring, analyzing, justifying, and predicting) that challenge an ELL to think.

Teaching Help

For two good websites that outline ways to enhance questioning using Bloom's taxonomy see www.teachers.ash.org.au/researchskills/dalton.htm (Dalton & Smith, 1986) and www.nwlink.com/~donclark/hrd/bloom.html (Clark, 1999). The latter gives a further detailed breakdown of Bloom's Learning Domains in terms of cognitive, affective, and psychomotor key words and how these can be used to foster an ELL's language learning.

Zehler (1994) provides a list of further strategies that teachers can use to engage ELLs at every stage. These include:

- asking questions that require new or extended responses;
- creating opportunities for sustained dialogue and substantive language use;
- providing opportunities for language use in multiple settings;
- restating complex sentences as a sequence of simple sentences;
- avoiding or explaining use of idiomatic expressions;
- restating at a slower rate when needed, but making sure that the pace is not so slow that normal intonation and stress patterns become distorted;
- pausing often to allow students to process what they hear;
- providing specific explanations of key words and special or technical vocabulary, using examples and non-linguistic props when possible;
- using everyday language;
- providing explanations for the indirect use of language (for example, an ELL student may understand the statement, "I like the way Mary is sitting" merely as a simple statement rather than as a reference to an example of good behavior).

1.3
Deciding on the Best ESOL Program

This section outlines the learning outcomes that ELLs typically accomplish in differing ESOL programs and the importance of the maintenance of first language development. Although school systems differ across America in the ways in which they try to deal with ELL populations, this section describes the pedagogical pros and cons of an array of ESOL programs and clarifies terminology used in the field.

There are several factors that influence the design of an effective ELL program. These include considerations regarding the nature of the ELL student demographics to be served, district resources, and individual student characteristics. The MLA Language Map at www.mla.org/map_main provides an interactive look into the distribution of languages spoken in the United States. The online maps are able to show numbers as well as percentages by state, district, and zip code. Over 30 languages may be geographically represented and compared. The MLA Language Map shows graphically that not all districts are the same. ELL populations differ across the country. Some areas may have an overwhelming majority of Spanish speaking ELLs whereas other districts may have an equally large numbers of ELL students but speaking 50–100 different languages. On the other hand, some districts may have very few ELLs while other districts experience an influx of ELLs of whose language and culture the area's schools have little knowledge (for example, Hmong in Marathon County in Wisconsin, Haitian Creole in Palm Beach, Broward, and Dade counties in Florida, and Somali/Ethiopian in Hennepin and Ramsey counties in Minnesota). Cultural and linguistic differences, as well as factors such as size, age, and mobility of community members, very much influence the types of ESOL instructional programs that school districts choose to develop. Refer to *English Language Learner Programs at the Secondary Level in Relation to Student Performance* (www.nwrel.org/re-eng/products/ELLSynthesis.pdf) for a wonderful research-based yet easy-to-read outline of how the implementation of different ELL programs in schools affects the language learning gains of ELLs.

As mentioned above, not all ELLs are the same. ELLs may enter a school with vastly different educational backgrounds. Some enter U.S. schools with a strong foundational knowledge in their first language. This means that they may have had schooling in their first language, have literacy skills in their first language, and/or have developed social everyday language competency as well as academic proficiency in their first language. Other ELLs may have had less or even no academic schooling in their first language. Many ELLs, especially refugees, may have attended school in their homeland only for it to have been interrupted by famine or war, or for other socioeconomic or political reasons. Some ELLs arrive in the United States with their families at a very young age and, although they speak their first language at home, they may have never developed reading or writing proficiency in it. As will be discussed in the next chapter, it is of great importance to uncover the nature of an ELL's first language development since this has a profound bearing on how an ELL manages to acquire English.

A third factor, according to the Center for Applied Linguistics (CAL, 1987, at www.cal.org), is the resources that a district has at its disposal. Some districts may have a cadre of qualified ESOL specialists working in schools, whereas other districts may only be able to use paraprofessionals and yet others draw on the surrounding community for help. Based on these constraints, one can classify different ESOL programs into what Baker (2001) terms strong and weak forms of bilingual education. Table 1.2 provides an overview of the merits of the many types of ESOL programs operating across the United States.

According to a report submitted to the San Diego County Office of Education (Gold, 2006), "there is no widely accepted definition of a bilingual school in published research in this country" (p. 37). As a rule of thumb, they are widely understood to be schools that promote bilingualism and literacy in two or more languages as goals for students (Baker, 2001; Crawford, 2004).

TABLE 1.2. Types of ESOL programs in the United States

Type of program	Target ELLs and expectations	Program description	What research says
Submersion	All ELLs regardless of proficiency level or length of time since arrival. No accommodations are made. The goal is to reach full English proficiency and assimilation	ELLs remain in their home classroom and learn with native speakers of English. The teacher makes no modifications or accommodations for the ELL in terms of the curriculum content or in teaching English	States such as Florida have in the past faced potential litigation because of not training teachers to work with ELLs or modifying curriculum and/or establishing ELL programs. In order to avoid submersion models, Florida has established specific ELL instructional guidelines (Consent Decree, 1990)
ESL class period	As above, though usually in school districts with higher concentrations of ELLs	Groups ELLs together, to teach English skills and instruct them in a manner similar to that used in foreign language classes. The focus is primarily linguistic and ELLs visit these classes typically 2 or 3 times per week	This model does not necessarily help ELLs with academic content. The effect is that these programs can tend to create "ESL ghettos." Being placed in such programs can preclude ELLs from gaining college-entrance applicable credits (Diaz-Rico & Weed, 2006)
ESL-plus (sometimes called submersion with primary language)	ELLs who are usually at speech emergence and/or intermediate fluency stage. The aim is to hasten ELL's ability to integrate and follow content classroom instruction	Includes instruction in English (similar to ESL class period and pull-out) but generally goes beyond the language to focus on content-area instruction. This may be given in the ELL's native language or in English. Often these programs may incorporate the ELL for the majority or all of the school day	According to Ovando & Collier (1998) the most effective ESL-plus and content-based ESL instruction is where the ESL teacher collaborates closely with the content teacher
Content-based ESL	As above	ELLs are still separated from mainstream content classes, but content is organized around an academic curriculum with grade-level objectives. There is no explicit English instruction	See above

continued overleaf

TABLE 1.2. *(continued)* Types of ESOL programs in the United States

Type of program	Target ELLs and expectations	Program description	What research says
Pull-out ESL	Early arrival ELLs. Usually in school districts with limited resources. Achieving proficiency in English fast is a priority so that the ELL can follow the regular curriculum	ELLs leave their home room for specific instruction in English: grammar, vocabulary, spelling, oral communication, etc. ELLs are not taught the curriculum when they are removed from their classrooms, which may be anything from 30 minutes to 1 hour every day	This model has been the most implemented though the least effective program for the instruction of ELLs (Collier & Thomas, 1997)
Sheltered instruction or SAIDE (specifically designed academic instruction in English). Sometimes called structured immersion	Targets all ELLs regardless of proficiency level or age. ELLs remain in their classrooms	This is an approach used in multilinguistic classrooms to provide principled language support to ELLs while they are learning content. Has same curriculum objectives as mainstream classroom in addition to specific language and learning strategy objectives	ELLs are able to improve their English language skills while learning content. Exposure to higher-level language through content materials and explicit focus on language fosters successful language acquisition (Brinton, 2003)
Transitional bilingual	Usually present in communities with a single large ELL population. Geared towards grades K–3. Initial instruction in home language and then switching to English by grade 2 or 3	ELLs enter school in kindergarten and the medium of instruction is in the home language. The reasoning behind this is to allow the ELL to develop full proficiency in the home language so that the benefits of this solid linguistic foundation may transfer over to and aid in the acquisition of English. Intended to move ELL students along relatively quickly (2–3 years)	Of all forms of traditional bilingual programs, the transitional model entails the least benefit to the ELL in terms of maintaining and building CALP in their home language

TABLE 1.2. *(continued)* Types of ESOL programs in the US

Type of program	Target ELLs and expectations	Program description	What research says
Maintenance bilingual	As above, but the ELL continues to receive language and content instruction in the home language along with English	As above, but are geared to the more gradual mastering of English and native language skills (5–7 years)	ELLs compare favorably on state standardized tests when measured against achievement grades of ELLs in transitional bilingual programs or ESL pull-out, ESL class period and ESL-plus programs (Hakuta *et al.*, 2000)
Dual language/ Two-way immersion	This model targets native speakers of English as well as native speakers of other languages, depending which group predominates in the community	The aim of this program is for both English native speakers and ELLs to maintain their home language as well as acquire another language. Curriculum is delivered in English as well as in the ELL's language. Instructional time is usually split between the two languages, depending on the subject area and the expertise of the teachers	Dual language programs have shown the most promise in terms of first and second language proficiency attainment. Research results from standardized assessments across the United States indicated that ELLs can outperform monolingual English children in English literacy, mathematics, and other content curriculum areas. Has also many positive social and individual affective benefits for the ELL (Genesee, 1999)
Heritage language	Targets communities with high native population numbers, e.g. Hawai'i, Native Americans in New Mexico. Community heritage language maintenance is the goal	In heritage language programs, the aim can be to help revitalize the language of a community. Sometimes English is offered as the medium of instruction in only a few courses. Usually the majority of the curriculum is delivered in the home language	Language diversity can be seen as a problem, as a right, or as a resource. Heritage language programs are operationalized through local, state, and federal language policies as emancipatory (Cummins, 2001)

1.4
Teaching for English Language Development

This section explains the very practical implications of research in the phenomenon of bilingualism for classroom teachers as it relates to a context where many ELLs are learning English as their second, third, or even fourth language. One very important objective of this section is to help teachers understand how they can positively and purposefully mediate an ELL's language development in English.

A very prevalent concept of academic English that has been advanced and refined over the years is based on the work of Jim Cummins (1979; 1980; 1986; 1992; 2001). Cummins analyzed the characteristics of children growing up in two language environments. He found that the level of language proficiency attained in both languages, regardless of what they may be, has an enormous influence on and implications for an ELL's educational success. One situation that teachers often discover about their ELLs is that they arrived in the United States at an early age or were born in the United States but did not learn English until commencing school. Once they begin attending school, their chances for developing their home language are limited, and this home language is eventually superseded by English. This phenomenon is often referred to as limited bilingualism or subtractive bilingualism. Very often ELLs in this situation do not develop high levels of proficiency in either language. Cummins has found that ELLs with limited bilingual ability are overwhelmingly disadvantaged cognitively and academically from this linguistic condition. However, ELLs who develop language proficiency in at least one of the two languages derive neither benefit nor detriment. Only in ELLs who are able to develop high levels of proficiency in both languages did Cummins find positive cognitive outcomes.

The upshot of this line of research in bilingualism seems counterintuitive for the lay person, but it does conclusively show that, rather than providing ELLs with more English instruction, it is important to provide ELLs with instruction in their home language. By reaching higher levels of proficiency in their first language, an ELL will be able to transfer the cognitive benefits to learn English more effectively.

Of course, we don't live in a perfect world, and it is not always feasible to provide instruction in an ELL's home language, so it behooves all teachers to be cognizant of the types of language development processes that ELLs undergo. Cummins (1981) also posited two different types of English language skills. These he called BICS and CALP. The former, basic interpersonal communication skills (BICS), correspond to the social, everyday language and skills that an ELL develops. BICS is very much context-embedded in that it is always used in real-life situations that have real-world connections for the ELL, for example in the playground, at home, shopping, playing sports, and interacting with friends. Cognitive academic language proficiency (CALP), by contrast, is very different from BICS in that it is abstract, decontextualized, and scholarly in nature. This is the type of language required to succeed at school or in a professional setting. CALP, however, is the type of language that most ELLs have the hardest time mastering exactly because it is not everyday language.

Even after being in the United States for years, an ELL may appear fluent in English but still have significant gaps in their CALP. Teachers can be easily fooled by this phenomenon. What is needed is for teachers in all content areas to pay particular attention to an ELL's development in the subject-specific language of a school discipline. Many researchers (Hakuta *et al.*, 2000) agree that an ELL may easily achieve native-like conversational proficiency within two years, but it may take anywhere between five and ten years for an ELL to reach native-like proficiency in CALP.

Since Cummins's groundbreaking research, there has been a lot of work carried out in the area of academic literacy. An alternative view of what constitutes literacy is provided by Valdez (2000), who supports the notion of *multiple literacies*. Scholars holding this perspective suggest that efforts to teach academic language to ELLs are counterproductive since it comprises multiple dynamic and ever-evolving literacies. In their view, school systems should accept multiple ways of communicating and not marginalize students when they use a variety of English that is not accepted in academic contexts (Zamel & Spack, 1998).

However, one very important fact remains. As it stands now, in order to be successful in a school, all students need to become proficient in academic literacy.

A third view is one that sees academic literacy as a dynamic interrelated process (Scarcella, 2003), one in which cultural, social, and psychological factors play an equally important role. She provides a description of academic English that includes a phonological, lexical (vocabulary), grammatical (syntax, morphology), sociolinguistic, and discourse (rhetorical) component.

Regardless of how one defines academic literacy, many have criticized teacher education programs for failing to train content-area teachers to recognize the language specificity of their own discipline and thus being unable to help their students recognize it and adequately acquire proficiency in it (Bailey *et al.*, 2002; Kern, 2000).

Ragan (2005) provides a simple framework to help teachers better understand the academic language of their content area. He proposes that teachers ask themselves three questions:

- What do you expect ELLs to know after reading a text?
- What language in the text may be difficult for ELLs to understand?
- What specific academic language should be taught?

Another very useful instructional heuristic to consider when creating materials to help ELLs acquire academic literacy was developed by Cummins and is called Cummins' Quadrants. In the Quadrants, Cummins (2001) successfully aligns the pedagogical imperative with an ELL's linguistic requirements. The four quadrants represent a sequence of instructional choices that teachers can make based on the degree of contextual support given to an ELL and the degree of cognitive demand placed on an ELL during any given instructional activity. The resulting quadrants are illustrated in Table 1.3.

TABLE 1.3. Cummins' Quadrants

Quadrant I: High context embeddedness, and Low cognitive demand (easiest)	Quadrant III: High context embeddedness, and High cognitive demand
Quadrant II: Low context embeddedness, and Low cognitive demand	Quadrant IV: Low context embeddedness, and High cognitive demand (most difficult)

Quadrant I corresponds to pedagogic activities that require an ELL to use language that is easy to acquire. This may involve everyday social English and strategies that have a high degree of contextual support (i.e. lots of scaffolding, visual clues and manipulatives to aid understanding, language redundancies, repetitions, and reinforcements) or this may include experiential learning techniques, task-based learning, and already familiarized computer programs. Activities in this quadrant also have a low degree of cognitive demand (i.e. are context embedded). In other words, they are centered on topics that are familiar to the ELL or that the ELL has already mastered and do not require abstract thought in and of themselves.

Quadrant IV corresponds to pedagogic activities that require the ELL to use language that is highly decontextualized, abstract, subject-specific, and/or technical/specialized. Examples of these include lectures, subject-specific texts, and how-to manuals. The topics within this quadrant may be unfamiliar to the ELL and impose a greater cognitive demand on the ELL. Academic language associated with Quadrant IV is difficult for ELLs to internalize because it is usually supported by a very low ratio of context-embedded clues to meaning (low contextual support). At the same time, it is often centered on difficult topics that require abstract thought (high cognitive demand). It is important for the teacher to (1) elaborate language, as well as (2) provide opportunities for the ELL to reflect on, talk through, discuss, and engage with decontextualized oral or written texts. By doing this the teacher provides linguistic scaffolds for the ELL to grasp academically.

Quadrants II and III are pedagogic "go-between" categories. In Quadrant II, the amount of context embeddedness is lessened, and so related development increases the complexity of the language while maintaining a focus on topics that are easy and familiar for the ELL. In Quadrant III, language is again made easier through the escalation of the level of context embeddedness to support and facilitate comprehension. However, Quadrant III instruction allows the teacher to introduce more difficult content-area topics.

When a teacher develops lesson plans and activities that are situated within the framework of Quadrant I and II, the ELL engages in work that is not usually overwhelming. In low-anxiety classrooms, ELLs feel more comfortable to experiment with their language to learn more content. As an ELL moves from level 1 of English language development (preproduction) to level 3 (speech emergence), a teacher may feel that the time is right to progress to creating lesson plans and activities that fit pedagogically into Quadrants III and IV. A gradual progression to Quadrant III reinforces language learning and promotes comprehension of academic content. According to Collier (1995):

> A major problem arising from the failure of educators to understand the implications of these continuums is that ELLs are frequently moved from ESOL classrooms and activities represented by Quadrant I to classrooms represented by Quadrant IV, with little opportunity for transitional language experiences characterized by Quadrants II and III. Such a move may well set the stage for school failure. By attending to both language

dimensions (level of contextual support and degree of cognitive demand) and planning accordingly, schools and teachers can provide more effective instruction and sounder assistance to second-language learners. (p. 35).

The degree of cognitive demand for any given activity will differ for each ELL, depending on the ELL's prior knowledge of the topic.

1.5
Not All ELLs are the Same

The United States continues to be enriched by immigrants from countries the world over. Many cities have ethnic enclaves of language minority and immigrant groups and these populations are reflected in school classrooms. This section outlines the background characteristics of ELLs that teachers need to be aware of when planning or delivering instruction. Certainly, ELLs bring their own strengths to the task of learning but they also face many challenges. Equally, these diverse backgrounds impact classroom practices culturally in terms of how ELLs behave in classrooms, how they come to understand curriculum content, and how their interactions with others are affected (Zehler, 1994). The following affords a glimpse of their diversity:

María is seven years old and is a well-adjusted girl in second grade. She was born in Colombia, but came to the United States when she was four. Spanish is the medium of communication at home. When she entered kindergarten, she knew only a smattering of English. By grade 2 she had developed good basic interpersonal communication skills (BICS). These are the language skills needed to get by in social situations. María sounded proficient in English; she had the day-to-day communication skills to interact socially with other people on the playground, in the lunchroom, and on the school bus. Of course, all these situations are very much context-embedded and not cognitively demanding. In the classroom, however, María had problems with her cognitive academic language proficiency (CALP). This included speaking, reading, and writing about subject-area content material. It was obvious to her teacher that Maria needed extra time and support to become proficient in academic areas but, because she had come to the United States as a four-year-old and had already been three years in the school, she was not eligible for direct ESOL support. Collier and Thomas (1997) have shown that, if young ELLs have no prior schooling or have no support in native language development, it may take seven to ten years for them to catch up to their peers.

Ismael Abudullahi Adan is from Somalia. He is 13 and was resettled in Florida as a refugee through the Office of the United Nations High Commissioner for Refugees (UNHCR; see www.unhcr.org/home.html). As is the case with all refugees in the USA, Ismael's family was matched with an American resettlement organization (see www. refugees.org/). No one in his family knew any English. They were subsistence farmers in Somalia and, because of the civil war in Somalia, Ismael had never attended school. The resettlement organization helped the family find a place to live, but financial aid was forthcoming for only six months. While all members of the family were suffering degrees of war-related trauma, culture shock, and emotional upheaval, as well as the stress and anxiety of forced migration, Ismael had to attend the local school. Everything was foreign to him. He had no idea how to act as a student and all the rules of the school made no sense to him. All Ismael wanted to do was work and help his family financially; he knew that at the end of six months financial aid from the government would stop and he worried about how his family was going to feed itself. He is currently placed in a sheltered English instruction class at school.

José came to the United States from Honduras with his parents two years ago. He is now 14. His parents work as farm laborers and throughout the year move interstate depending where crops are being harvested. This usually involves spending the beginning of the calendar year in Florida for strawberry picking, late spring in Georgia for the peach harvest, early fall in North Carolina for the cotton harvest, and then late fall in Illinois for the pumpkin harvest. When the family first came to the United States from Honduras as undocumented immigrants, José followed his parents around the country. His itinerancy did not afford him any consistency with schooling. Last year, his parents decided to leave José with his uncle and aunt in North Carolina so that he would have more chances at school. Now he doesn't see his parents for eight months out of the year. He misses them very much. At school José has low grades and has been retained in grade 8 because he did not pass the North Carolina High School Comprehensive Test. He goes to an ESOL pull-out class once a day at his school.

Andrzej is 17 years old. He arrived with his father, mother, and 12-year-old sister from Poland. They live in Baltimore where his father is a civil engineer. The family immigrated the year before so that Andrzej's mother could be closer to her sister (who had married an American and had been living in the United States for the past 10 years). Andrzej always wanted to be an engineer like has father, but now he isn't sure what he wants to do. His grades at school have slipped since leaving Poland. He suspects that this is because of his English. Even though he studied English at school in Poland, he never became proficient at writing. Because he has been in the United States for more than a year, he no longer receives ESOL support at school. His parents, however, pay for an English tutor to come to his house once a week.

The above cases reflect the very wide differences in the ELL population in schools today. One cannot assume that every ELL speaks Spanish or that all ELLs entered the country illegally. The ELL population in a school may include permanent residents, naturalized citizens, legal immigrants, undocumented immigrants, refugees, and asylees. Of this foreign-born population, 4.8 million originate from Europe, 9.5 million from Asia, 19 million from Latin America, 1.2 million from Africa, and 1 million from other areas including Oceania and the Caribbean (U.S. Census Bureau, 2005).

Stages of Cultural Adjustment

What the above cases of María, Ismael, José, and Andrzej also identify is that since the nation's founding immigrants have come to the United States for a wide variety of reasons. These may include one or any combination of economic, political, religious, and family reunification reasons. Depending on the reason for coming to the United States, an ELL might be very eager to learn English since they might see having English proficiency as the single best means to "get ahead" economically in their new life, or they might resist learning English because they see this as an erosion of their cultural and linguistic identity. A teacher may find an ELL swaying between these two extremes simply because they are displaying the characteristics and stages of *cultural adjustment*.

The notion of cultural adjustment or, as it is sometimes called, "culture shock" was first introduced by anthropologist Kalvero Oberg in 1954. The emotional and behavioral symptoms of each stage of this process can manifest themselves constantly or only appear at disparate times.

Honeymoon Stage

The first stage is called the "honeymoon" stage and is marked by enthusiasm and excitement by the ELL. At this stage, ELLs may be very positive about the culture and express being overwhelmed with their impressions particularly because they find American culture exotic and are fascinated by it. Conversely, an ELL may be largely passive and not confront the culture even though (s)he finds everything in the new culture wonderful, exciting, and novel. After a few days, weeks, or months, ELLs typically enter the second stage.

Hostility Stage

At this stage, differences between the ELL's old and new cultures become aggravatingly stark. An ELL may begin to find anything and everything in the new culture annoying and/or tiresome. An ELL will most likely find the behavior of those around him/her unusual and unpredictable and thus begin to dislike American culture as well as Americans. They may begin to stereotype Americans and idealize their own culture. They may experience cultural confusion and communication difficulties. At this stage, feelings of boredom, lethargy, restlessness, irritation, antagonism, depression, and feelings of ineptitude are very common. This occurs when an ELL is trying to acclimatize to the new culture, which may be very dissimilar to the culture of origin. Shifting between former cultural discourse practices and those of the new country is a problematic process and can take a very long time to overcome. If it is prolonged, an ELL may withdraw because of feelings of loneliness and anxiety.

Home Stage

The third stage is typified by the ELL achieving a sense of understanding of the new culture. The ELL may feel more comfortable living in the new country and experiencing the new culture. They may regain their sense of humor. In psychological terms, an ELL may start to feel a certain emotional balance. Although feelings of isolation may persist, the ELL may stop feeling lost and even begin to have a feeling of direction. The ELL re-emerges more culturally stable, being more familiar with the environment and wanting to belong. For the ELL, this period of new adjustment could initiate an evaluation of old cultural practices versus new ones.

Assimilation Stage

In the fourth stage, the ELL realizes that the new culture has positives as well as negatives to offer. Integration patterns and practices displayed by the ELL become apparent. It is accompanied by a more solid feeling of belonging. The ELL enjoys being in the new culture, functions easily in the new environment (even though they might already have been in the new culture for a few years) and may even adopt cultural practices of the new culture. This stage may be seen as one of amalgamation and assimilation.

Re-Entry Shock Stage

This happens when an ELL returns to the old culture for a visit and notices how many things have changed in the country as well as how they themselves have changed. Upon returning from the home country, an ELL will have developed a new sense of appreciation and of belonging to the new culture.

Worthy of note is the fact that the length of time an ELL spends in each of these stages varies considerably. The stages are neither discrete nor sequential and some ELLs may completely skip stages. They may even exhibit affective behaviors characteristic of more than one stage.

Cultural Practices at School

Whenever an ELL steps into a new school environment, the ELL will be sure to go through a process of cultural adjustment. For an ELL, the countless arrays of unspoken rules acquired in his/her culture of origin may not be suitable in the new school and a new set of practices needs to be discovered and internalized. These include, but are of course not limited to, school rules, what it means to be a "good" student, how to interact with fellow students and teachers, eating practices, bathroom practices, and even ways of learning. It would be fairly easy to learn new rules for living if such were made explicit and one were provided with lists of things to learn. However, most cultural rules operate at a level below conscious awareness and are not easily relayed to students.

Often ELLs find themselves in the position of having to discover these rules on their own. Shared cultural discourse practices can be seen as the oil that lubricates social interaction; however, what a community's cultural practices are, as well as the meanings that group members attach to their shared repertoire of cultural practices, are not always made explicit. Unfamiliarity with these cultural rules on the part of an ELL can cause a great deal of stress.

Many definitions regarding what culture is or is not abound. Diaz-Rico and Weed (2006) provide a very nice overview of the characteristics of culture. For them, culture is an adaptive mechanism, culture is learned, cultures change, culture is universal, culture provides a set of rules for living and a range of permissible behavior patterns, culture is a process of deep conditioning, culture is demonstrated in values, people usually are not aware of their culture, people do not know all of their own culture, culture is expressed verbally and non-verbally, culture no longer exists in isolation, and, last but very poignantly, culture affects people's attitudes toward schooling and it governs the way they learn. It can affect how they come to understand curriculum content and how they interact with fellow students.

Diaz-Rico and Weed (2006) offer a number of strategies to promote cultural pluralism and assuage potential exclusionary practices such as stereotyping, prejudice, and racism in the classroom. Ways to acknowledge different values, beliefs, and practices include accommodating different concepts of time and work rhythms, as well as different concepts of work space. Being open to culturally sensitive dress codes and inclusive of culture in school rituals are effective ways of promoting cultural pluralism. Considering different notions about work and play and maintaining an inclusive understanding of different health and hygiene practices as well as being tolerant of different religious practices and food and eating practices are critical in teaching acceptance. Most important to remember in relation to your ELL students are culturally based educational expectations (roles, status, gender), different discourse patterns, and your need to foster cultural pride and home–school communication.

One way to ease your ELL's cultural adjustment while demonstrating inclusiveness is to get to know where your ELLs come from and then incorporate aspects of their culture into your lessons. You could overtly ask your ELL about their home country, but this tactic may not provide you with the type of information you want since your ELL may not have the language proficiency in English to express abstract cultural concepts. Therefore, you should observe your ELL and how they behave, interview people from the same country, conduct a home visit, or visit the community in which the ELL lives. Of course, teachers are often constrained by time, so an alternative is to conduct internet research or buy appropriate books.

1.6
Culturally Responsive Pedagogy

As more and more students from diverse backgrounds populate 21st century class-rooms, and efforts mount to identify effective methods to teach these students, the need for pedagogical approaches that are culturally responsive intensifies. Today's classrooms require teachers to educate students varying in culture, language, abilities, and many other characteristics.

(Gollnick & Chinn, 2002 p. 21)

The question is: How does a teacher adequately respond to the multicultural classroom?

In 2000 Gay wrote that culturally responsive pedagogy is validating, comprehensive, multidimensional, empowering, transformative, and emancipatory. In other words, culturally responsive pedagogy necessitates that teachers tread outside their comfort circles. It is only natural for humans to see, understand, judge, make sense of, and canonize the world around them through their own discursive norms of practice. What this means in the context of education is that teachers make choices every day about what they will and will not teach. More importantly, teachers make choices as to how they will present and frame their curriculum choices. Of course this sends a subtle message to students: What curriculum matter is taught and how it is framed tends to legitimatize, validate, and endorse it over other potential curricular perspectives, which by default are marginalized.

Thus, teachers instruct in ways and about things that are familiar to them. They usually adopt and transmit the dominant voice in society, namely that of white middle-class America. The problem is, if a student is an ELL, (s)he is usually not white, middle-class, or American. This is where the practice of culturally responsive pedagogy can help. Look at the reflection vignette below. It shows how the media can tend to reinforce dominant societal perspectives, perspectives that are reinforced and repeated in school curricula and textbooks across the country.

Reflection Vignette

I was driving my 12-year-old son to school in the fall of 2003 when over the radio we heard a commercial for the movie *Alamo*. Coincidently, the previous day we had been to the movies and one of the trailers was for the same movie. Kevin Costner was one of the Texan heroes in the movie, and every time the movie trailer showed the Texans the screen was bright and full of smiling people. The music was light and they were obviously the "good guys." However, when the screen shot showed the Mexican antagonists, the screen was dark, with hues of blue and red, the background images were full of cannon sounds, and the faces were "mean-looking."

Back in the car, I asked my son, who at the time was focused on playing his Gameboy, "You're doing American history now in your social studies class, right?"

My son, recognizing that another of dad's teachable moments was upon him, just rolled his eyes and disgruntledly put down his Gameboy.

"Yes, why?" he said.

"What aspect of U.S. history are you learning about now?" I asked.

"We're learning about the westward colonization of North America."

"Did you hear that ad?" I asked.

"Sure."

"Let me ask you something. What do you think would happen if a bunch of Cubans came into the middle of Florida, bought up a cluster of farms, and then told the government they were not going to pay taxes?"

"I suppose the government would fine them," he said.

"Well, what would happen if those same Cubans then told the government that they were going to create their own country?"

"The government would send in the army and kick 'em all out and probably send them back to Cuba."

At that point, I could see a flash of realization cross my son's face. "Oh, I get it," he said, "the Cubans are the Texans."

In the United States the Alamo is usually constructed as part of a righteous war of independence against an autocratic foreign government, namely Mexico. Yet in Mexican schools the war surrounding the Alamo is constructed as an aggressive grab for land by non-Spanish speaking settlers. Who is right? Perhaps the question should be: Am I teaching curriculum matter in a way that alienates and inadvertently marginalizes my students? How would a Mexican ELL feel in your classroom if you taught a unit on the Alamo, or on the westward European settlement of North America, and Mexico and the Mexicans were portrayed as the baddies? At the very least it marginalizes an ELL's voice in the classroom and indirectly discredits his/her potential contribution of another perspective for the class to think about.

Using Gay's (2000) principles of culturally responsive pedagogy, how does a teacher make the curriculum more validating, comprehensive, multidimensional, empowering, transformative, and emancipatory?

The first step is to be conscious of our choice of language. Language is never neutral. What and how we say things in the classroom affects the way our students perceive curriculum matter. The second step is to be conscious of the images we present to the students. The third step is to engage in critical and reflexive thinking and writing tasks. By getting teachers to reflect critically on the language, images, and content of their teaching, we begin to open the door on *other* ways to think about teaching that are less ethnocentric. The fourth step is to learn the history and culture of the ELL groups in your classroom. The fifth step is to try and visit teachers who are successful at implementing culturally responsive pedagogy and, last, become an advocate in your own educational institution to reform ethnocentric discursive practices so that it becomes more inclusive. Richards, Brown, and Forde (2004) suggest the following activities to become more culturally responsive:

1. acknowledge students' differences as well as their commonalities;
2. validate students' cultural identity in classroom practices and instructional materials;
3. educate students about the diversity of the world around them;
4. promote equity and mutual respect among students;
5. assess students' ability and achievement validly;
6. foster a positive interrelationship among students, their families, the community, and school;
7. motivate students to become active participants in their learning;
8. encourage students to think critically;
9. challenge students to strive for excellence as defined by their potential;
10. assist students in becoming socially and politically conscious.

1.7
Not All Parents are the Same
Home–School Communication

Any school administrator and teacher will readily admit that the key to a school's success and indeed the key to a child's learning success is the active involvement of parents in the learning process. In the case of ELLs, parents are often at a loss because of barriers that prevent them from fully participating in the school community. Parents' hesitancy to involve themselves in their child's school arises from barriers such as the frustration they feel because of their own limited knowledge of English, their own possible lack of schooling, perceptions about power and status roles, or the anxiety they have because of different cultural norms such that they do not readily understand American school cultures or the cultural expectations, rights, roles, and responsibilities of teachers, parents, and students.

Schools can greatly enhance the effectiveness of ELL home–school communication and involvement by taking active steps to reduce these barriers. Careful planning is required to meet these challenges, though it can be done.

1. *Knowledge is King!* Get as much background information as is possible. Information useful to schools and teachers includes home language, home cultural/ethnic values, parental attitudes towards education, work schedules of parents, English proficiency, and the circumstances under which they have come to be in the United States (e.g. are they refugees, itinerant migrants, political asylees, second or third generation heritage speakers?). Depending on the information a school receives, a classroom teacher may make informed decisions about bilingual aide support, translation support, and changing school cultural practices that raise rather than bring down barriers to ELL home–school communication and parental involvement.

2. *Communicate as if it is going out of style!* The importance of fostering ELL parental involvement centers foremost on fostering and maintaining good lines of communication between the school/teacher and the home/parents. An important facet that frames parents' participation

in schools is their perceptions of school personnel. Is the school inviting and welcoming? Are teachers and the administration approachable? Are teachers empathetic to ELL parental concerns, wishes, contributions, values, and cultural practices? How often are they invited to attend school functions? Do teachers follow through on their communications? Do teachers make an effort to talk directly and in person with parents? Are parents allowed to visit often and learn what goes on in the classroom? Do teachers take the time to explain the whats, whys, and hows of their teaching and the ELL child's learning?

3. *It's not just about educating the ELL!* If schools want to enlist the support and help of ELL parents, then both the administration of a school and its teachers need to be prepared to extend their instruction beyond the ELL student to the ELL parent—beyond the classroom and into the ELL home. In other words, in order to break down the types of barriers that inhibit ELL parents from school involvement, steps need to be taken to educate the parents in matters concerning English language, as well as U.S. school customs. What would such steps look like? In an article published in *Essential Teacher* (2004), Bassoff says it centers solely on *access, approachability,* and *follow-through.*

Ideas: On Fostering Access

- Create, endorse, and implement an ELL parent–school participation program/policy.
- Have an ELL parent representative on school committees.
- Make the school a place to foster ELL community events.
- Provide access to the school library to aid ELL parents' learning of English.
- Translate all school communications into the home language.
- Make sure all written communication reaches the ELL parent.
- Foster in-school support groups for ELL parents.
- Advocate that your school district establish an "Intake Center" for new arrivals that will help ELL newcomers with school registrations, placement, testing, and information services.
- Allow ELL parents to come to school professional development opportunities.
- Provide ELL parent education workshops and orientation opportunities.
- Advertise the contact information of bilingual school staff.

Ideas: On Fostering Approachability

- Use ELL parents as sources of information.
- Invite ELL parents to school.
- Use parents to raise multicultural awareness in the school and classroom; multiculturalism is a two-way street—foster inclusion through the provision of multicultural workshops, presentations, and events to mainstream monolingual school personnel and students.
- Multicultural appreciation events could include ethnic music and dance performances, art displays, drama shows, science fairs, and festival evenings, all accompanied by talks from ELL parents or ELL community leaders.
- Be amenable and open to different ways about thinking about education—show this through inclusive classroom practices, activities, realia, and visuals.
- Embed multicultural routines in everything and all the time.
- Foster ELL literacy family evenings.
- Establish native language parent groups.

Ideas: On Achieving Good Follow-Through

- Give mainstream students service-learning opportunities to help ELL parents/families adjust to U.S. life.
- Foster ELL parent network circles.
- Provide classes that help ELL parents to meet their children's education needs.
- Have the school library purchase a wide range of fiction and non-fiction bilingual books.
- Take the time to learn about the culture, language, and education system of the ELLs' home countries and apply what you learn in your classroom.
- Create virtual spaces to post ongoing information for ELL parents as well as WWW links to useful websites.[1]

1.8
English Language Learners with Special Needs

We want to highlight an important subset of the ELL population that is often disadvantaged because its members fall simultaneously into two underrepresented groups: special needs and ELL. They are underprivileged because many teachers within these separate discipline areas have not been trained to work with this population of students—ESOL teachers with special needs students, or special needs teachers with ELLs.

In 1984 the National Office for Educational Statistics reported that 500,000 students in the United States were English language learners with exceptionalities. Today, more than 20 years later, it is projected that there are more than 1 million ELLs with special needs in the United States (Baca & Cervantes, 2004).

Despite an abundance of legislative initiatives (*Civil Rights Act—Title VI* in 1963, *Title VII of the Elementary and Secondary Education Act* (ESEA) reauthorized in 1974, 1978, 1984, and 1998, *Lau v. Nichols* in 1974, and the *Equal Educational Opportunity Act*, extending the Lau decision to all schools, *President's Committee on Mental Retardation* in 1970, the *Education for All Handicapped Children Act* in 1975, the *Bilingual Education Act* in 1984, reauthorization of the ESEA in 1994 coupled with a Presidential Executive Order in 2000, the *Individuals with Disability Education Act* (IDEA) of 1997 and *Title II* of the *No Child Left Behind* (NCLB) *Act* 2002), inappropriate referrals, assessments, and the institutionalization of inappropriate instructional processes remain crucial issues in the education of ELL special needs children.

A colleague of ours once told the story of when he first came to the United States. His son was seven years old and at the end of the summer in 2005 was ready to be placed in grade 2. In Florida, the parents of every newly enrolled student are obliged to fill out a home language survey form. Our colleague was raising his children bilingually and both his children were equally fluent in English and German. When asked on the form what languages were spoken at home, he wrote German and English. A week later, his son innocuously said at the dinner table that he enjoyed being pulled out of the classroom, whereupon both parents asked the son what he meant. "Why I love being in the ESOL class with all the kids who speak other languages." Little did my colleague know that, because he had written German on the home language survey, the school was legally bound to place his son in ESOL classes. The upshot of the story was that our colleague went to the school and explained to the administration that his son was a balanced bilingual speaker and having him in ESOL classes was unnecessary. The administration told him that there was nothing they could do because the home survey was filled out as it was. Ultimately, my colleague had to disenroll his son, re-enroll him in the same school, and fill out the home survey again (this time just putting English as the home language) to finally have him pulled from the ESOL classes. The reason this story is related is because parents and teachers are all too familiar with the fact that, within education environments, rule-driven practices, acronyms, and terminologies abound that more often than not pigeon-hole students into predetermined roles and assign these students to inevitable and predictable expectations. Unfortunately, ELLs with special needs have fallen prey to this stereotyping. There is, however, an ever-increasing but incomplete body of research that spotlights instructional strategies for ELLs with special needs that teachers may draw upon to help them in their efforts to identify, instruct, and assess. The following section summarizes some of the more important aspects of this research. The following two points may act as instructional guides:

- Students with mild to severe disability levels benefit from native language instruction (de Valenzuela & Niccolai, 2004).
- Instruction needs to be enriching and not remedial, empower language learners, recognize the learners' culture and background, provide learners with authentic and meaningful activities, connect students to real-life experiences, begin with context-embedded material that leads to the use of context-reduced material, and provide a literacy/language-rich environment (Echeverria and McDonough, 1993).

But how can we translate the above into effective classroom practice?

There are various pedagogic models that have been developed based on theoretical frameworks, research findings, and recommended practices appropriate for ELLs with special needs (Ruiz, 1995a,b). Ortiz (1984) describes four basic types of pedagogic models that offer structured institutional support for ELLs with special needs to achieve more accomplished social and academic skill levels. These models are:

1. *Coordinated services model*—assists the ELL with special needs with a monolingual English speaking special education teacher and a bilingual educator.
2. *Bilingual support model*—bilingual paraprofessionals are teamed with monolingual English speaking special educators and assist with the individualized education plans of ELLs with special needs. Wherever noted on the individualized education program (IEP), the bilingual paraprofessional provides home language instruction concurrently with the teacher providing content expertise.
3. *Integrated bilingual special education model*—consists of one teacher who is certified in both bilingual education and special education, where the teacher is able to assist with level-appropriate English language instruction as the learner develops in proficiency.
4. *Bilingual special education model*—in this model all professionals interacting with the ELL special needs student have received bilingual special education training and are qualified to provide services that meet the goals outlined in any IEP.

Another model, the Optimal Learning Environment (OLE) Project (Ruiz, 1989), is based on a constructivist philosophy and works within a holistic–constructivist paradigm, focusing on the extensive use of interactive journals, writers' workshops, shared reading practices, literature conversations, response journals, patterned writing, as well as the provision of extended assessment time. The aim of the strategies is to build on a student's schema and interest.

The benefits of such models highlight the individualized and diverse needs of language learning students with special needs. As yet, guaranteeing unambiguous benefits across the board is not possible precisely because of the dearth of empirical research on instructional planning and curriculum design in this area. A very real consequence of this situation is the paucity of curricular materials available specifically geared to bilingual special education. Both fields of education have propagated methods on preparing either English language learners or special needs students. The main point to be internalized here is that materials must be integrated and specifically designed for English language learners *with* special needs. It is not enough that they receive "half of each curriculum" (Collier, 1995). Lack of curricular materials and trained personnel is still cited as the greatest barrier to providing services to English language learners with special needs.

So, what can teachers do to facilitate language learning for ELL students with a special need?

Of course, implementing well-informed instructional practices is one thing, but awareness raising, understanding of difficulties, and knowledge of differences and disorders are also an integral part of assisting the English language learner with disabilities.

In conclusion, we offer Hoover and Collier's (1989) recommendations as a point of departure to think about teaching ELLs with special needs:

1. Know the specific language abilities of each student.
2. Include appropriate cultural experiences in material adapted or developed.
3. Ensure that material progresses at a rate commensurate with student needs and abilities.
4. Document the success of selected materials.
5. Adapt only specific materials requiring modifications, and do not attempt to change too much at one time.
6. Try out different materials and adaptations until an appropriate education for each student is achieved.
7. Strategically implement materials adaptations to ensure smooth transitions into the new materials.
8. Follow some consistent format or guide when evaluating materials.
9. Be knowledgeable about particular cultures and heritages and their compatibility with selected materials.
10. Follow a well-developed process for evaluating the success of adapted or developed materials as the individual language and cultural needs of students are addressed. (Hoover & Collier, 1989: 253)

Conclusion

Understanding your English language learners can be daunting. They are different; they probably come from very different home environments from you, their teachers. Some of your students may be third-generation American and yet others may be newly arrived undocumented immigrants.

After reading Part 1, we don't expect you to now know everything there is to know about ELLs. We did not set out to provide you in these few short pages with an all-inclusive research-informed, all-encompassing treatise on ELLs in education. We have been circumspect, to be sure, in trying to introduce you to ELLs. There are plenty of ELL-specific books for that. It *was* our intent, however, to raise your awareness about the educational implications of having ELLs in your classroom. Our goal with this is to start drawing a picture of who an English language learner is and from this position help you think about the educational possibilities for your class.

Parts 2, 3, and 4 of this book are devoted exclusively to completing this picture. Not in a global sense, but finely etched within the parameters of your own content area.

What will be introduced to you in the pages to come will undoubtedly refer back to some of the points raised in Part 1. We have no intention of offering you static teaching recipes; instead we offer something akin to ideas, understandings, and skills that you can transfer to your own classrooms. Last, we refer you to Part 4 of this book, which offers you avenues for future professional development.

Part 2
Influences on the Mathematical Attainment of English Language Learners

2.1
Overview
Influences on the Mathematical Attainment of English Language Learners

Jamison Middle School is a neighborhood school that has experienced a shift in its student population since it opened 15 years ago. Originally, the student population was homogenous with mostly White students from middle-class families who lived in the surrounding neighborhoods. However, over the last few years, the student population has become both culturally and linguistically diverse. Despite the changes in the student population, the teaching staff has remained stable and the majority of the teachers speak only English. Teachers are grappling with methods to meet the needs of their increasingly diverse student population. Teachers are constantly asking themselves questions such as "How can I teach students who do not understand the language that I am using?", "What can I do to prepare these students to be successful mathematically?", and "What are effective strategies for helping my English language learners?"

John Thomas, a seventh grade mathematics teacher, is concerned about the number of ELLs enrolled in his classes. He believes they should be immersed in English prior to taking subject matter courses. On more than one occasion, Mr. Thomas has expressed publicly that he thinks it is absurd for these students to be placed in his mathematics classroom. "How can anyone expect me to teach them when I can't communicate with them? The students don't speak English and I don't speak their native language." Because his concerns have remained unanswered, he resigned himself to dealing with these students. He ultimately decided that he cannot devote additional time to his ELLs because it would take his attention away from other students in his class. As a result, he provides ELLs with copies of the assignment but does not attempt to engage them in any classroom activities.

Carly Smith, an eighth grade mathematics teacher, has many of the same concerns as Mr. Thomas, but decided that she must teach all students in her class regardless of their backgrounds or language proficiency. Despite the challenges in teaching students with limited English proficiency, she knows her ELLs are capable of learning and she wants to ensure that they develop the mathematics background and understanding to keep their future educational options open.

Although she does not speak the students' native language, she uses pictures and gestures to communicate with them. She includes ELLs in all aspects of her classroom activities. Each day she monitors their progress to determine how they make sense of such activities. She has asked other students to serve as peer mentors and she monitors the interactions between ELL students and their English speaking partners. As part of her classroom instruction, she uses manipulatives, focuses on students' vocabulary development, and encourages them to use their new vocabulary whenever possible.

In which of the two classrooms do you believe an ELL will have an opportunity to learn mathematics? In what ways might teacher decisions influence the schooling experiences of ELLs?

The concerns identified by the teachers depicted in the vignette are not unlike those of many mathematics teachers. In addition to teaching topics that students may find difficult, we have to communicate with and engage students who have limited English proficiency. We need to recognize the challenges that ELLs experience in the classroom. How does one learn subject matter when the language used for instruction is not one's native language? In addition to learning in a linguistically and culturally unfamiliar environment, ELLs attempt to build meaning without the background knowledge (e.g. mathematics vocabulary, cultural references in word problems) that their peers use to make assumptions and process new information. Clearly, these classroom situations might be frustrating to both ELLs and their teachers.

Meeting the needs of ELLs can be particularly challenging for mathematics teachers given that understanding mathematics requires a breadth of communication skills (e.g. speaking, listening, reading, and writing) (Thompson, Kersaint, Richards, Hunsader, & Rubenstein, 2008). In fact, mathematics itself is considered a language (Usiskin, 1996). The language of mathematics is inherently complex as it combines common everyday words with technical mathematics vocabulary and has its own syntax, semantics, and discourse features. These complexities, coupled with the fact that many ELLs do not have a working knowledge of American culture to serve as schema for new learning, lead to the challenges that might exist for ELL students in mathematics classrooms.

The National Council of Teachers of Mathematics (NCTM) has played a significant role in establishing a vision for mathematics teaching and learning through its publication of standards documents (Martin, 2007; NCTM, 1991, 2000). In these documents, NCTM asserts that instruction should be tailored to address the needs of *all* students, including those with limited English proficiency. NCTM (2000) states that "equity requires accommodating differences to help everyone learn mathematics" (p. 13). Within this statement is the recognition that some students may need additional assistance to meet high expectations.

Students who are not native speakers of English, for instance, may need special attention to allow them to participate fully in classroom discussions. Some of these students may also need assessment accommodations. If their understanding is assessed only in English, their mathematics proficiency may not be accurately evaluated. (NCTM, 2000: 13)

Part 2 of this book examines factors that influence the mathematical attainment of ELLs who are mainstreamed in mathematics classrooms. The chapters here address factors that influence the learning of mathematics by ELLs and report research findings that attest to how these factors contribute to ELLs' ability to learn mathematics.

To begin our discussion, in Chapter 2.2 we present an overview of the current goals and standards for teaching mathematics outlined by the NCTM. This discussion is helpful as it highlights the importance of providing *all* students an equitable and high-quality mathematics education and provides a frame for thinking about issues that may influence our ability to provide ELLs with the access and opportunities to learn mathematics.

Chapter 2.3 addresses difficulties ELLs might experience with mathematics language as they are also in the process of learning English. Specifically, this chapter illustrates the nuances of the language of mathematics that may produce additional challenges to students who are learning a new language while also learning mathematics, a possible third language.

Chapter 2.4 addresses features of the mathematics learning environment that are necessary to ensure that students, including ELLs, are provided ample opportunities to learn. Issues addressed in this chapter include tasks used to develop mathematics understanding, classroom discourse, the learning environment, and teacher preparedness to work with ELLs.

Chapter 2.5 highlights culturally laden aspects of mathematics that may influence students' ability to make sense of what they are learning. It demonstrates that mathematics is not culture-free and that it is important for teachers to be culturally aware in order to make instruction inclusive and relevant to all students.

Chapter 2.6 addresses assessment issues that may influence conclusions drawn about what ELLs know and are able to do. These issues are particularly important because decisions based on assessment results influence students' opportunity to learn advanced mathematics. As a result, it is important that we obtain appropriate and accurate measures of student knowledge.

Finally, Part 2 ends with a discussion of recommendations for improving the teaching and learning of ELLs.

Collectively, the information provided in these chapters helps teachers understand possible influences on ELLs' ability to learn mathematics while they simultaneously learn a new language. These chapters do not offer instructional strategies to use when teaching ELLs. That is addressed in Part 3. Rather, the chapters in Part 2 provide research-based knowledge about ELLs and their experiences in mathematics classrooms. The final chapter in this section, Chapter 2.7, identifies recommendations for improving the mathematics preparation of ELLs as identified by the available literature. In Part 3, instructional strategies linked to this research are provided to assist mathematics teachers as they attempt to meet the needs of their ELLs.

2.2
Providing an Equitable Mathematics Education to English Language Learners
Mathematics Education Standards

In order to provide English language learners (ELLs) an equitable and high-quality mathematics education, it is important to understand current expectations for *all* students to ensure that ELLs are provided the same opportunity and access to learn mathematics as their peers. In this chapter, we discuss the vision for school mathematics espoused by the National Council of Teachers of Mathematics (NCTM), the professional organization that represents the goals and expectations of the pre-K–12 mathematics education community.

Since the early 1980s, the NCTM has provided a comprehensive vision for mathematics instruction that represents a significant shift from practices commonly used for teaching and learning mathematics. In *Curriculum and Evaluation Standards for School Mathematics*, NCTM identified five goals for all students:

> (1) that they learn to value mathematics, (2) that they become confident in their ability to do mathematics, (3) that they become mathematical problem solvers, (4) that they learn to communicate mathematically, and (5) that they learn to reason mathematically. (NCTM, 1989: 5)

In 2000, NCTM built on its earlier documents (NCTM, 1989, 1991, 1995) and on reform efforts for over a decade to update its vision for a mathematics curriculum for the twenty-first century. In *Principles and Standards for School Mathematics*, NCTM identified six principles that emphasize a high-quality mathematics education for all students (see Table 2.1). These principles are intended to describe the features of a high-quality mathematics education.

The *equity principle* challenges assumptions that only some students with particular backgrounds are capable of learning robust mathematics. It highlights the need to provide an *equitable* (which is not to be confused with an *equal*) opportunity for *all* students to learn mathematics. An equitable access to high-quality mathematics education recognizes that some students, such as ELLs, might need additional support to meet established high expectations.

TABLE 2.1. NCTM principles for school mathematics

Equity	Excellence in mathematics education requires equity—high expectations and strong support for all students
Curriculum	A curriculum is more than a collection of activities; it must be coherent, focused on important mathematics, well articulated across the grades
Teaching	Effective mathematics teaching requires understanding what students know and need to learn and then challenging and supporting them to learn it well
Learning	Students must learn mathematics with understanding, actively building new knowledge from experience and prior knowledge
Assessment	Assessment should support the learning of important mathematics and furnish useful information to both teachers and students
Technology	Technology is essential in teaching and learning mathematics; it influences the mathematics that is taught and enhances students' learning

Source: National Council of Teachers of Mathematics (2000: 11).

The *curriculum principle* highlights the role that the school mathematics curriculum plays in providing access and opportunity to learn mathematics. An effective mathematics curriculum addresses important mathematics that prepares students to function in various settings, including home, school, and work. This requires the use of a coherent and well articulated curriculum. According to *Principles and Standards*, "A coherent curriculum effectively organizes and integrates important mathematical ideas so that students can see how the ideas build on, or connect with, other ideas, thus enabling them to develop new understandings or skills" (NCTM, 2000: 15). Additionally, the mathematics addressed in the curriculum should help students understand how mathematics is used to represent and solve problems within and beyond the mathematics classroom. A curriculum that is well articulated across grades allows the subject matter to grow and allows for the deep examination of mathematics content.

The *teaching principle* highlights the extent to which teachers and instruction shape students' mathematical learning. What mathematics students know and how they know it are dependent on the approaches used for teaching mathematics. The learning environment established by the teacher can support (or hinder) student learning. Teachers make curricular, pedagogical, and daily classroom decisions that influence students' experiences with and dispositions toward mathematics. Effective teachers recognize the role they play in the long-term mathematical education of students. They structure and use learning activities and tasks that have potential for enhancing students' understanding of mathematics. They orchestrate classroom discourse in ways that support the development of student knowledge. Finally, they continue to grow professionally as they work to refine instructional practices.

The *learning principle* emphasizes that students are expected to learn mathematics with understanding. That is, it clarifies that the rote learning of mathematics is not sufficient to meet the demands and requirements of the twenty-first century. As a result, instruction is expected to focus on the development of conceptual understanding of mathematics in addition to the development of procedural understandings. Students with conceptual understanding of mathematics are able to apply their knowledge in various settings and to solve various routine and novel problems. They not only understand the underpinning of particular mathematics topics, they are able to connect and relate mathematical ideas. What and how students learn depends on the environment in which they learn and the experiences that are provided to facilitate learning. Current thinking about best approaches to support learning suggests that students learn best in environments that support social interaction and active engagement.

The *assessment principle* highlights the essential role that assessments play in student learning. Assessments provide insights about what students know and are able to do, and guide instructional and curricular decisions. It is important to use a variety of assessment tools and techniques to obtain information about what students are learning and to make appropriate decisions about best approaches to facilitate further learning.

Finally, the *technology principle* acknowledges the ubiquitous role of technology in society and recommends its use to support students' learning of mathematics. Technology enhances mathematics learning by allowing students to access new mathematics topics and to study mathematics topics more deeply. When technology is used to support mathematics learning, students are provided opportunities to extend their knowledge by focusing on problem solving and reasoning. It enriches the range and quality of possible investigations in a mathematics class and its use provides a means of viewing mathematical ideas from multiple perspectives.

Guided by these principles, NCTM (2000) produced a set of content and process standards for the pre-K–12 mathematics curriculum. Content standards address five content areas and represent the understandings, knowledge, and skills that students should know and be able to demonstrate; the process standards highlight and describe how students should acquire that content knowledge (see Table 2.2).

Mathematics instruction envisioned by the standards is likely different from methods often used to teach mathematics (see Hiebert *et al.*, 2003; Stigler & Hiebert, 1999). Typically, teachers present a brief lecture in which they model procedures for students. Students, in turn, practice the procedures as part of seatwork or homework. This scenario places the mathematics knowledge squarely in the hands of the teachers and emphasizes obtaining correct answers as the goal for instruction. Although often used, this type of instruction has failed a large segment of the student population, as reported in national and international assessments (Kloosterman & Lester, 2007; Schmidt, McKnight, & Raizen, 1997).

In contrast, NCTM envisions a learning environment in which the teacher and the students are both contributors to knowledge development. That is, students engage in discussions with the teacher and with peers in a learning community; they negotiate meaning, debate ideas, and reach consensus about mathematics as they actively engage in mathematical experimentation and investigations. Teachers scaffold student learning experiences by building on prior knowledge and making connections among mathematics topics. The learning experiences supported by this type of instruction emphasize teaching within a student's "zone of proximal development." According to Vygotsky (1978), the zone of proximal development is "the distance between the actual developmental level as determined by independent problem solving and the level of potential development as determined through problem solving under adult guidance, or in collaboration with more capable peers" (p. 86). This suggests that, if instruction is provided below students' level of ability, they will likely lose interest; if instruction is provided beyond students' level of ability, they will likely become frustrated as learning of the intended concepts appears unattainable. Teachers monitor students' progress and continuously assess students' learning experiences and outcomes. The ability to communicate is an integral part of such a learning environment because discourse is a vehicle to make meaning and to share and discuss how solutions are obtained.

Summary

Given the needs of today's students to function in the twenty-first century, it is imperative that students receive a high-quality mathematics program. *Principles and Standards* (NCTM, 2000) guides instruction that supports the mathematical learning of all students. It is essential that mathematics teachers consider how the classroom environment and instruction influence what, how, and how much students learn, regardless of their English language proficiency.

TABLE 2.2. NCTM mathematics content and process standards

Instructional programs from pre-Kindergarten through grade 12 should enable all students to:

Content Standards

Number and Operations	understand number, ways of representing numbers, relationships among numbers and number systems; understand meaning of operations and how they relate to one another; compute fluently and make reasonable estimates.
Algebra	understand patterns, relations, and functions; represent and analyze mathematics situations and structures using algebraic symbols; use mathematical models to represent and understand quantitative relationships; analyze change in various contexts.
Geometry	analyze characteristics and properties of two- and three-dimensional geometric shapes and develop mathematical arguments about geometric relationships; specify locations and describe spatial relationships using coordinate geometry and other representational systems; apply transformations and use symmetry to analyze mathematical situations; use visualization, spatial reasoning, and geometric modeling to solve problems.
Measurement	understand measurable attributes of objects and the units, systems, and processes of measurement; apply appropriate techniques, tools, and formulas to determine measurements.
Data Analysis and Probability	formulate questions that can be addressed with data and collect, organize, and display relevant data to answer them; select and use statistical methods to analyze data; develop and evaluate inferences and predictions that are based on data; understand and apply basic concepts of probability.

Process Standards

Problem Solving	build new mathematics knowledge through problem solving; solve problems that arise in mathematics and other contexts; apply and adapt a variety of appropriate strategies to solve problems; monitor and reflect on the process of mathematical problem solving.
Reasoning and Proof	recognize reasoning and proof as fundamental aspects of mathematics; make and investigate mathematical conjectures; develop and evaluate mathematics arguments and proofs; select and use various types of reasoning and methods of proof.
Communication	organize and consolidate their mathematical thinking through communication; communicate their mathematical thinking coherently and clearly to peers, teachers, and others; analyze and evaluate the mathematical thinking strategies of others; use the language of mathematics to express mathematics ideas precisely.
Connections	recognize and use connections among mathematical ideas; understand how mathematical ideas interconnect and build on one another to produce a coherent whole; recognize and apply mathematics in contexts outside of mathematics.
Representation	create and use representations to organize, record, and communicate mathematical ideas; select, apply, and translate among mathematical representations to solve problems; use representations to model and interpret physical, social, and mathematical phenomenon.

Source: National Council of Teachers of Mathematics (2000).

2.3
The Nature of Mathematics Language

Language is the primary vehicle for learning, instruction, and overall intellectual development. It is not only a means for communicating information, it is also a vehicle for helping learners broaden and deepen their understanding of important ideas. Unlike other subjects, mathematics itself is a language and has a "register." The mathematics register refers to a subset of language composed of meaning appropriate to the communication of mathematical ideas. It includes the vocabulary used to express these ideas and the structures of sentences in which these vocabulary terms appear, and is distinctively different from other content-area registers. Specifically, the mathematics register includes unique vocabulary, syntax (sentence structure), semantic properties (truth conditions), and discourse (text) features. Researchers and educators have revealed many of the challenges associated with understanding the language of mathematics (e.g. Anstrom, 1999; Crandall, Dale, Rhodes, & Spanos, 1985; Dale and Cuevas, 1992; Kessler, Quinn, & Hayes, 1985; Rubenstein & Thompson, 2001; Spanos, Rhodes, Dale, & Crandall, 1988; Thompson & Rubenstein, 2000). The difficulties fall into five broad categories—vocabulary, symbolic representations, syntax, semantics, and linguistic features of discourse—that are discussed below.

Vocabulary

Vocabulary is identified as the most important aspect of second language competence when learning academic content (Kessler, Quinn, & Hayes, 1985). To process information in mathematics, students must understand specialized words unique to mathematics (e.g. *hypotenuse*, *parallelogram*) as wells as words with special meaning for the mathematics register (e.g. *similar*, *average*, *mean*, *plane*). In fact, the language of mathematics contains several types of vocabulary that may influence student understanding:

- English words with a different meaning in mathematics (e.g. *positive, negative, table, rational, volume, limit, supplementary*);
- technical or specialized mathematics terms (e.g. *hypotenuse, divisor, trapezoid*);
- terms with multiple meanings within mathematics (e.g. *median, base*);
- compound phrases that are used to represent new concepts (e.g. *least common denominator, square root, inverse variation*);
- terms that are homonyms with common English words (e.g. *plane* vs. *plain, arc* vs. *ark, sum* vs. *some*);
- words with different meanings in different content registers (e.g. *radical* in social studies and in mathematics; *solution* in science and in mathematics) (adapted from Thompson, Kersaint, Richards, Hunsader, & Rubenstein, 2008).

Additionally, multiple terms may be used to convey the same mathematics concept:
- addition (e.g. *combine, add, plus, sum, and, increased by*);
- subtraction (e.g. *less, minus, decrease, difference, less than*).

Learning vocabulary is particularly challenging for ELLs who must make sense of presented information and who may not be familiar with the meaning of phrases assumed to be "taken as shared." That is, ELLs with a limited vocabulary may find language difficult when an unfamiliar synonym is used to communicate a familiar idea. Although variation in language usage makes for more interesting conversation or text, the variation in language can be problematic for those who are in the process of learning a new language. For ELL students at levels 1 or 2 (preproduction or early production), it may be more helpful to use social language in describing mathematics terms as these students are still attempting to learn basic interpersonal communication skills (BICS); although we may write the mathematics term so that students become familiar seeing it, we will need to use social language to help students make sense of that term. In contrast, ELL students at level 4 (intermediate fluency) are more prepared to deal with academic aspects of mathematics language as they are ready to acquire cognitive academic language proficiency (CALP); these students are in a better position to deal with abstract words in describing mathematics terms.

Symbols

In addition to the comprehension of words, symbols are used in mathematics to express concepts and processes. Students must identify the functionality of each symbol and understand the rules that govern its usage. Rubenstein and Thompson (2001) identified several challenges regarding the use of symbols to convey mathematical ideas. Specifically, mathematics symbols may:

- require several words to verbalize their meaning.

  E.g. $\geq$ is verbalized as *is greater than or equal to*; $\subset$ is verbalized as *is a subset of*.

- be verbalized in multiple ways.

  E.g. $a \times b$ can be verbalized as *a times b*, *the product of a and b*, and *multiply a and b*.

- have several meanings depending on the context.

  E.g. subscripts—the subscripts in $m = \dfrac{y_2 - y_2}{x_2 - x_1}$ indicate how the coordinates from two

ordered pairs are to be used—the subscript in the expression $\log_2 64$ represents the base of an exponent—the subscript in 14_5 represents the number written in base 5.

- be represented with different symbols.

    E.g. multiplication—8×2, $8(2)$, and $8 \cdot 2$.

- be implicit but central to meaning.

    E.g. addition—64 represents $60 + 4$, $1\frac{2}{3}$ represents $1 + \frac{2}{3}$; multiplication—$5(x + 3)$ represents 5 times the quantity $x + 3$, 5^2 represents 5×5.

    When using technology, parentheses that are implicit must be made explicit in order to evaluate an expression correctly, such as in the square root symbol and the fraction bar:

$$\sqrt{x-9} \quad \text{and} \quad \frac{1}{x-1}$$

So, students must not only recognize the symbols, but they must also learn to associate them with particular concepts and the words used to express those concepts.

Syntax

Other language issues are associated with the syntax of mathematics communications, particularly as they appear in word problems. For example, the surface syntax of a word problem may not result in a correct mathematical or algebraic representation. Consider the following problem: "The number a is 5 more than the number b." When students are asked to translate this sentence into its symbolic representation, they might write $a + 5 = b$ to represent the placement of the values in the sentence rather than an appropriate representation $a = b + 5$. This inversion error typically results from an expectation of a one-to-one correspondence between the words in the problem and an algebraic equation. This translation error is not unique to ELLs as English speaking students have been found to have the same difficulty (see for example, Clement, Lochhead, & Monk, 1981; Kaput & Sims-Knight 1983; Philipp, 1992).

Another area of difficulty is the use of *logical connectors* to link abstract ideas and concepts. Logical connectors are phrases used in combination to indicate a relationship between two or more propositions (e.g. *if . . . then, if and only if, because*) (Kessler, Quinn, & Hayes, 1985). To function successfully in mathematics environments, students must recognize these connectors, the situations in which they appear, and the situations signaled by them (i.e. similarity, contradiction, cause and effect, reason or result, chronological or logical sequence). In addition,

> Structures such as *greater than, less than, n times as much as, as . . . as* are often confusing at the syntactic level because they require that the student master complex patterns that relate to specific meanings in a variety of ways.
>
> Consider, for example, the fact that the following sentences are paraphrases of one another:
>
> 1. Triangle A is as large as Triangle B.
> 2. Triangle A and B are equal in size.
> 3. Triangle A and Triangle B are the same in size.
>
> The same problem . . . exists with the syntactic patterns required by prepositional phrases and passive voice. Consider, for example, sentences 4–6.
>
> 4. Four divided into nine equals nine-fourths.

5. Nine divided by four equals nine-fourths.
6. If nine is divided by four, nine-fourths results.

As with the comparative structures in 1–3, sentences 4–6 are paraphrases that require a rather advanced facility with two-word verbs ending in prepositional particles and corresponding passives. The potential for confusion becomes evident when one considers that textbook writers and instructors are apt to employ a variety of patterns in their exercises and lectures that, although stylistically desirable, are beyond the competence of a sizable number of students, both native and foreign. (Spanos, Rhodes, Dale, & Crandall, 1988: 225)

Moreover, ELLs seldom encounter the use of passive voice as part of conversation, yet many sentences in mathematics are written and presented using the passive voice (e.g. "If a weight is placed on the scale" vs. "If you place the weight on the scale"). When mathematics teachers have ELLs in their classroom, they need to imagine themselves wearing two hats—the hat of the mathematics teacher teaching content and the hat of the mathematics teacher helping students focus on the language of mathematics. As they design instruction, each lesson should likely have content objectives as well as language objectives so that important language is explicitly developed.

Semantics

Semantics refers to the process of making meaning from language. In mathematics, a student's ability to make inferences may depend on his or her knowledge of how references are used (Dale & Cuevas, 1992). For example, students may encounter difficulty with references used in problem statements. Consider the following statement: *8 times a number is 30 more than 6 times the number.* Students may fail to recognize that the number referred to by the phrases *a number* and *the number* are in fact the same number. Thus, both phrases are represented by the same variable when the sentence is represented symbolically. Another inherent difficulty with making meaning in mathematics is the fact that similar terms may have different functions depending on the context. Several examples are provided below:

Square

- the *square* of the number 4 indicated by $4^2 = 16$
- the *square* root of a number 4 indicated by $\sqrt{4} = 2$
- a geometric figure that is a *square*

Base

- the area of a triangle = ½ (*base* × height), where *base* refers to the length of a side
- the volume of a prism = area of the *base* × height, where *base* refers to one of the parallel faces of the prism
- the *base* 2 in the expression 2^3

Range

- the *range* of a relation (the set of second numbers of the ordered pairs)
- the *range* of a set of data (the difference between the greatest and least value)

Clearly these issues related to semantics reveal the need to help ELLs make sense of the words and phrases they encounter in the mathematics classroom.

Linguistic Difficulties Associated with Mathematical Discourse (Oral and Written)

"Discourse Features refers to the 'chunks' of language—sentences or groups of sentences or paragraphs—that function together as textual units, each with a specific meaning and purpose of mathematics" (Dale & Cuevas, 1992: 337–338). Discourse has two components—understanding oral language and understanding written language (text). To make meaning in the mathematics classroom, ELLs must combine their understanding of the English language with the mathematical background needed to address and process cognitively complex information.

Students may find mathematical discourse difficult because it lacks redundancy or paraphrasing, a common feature in oral discourse and other written material. In addition, a large amount of content may be presented by a relatively small amount of text or by a combination of words or symbols that are used to present a mathematical idea. Imagine that an ELL reads the following passages in a mathematics text. In what ways would the ELL be able to make sense of the information presented? What meaning would they take from the text?

> Algebra—a function in the form $y = kx$, where $k \neq 0$, is a direct variation. The constant of variation k is the coefficient of x. The variables y and x are said to vary directly with each other. (Bellman, Bragg, Charles, Handlin, & Kennedy, 2004: 263)

> Geometry—a perpendicular bisector of a triangle is a line, segment, or ray that passes through the midpoint of the side and is perpendicular to that side. (Boyd, Cummins, Malloy, Carter, & Flores, 2004: 238)

In both examples, students are inundated with information that they need to connect to make meaning of the concepts. Yet no information is provided in the text to help them make sense of any particular word. Chapter 3.3 focuses on strategies teachers can use to help students deal with learning technical aspects of mathematics language.

Written mathematics discourse may be particularly troublesome for ELLs on account of a number of features (Dale & Cuevas, 1992). ELLs may experience difficulty with written discourse because the ability to solve word problems is dependent on an understanding of the linguistic and mathematics dimensions of meaning as well as the ability to plan solution strategies that draw on both cognitive and metacognitive functioning (Kessler, Quinn, & Hayes 1985). Research findings indicate that the language used in mathematics word problems often confuses students because it contains a mixture of social language (BICS) and academic language (CALP). This mixture causes confusion when words that have multiple meanings are used differently in different types of discourse. Further, students may experience difficulty with abstract mathematics ideas such as numbers, functions, values, and variables when they are couched in terms of natural language, particularly in problems presented with apparent ambiguities to someone learning a new language. Consider the problem that follows:

> Ms. Jones plans to place a fence around her vegetable garden. The dimension of the rectangular garden is 3 yards by 6 yards. The fencing costs $2.75 per yard with a tax rate of 7%. What can Ms. Jones expect to pay for fencing that encloses her garden?

There are several mathematics concepts that are implicit in this problem. First, the word *around* is intended to alert the reader that the mathematical concept being addressed is *perimeter*. Second, the word *rectangular* is a cue that to determine the perimeter the student must consider all sides of a four-sided figure with special characteristics to obtain a total amount of needed fencing (18 yards). Finally, students must know that the use of the word *tax* represents the need to consider additional payment above and beyond the cost of the fencing. ELLs may not recognize these subtleties if they are not familiar with the vocabulary and have difficulty making sense of the words presented in the problem. In solving this problem, ELLs may attempt to make sense of this problem by using a different interpretation of words. For example, they may see the word *around* and connect it to other uses of that word; *around* is often used to imply an approximation in natural language and in mathematics. In addition, ELLs in classes where the teacher focuses on key words may see the word *by* and assume that there is a need to multiply 3 and 6 (in this case obtaining a correct response for the perimeter, but for a wrong reason). As discussed earlier, vocabulary plays an important role in understanding mathematics. However, memorizing vocabulary or "key words" is not sufficient for students to make meaning because the meaning of words in mathematics is often determined by context. For example, the word *more* is often associated with addition; however the response to the question "how many more?" typically requires subtraction.

Crandall, Dale, Rhodes, and Spanos (1985) identify other discourse features that may hinder ELLs' ability to comprehend mathematics. First, if the cultural context of word problems is unfamiliar, students may have difficulty interpreting the intent of the problem and subsequently solving it. That is, students' personal experiences may mismatch the linguistic expression used to state the problem. For example, "students who are unfamiliar with an economic system that encourages competition and private enterprise are likely to misunderstand such business concepts as discounts, mark ups, wholesale, and retail" (p. 232). Second, students may not be familiar with the use of colloquial statements that are used in word problems, making interpretations difficult (e.g. someone being "in the red"). Third, students may also apply restricted experiences to mathematics problems in inappropriate ways. For instance, when solving a problem involving sales tax, a student might not be able to reconcile the difference between the rate in the problem and the rate in their home town. As a result, they use the familiar value rather than the information presented in the text. Fourth, students may struggle with the lack of practical applications or may not relate to the situation or context presented in a problem. Lastly, a student may apply the meaning of words literally. For example, a student may incorrectly interpret the direction "make a table" to mean "draw a picture of a table." Depending on their language proficiency, ELLs may not distinguish between the use of the word *table* in everyday language and its use in mathematics. In some languages, two different words are used. For example, in Spanish the word *mesa* refers to the dinner table and the word *tabla* refers to a table of values in mathematics.

Gorgorió and Planas (2001) illustrate difficulties a student had when the language of instruction (Catalan) was not the student's home language (Urdu). The students were presented with the following problem:

> Two friends, Maria and Mohammed, go down the stairs by jumping. Both of them begin with the left foot. Maria jumps 4 steps each time. Mohammed jumps 3 steps each time. How many steps do the stairs have to have at least, if there is a step on which Maria and Mohammed have to land with the same foot? Will the foot be the right foot or the left foot? (p. 24)

When asked to solve the problem, a student responded that the problem was impossible to solve. The teacher was initially baffled by this statement. However after a conversation with the student, the teacher realized the student was thinking of a stepladder, which would render the problem senseless in the real word. In the language of instruction, Catalan, there are two different words for stepladder and stairs; however the students only knew the translation for the first and attempted to make sense of the problem using that translation. Although this situation did not involve English, one can easily recognize that similar difficulties might occur in classrooms in which English is the language of instruction.

Summary

The examples provided in this chapter illustrate a range of challenges that ELLs might encounter as they try to make sense of the language of mathematics; these situations are not dependent on their classroom experiences. Teachers who are aware of these potential difficulties can adapt instruction in ways that help ELLs, and other students for that matter, make sense of presented information.

2.4
Mathematics Teaching and Learning

Instruction that supports the goals and expectations articulated in the National Council of Teachers of Mathematics standards document (NCTM, 2000) represents a significant shift from instructional practices commonly used for teaching mathematics. In many mathematics classrooms, instructional practices are teacher-centered and place students in a passive role as recipients of information. NCTM (2007) provides a more dynamic vision for mathematics teaching in which students are actively engaged in doing and thinking about mathematics, justifying and explaining their thinking, and making judgments about ideas presented by others. The mathematics tasks used in the classroom, the ways in which classroom discourse is facilitated, and the learning environment that is established all play a role in how mathematics is taught and what mathematics is learned. In this chapter, we discuss these classroom dimensions as they relate to ELLs. In addition, we discuss how teachers' expectations and preparedness to work with ELLs influence their ability to engage ELLs in mathematics classes.

Tasks

The mathematics tasks and materials used to engage students and support mathematics learning provide a foundation upon which students build their mathematics understandings. Tasks used to facilitate learning convey direct and indirect messages about what mathematics is, what is important to know about mathematics, what doing mathematics entails, and what is valued about learning mathematics. Broadly speaking, tasks represent the various lessons and activities that students may encounter as they study mathematics, including the types of questions, exercises, problems, and investigations that provide a context for cognitive development. Teachers guide students' learning based on the decisions they make about what tasks to use and how to use such tasks. According to NCTM (1991),

The teacher of mathematics should pose tasks that are based on—
- sound and significant mathematics;
- knowledge of students' understandings, interests, and experiences;
- knowledge of the range of ways that diverse students learn mathematics;

and that

- engage students' intellect;
- develop students' mathematical understandings and skills;
- stimulate students to make connections and develop a coherent framework for mathematical ideas;
- call for problem formulation, problem solving, and mathematical reasoning;
- promote communication about mathematics;
- represent mathematics as an ongoing human activity;
- display sensitivity to, and draw on, students' diverse background experiences and dispositions;
- promote the development of all students' dispositions to do mathematics. (p. 25)

Most important, students should engage in worthwhile mathematics tasks that involve higher-level demand, that focus on the development of conceptual knowledge, and that engage them in "doing" mathematics. Tasks that focus primarily on routine computational procedures limit students' knowledge. In contrast, tasks that require students to investigate, reason, think conceptually, and make connections among mathematics topics lead to a deeper level of mathematical understanding. Students who are not provided opportunities to engage in meaningful and challenging mathematics tasks lack the opportunity to think about and use mathematics in ways that make sense.

Research in urban middle schools as part of the QUASAR (Quantitative Understanding: Amplifying Student Achievement and Reasoning) project found that teachers could engage students in a curriculum with challenging tasks that permitted thinking, reasoning, and problem solving (Stein, Grover, & Henningsen, 1996). The QUASAR project resulted in positive gains in mathematics achievement for all groups of students, including bilingually educated Latino students (Lane, Silver, and Wang, 1995). All students benefited almost equally from reformed mathematics education and developed their reasoning and critical thinking skills in mathematics. The mathematics tasks used in QUASAR classrooms required students to use multiple strategies to obtain solutions, depict their work using various representations, and explain their solution strategies. Mathematics procedures were often connected to the underlying concepts and students were engaged in activities identified by the researchers as "doing mathematics." ELLs, like other students, must engage in tasks that require high levels of cognitive complexity if they are to meet the established standards for learning.

Henningsen and Stein (1997) identified five factors that appear to be associated with maintaining student engagement with high-level and cognitively challenging mathematics tasks:

- Tasks are selected that build on students' prior knowledge.
- Teachers support and scaffold student learning.
- An appropriate amount of time is provided to complete the tasks.
- Students have opportunities to witness the modeling of high-level performance.
- Teachers focus on obtaining student explanation and meaning.

To maintain the focus on the cognitive complexity of tasks, it is important that instruction does not shift from a focus on understanding to a focus on obtaining a correct solution. Tasks used to develop students' understanding should provide them opportunities to investigate mathematics ideas, make and test conjectures, reason, debate, identify misunderstandings, explain thinking, and evaluate the thinking of others. Though important, obtaining the correct solution should not be misconstrued as mathematics understanding. In general, students, including ELLs, should engage in tasks that represent authentic problems, not just those that are provided to reinforce through practice the learning of taught procedures. Teachers support the mathematical development of ELLs by adapting tasks or the implementation of tasks in ways that provide linguistic support.

Classroom Discourse

Students' opportunities for learning are maximized when they are engaged in an interaction- and language-rich classroom focused on developing students' understanding of the content (McNair 2000). According to NCTM (1991),

> *Discourse* refers to the ways of representing, thinking, talking, and agreeing and disagreeing that teachers and students use to engage in those tasks. The discourse embeds fundamental values about knowledge and authority. Its nature is reflected in what makes an answer right and what counts as legitimate mathematical activity, argument and thinking. Teachers, through the ways in which they orchestrate discourse, convey messages about whose knowledge and ways of thinking and knowing are valued, who is considered able to contribute and who has status in the group. (p. 20)

This vision for classroom discourse requires a setting that provides opportunities for students to engage in discussions about important mathematics and to observe patterns, make meaning, share findings, justify reasoning, debate areas of disagreement and reach consensus about appropriate approaches and solution strategies. However, such instruction is not typically used in classrooms in which "teaching by telling" is the mode of instruction and the teacher asks all or most of the questions.

The type of discussion facilitated by the teacher plays a significant role in what students learn. Engaging students in discussions is not sufficient to ensure significant learning. The discussion needs to be orchestrated in ways that enhance understanding of the content, provide answers to "why" and "how" questions, and encourage students to reflect on their own thinking processes. Mathematics discussion must include the mathematical subject and purpose and be framed to provide maximum learning opportunities for students (McNair, 2000). The *subject* refers to the mathematics content to be learned (e.g. numbers, shapes, spaces, variables, and the patterns and relationships between them). The *purpose* refers to the intent for engaging in the study of a particular mathematics topic (e.g. to solve a problem). The *mathematical frame* is the design of learning experiences that engage students in searching for patterns, generalizing and formalizing procedures, making connections, using logical reasoning and proofs, and communicating their ideas. Teachers who encourage classroom discourse recognize that there may be challenges inherent in asking ELLs to communicate their mathematical understanding. Mathematics understanding, as used here, does not refer to students' ability to mimic or replicate a previously taught process. Instead, it refers to students' ability to link information to prior knowledge, to explain their understanding in ways that are comprehensible to others, and to apply that knowledge in new situations. Demonstrating this type of understanding may be difficult for ELLs. Even native speakers of English may have difficulty expressing their thoughts. However, such communication is a more problematic issue for ELLs because teachers and others may confound how people use mathematics language with actual knowledge of mathematics. People who sound like they know what they are talking about are judged to have knowledge, while those who don't express themselves well are judged not to have such knowledge. However, if the best practices begin not only with where students are academically, then teachers of [ELLs] need to begin not only with what students understand but also with how they can express their understandings. (Secada & Carey, 1990: 5)

When engaging ELLs and other students in mathematics discourse, teachers must accept different approaches to engaging in the conversation as well as the various views students bring to the classroom (Moschkovich, 1999). ELLs in particular should be permitted to use a variety of language resources, including the use of their first language, gestures, drawings, and the like to convey their intended message. Research by Diaz-Rico and Weed (1995) showed that, in peer interaction, students use four communication strategies that contribute to the occurrence of comprehensible input: (1) embedding language within a meaningful context; (2) modifying language presented to non-native peers; (3) using paraphrase and repetition judiciously; and (4) negotiating meaning consistently. Clearly, the opportunities that ELLs have to engage in mathematics discourse influence their ability to learn.

Brenner (1998) and Moschkovich (1999, 2002) have investigated the nature of mathematics classroom discourse when the students have linguistically and culturally diverse backgrounds. Moschkovich (1999) observed discussions in a computer-based dynamic instructional environment, noting which teaching techniques improved ELLs' participation in the mathematics discussions about the geometric shapes and figures in a tangram puzzle. She found that teachers improved ELLs' participation in discussions by employing techniques such as utilizing objects to encourage students to talk about their properties and characteristics, giving sufficient time for group discussions (student-to-student discussions), asking students to repeat their statements using different expressions in order to clarify intended meaning, and using "revoicing" (reformulating the students' statements using formal mathematical terms) in order to show acceptance of the ELLs' responses and thus encourage their participation in discussions. Rather than correcting ELLs' linguistic mistakes and concentrating on language development, the focus is placed on whether students demonstrated conceptual understanding.

In another study, Moschovich (2002) explored ELLs' learning in discourse-rich classrooms. She found that bilingual students are capable of communicating meaning and competence in mathematics by using gestures, objects, or everyday examples as resources, or simply by using their first language. She also asserted that when ELLs engage in classroom discourse they are provided opportunities to develop their second language as well as their mathematics knowledge.

Brenner (1998) evaluated the mathematical communication in two algebra classes with large populations of ELLs, mostly Hispanic students. In classrooms in which small-group discussions were encouraged and computers were employed to stimulate discussions, she found that more successful mathematical communication was exhibited, which later spread to a large-group setting. The ELLs in the class in which instruction was primarily whole-class were reluctant to speak aloud in front of a large group, but were willing to engage in small-group discussions. Small-group interactions provided additional cognitive and language support and allowed students to influence each others' learning of mathematics. The learning environments described by Brenner and Moschkovich are designed to focus on and develop students' conceptual understanding of mathematics rather than focus on students' linguistic shortcomings or difficulties.

Learning Environment

The established learning environment plays a significant role in students' opportunity to learn (Kersaint, 2007). To achieve the goals outlined by the standards, ELLs need access to classroom environments that build on the background and knowledge they bring to the classroom, honor their first language while simultaneously supporting the development of their second language, and provide ample opportunities for students to show what they know. Because ELLs are main-streamed into mathematics classes, it is important that mathematics teachers consider methods to meet these students' needs. Expectations for learning and the quality of instruction contribute substantially to the learning opportunities of ELLs and influence their ability to develop mathematical knowledge. Indeed, ELLs placed in Mr. Thomas' mathematics class (see the vignette in Chapter 2.1) will have limited opportunities to learn mathematics. In fact, their experiences in such a classroom may alienate them from mathematics because they see no benefit to attending this class. In contrast, ELLs placed in Ms. Smith's class are given opportunities to learn language while learning mathematics. Her accommodations in terms of pictures, gestures, and interactions with peers communicate clear expectations that ELLs must engage in the learning process. If teachers expect ELLs to meet a high level of academic success, they must use teaching behaviors and instructional approaches that enhance and optimize opportunities for students to learn. Unfortunately, in our experiences we find that it is not uncommon for ELLs to be ignored in classrooms. (See also videos of ELLs talking about their classroom experiences, found in Teaching English Language Learners at www.celt.sunysb.edu/ell/default.php.) We should not assume that Mr. Thomas or teachers like him are insensitive to the needs of ELLs. Instead, we should recognize that many teachers do not engage ELLs because they do not have the tools and preparation needed to permit them to work effectively with these students.

Several studies have linked teacher expectations to ELLs' mathematics achievement (Rhine, 1995a, 1995b, 1999). Rhine analyzed the tutoring sessions of intermediate-grade teachers who taught classes that included ELLs and examined teachers' expectations of ELLs' performance in mathematics. He videotaped interactions between teachers and students during tutoring sessions and used recall interviews with teachers to ask them about decisions they made. From analysis of the videotaped sessions, Rhine found that teachers tended to teach differently when ELLs were present in a group. When asked to make predictions of students' achievement on tests, teachers tended to underestimate the mathematics background and mathematics potential of ELLs as compared to their English speaking peers.

Many researchers have studied the nature of discourse in the mathematics classroom environment (see for example Jacobson & Lehrer, 2000; Lampert & Blunk, 1998; McNair, 2000). Although the results are not specific to ELLs, the findings have implications for all mathematics learners. The two features of mathematics classes that appear to influence student learning are the tasks used and the structure used for learning (e.g. small-group vs. whole-class interaction). Research findings suggest that teachers' expectations of ELLs may be low because they erroneously associate a lack of English language proficiency with a concurrent lack of mathematics knowledge. Like other students, ELLs vary in their command of the English language and in their mathematics proficiency. Recognizing this fact is particularly important when considering the development of students' conceptual understanding and communication in accordance with the reforms recommended by NCTM (2000) and the requirements to educate and provide access to mathematics for *all* students.

Teacher Preparedness to Work with ELLs

Despite the growing number of ELLs in our nation's schools, the demographic characteristics of the teaching force have remained rather consistent. According to 2003–2004 data obtained by the National Center for Education Statistics (NCES) (Strizek, Pittsonberger, Riordan, Lyter, & Orlofsky, 2006), the teaching force was 83 percent non-Hispanic White, 8 percent non-Hispanic Black, 6 percent Hispanic, approximately 1 percent non-Hispanic Asian, and less than 1 percent non-Hispanic Native Hawaiian or other Pacific Islander. This suggests that the majority of teachers do not have a cultural or linguistic background that is similar to that of most ELLs. This lack of cultural and linguistic connections raises questions about teacher preparedness to work with these students. During the 1999–2000 school year, 41 percent of the nation's teachers had ELLs in their classrooms, but only 13 percent of those teachers reported that they received any instruction or professional development to prepare them to educate ELLs (NCES, 2002, as cited in Watson, Miller, Driver, Rutledge, & McAllister, 2005). Reeves (2006) surveyed 279 teachers; they generally reported a lack of adequate training to work with ELLs. More than half were not interested in receiving such training. This finding is particularly troubling because the ELL population is expected to increase and to permeate locations beyond the coastal United States.

One would expect that teachers receive professional development related to working with ELLs as part of preservice or in-service teacher education programs. However, recent findings suggest that this may not be the case (Meskill, 2005; Watson et al., 2005). Watson et al. (2005) found that issues of ELLs were not given much attention in textbooks used in content-specific education methods courses. They examined several of the most widely used textbooks in teacher education courses, including mathematics education, to determine the extent to which the texts address issues related to ELLs. They found the percentage of ELL content per text to be 3 percent or less. Based on this finding, one can conclude that little attention is given to the needs of these students unless teacher education professors supplement their curricula to address ELL issues or education programs offer courses specifically designed to address ELL issues. Regarding in-service education, there is evidence that professional development exists to prepare teachers to work with ELLs (see for example Echevarria, Vogt, & Short, 2004). However, there is a need for more research about the variability and quality of programs that are offered, particularly as they relate to the preparation of content-area teachers.

This lack of content-specific pedagogical preparation to work with ELLs could explain why many teachers find it difficult to teach ELLs who are mainstreamed in their content classes. In their survey of 5,300 California teachers, Gandara, Maxwell-Jolly, and Driscoll (2005) identified several challenges that teachers who taught ELLs experienced:

- *Difficulty communicating with students and parents.* They were particularly concerned with their inability to engage parents of ELLs in the school process; they could not inform parents of students' progress or rely on parents to assist with homework.
- *Insufficient time to teach both subject matter and language.* High school teachers in particular were concerned that students did not have sufficient time to meet graduation requirements, particularly if they enrolled in school in the latter years of high school.
- *Variable academic levels among ELLs in their classrooms.* In any given classroom, ELLs with various levels of English language proficiency, cultural experience, and subject matter knowledge are found.
- *Lack of resources (e.g. ELL-friendly textbooks or assessments).* Teachers had to rely on the same materials and assessments that they used with their English speaking students and deemed these materials inappropriate for ELLs. In fact, teachers with more preparation for working

with ELLs were more likely to report inadequacies of instructional programs and classroom resources. These teachers cited a lack of appropriate "tools and materials" and lack of adequate support from educational policies.

- *Insufficient in-service training.* Forty-three percent of the teachers whose classes were composed of 50 percent or more ELLs reported they had received no more than one in-service professional development session that addressed instruction of ELLs during the five years prior to completing the survey. In addition, those who had participated in professional development programs reported that they found them inadequate.
- *Insufficient support.* Teachers expressed the need for additional support. Secondary teachers, in particular, wanted more opportunities for teacher collaboration, better materials, and more paraprofessional help.
- *Low percentage of in-service time that could be devoted to instruction of ELLs.*

Successful teachers of ELLs were found to have the following characteristics: ability to communicate with students; ability to engage students' families; knowledge of language uses, forms, and mechanics and how to teach them; and a feeling of self-efficacy with regard to teaching ELLs. Teachers with greater preparation for working with ELLs, gained as part of their teacher education programs (pre- or in-service), reported greater confidence in their ability to work with ELLs. The results from this study identify some of the challenges associated with teaching ELLs and provide some indication that the preparation teachers have to work with ELLs influences their ability to be effective in classrooms with ELLs present.

Summary

Throughout this chapter, we discussed various factors that influence the type of instruction ELLs experience in mathematics classrooms. The tasks used to develop mathematical knowledge influence the type of understandings students develop (i.e. procedural vs. conceptual), their experiences with mathematics, and their assumptions about what is important about mathematics. Like other students, ELLs are expected to engage in classrooms where they are challenged to obtain deeper understanding of mathematics content. This is possible in acquisition- and language-rich classrooms that allow them to learn mathematics while simultaneously learning English. Teachers establish a learning environment that encourages students' mathematics development by facilitating classroom discourse in ways that encourage student participation and that help students recognize the importance of contributing to their own learning and the learning of their peers. Learning environments that support ELLs' understanding of mathematics are developed by teachers who seek out methods and approaches to enhance ELLs' learning experiences.

2.5
Cultural Influences on Mathematics Learning and Engagement

Many educators mistakenly assume that the transition from social language to academic language is easier for ELLs in mathematics than in other subjects. However, this is not the case in classrooms that use language-rich curricula or that focus on communication and understanding. It is also erroneous to assume that mathematics concepts and symbols are culture-free. Although mathematics is a universal language in many ways, the notation, algorithms, and approaches used for teaching and learning mathematics vary. These differences in approaches to mathematics may lead to misinterpretations and confusion for both teachers and students. Teachers who acknowledge mathematics as culturally laden take the time to understand and validate alternative approaches used for algorithms and procedures that often seem quite different from those they are accustomed to using.

Cultural Links to Mathematics Content and Processes

ELLs might experience some difficulties with mathematics topics because of their past mathematics schooling experiences. That is, they might be challenged by the need to interpret how mathematics is presented and taught in their new environment. Some difficulties students might encounter with mathematics as they transition to school mathematics in the United States include:

- *Numerals*: Numerals are not universally interpreted the same, particularly when it comes to the use of notations (e.g. commas and periods) in numbers. In many South American and European countries, commas and periods are used with meanings opposite to their U.S. meaning. That is, commas are used where periods would be used in the United States and periods are used where commas would be used. For instance, in the U.S. *2,670* means two thousand, six hundred seventy; but for students from South American or European countries this numeral might be interpreted as two and six hundred seventy thousandths. Likewise, in the U.S. system *5.342* means five and three hundred forty-two thousandths; but South American or European students might interpret this numeral as five thousand, three hundred forty two. In addition, students who read from right to left in their native language (e.g. Arabic or Chinese) might have difficulty reading numerals correctly, perhaps reading *65* as fifty-six (Secada, 1983). So, teachers need to take special care to ensure that students who received education in other countries are clear about the manner in which numerals are written in the United States.

- *Money*: ELLs may find working with money difficult. The value of American coins cannot be assumed based on size: a dime is smaller in size than a nickel but is greater in value. In addition, the values of coins are not written on the coins in numerals so students do not have a reference for the intended values. Even English-speaking students from other countries (e.g. England, Australia, and New Zealand) may find the U.S. system of bank notes difficult. U.S. bills are all the same color and size. In many other countries, bills of different denominations have different sizes and colors so that users can easily distinguish their values.

- *Fractions*: Many ELLs come from environments that emphasize decimals over fractions. As a result, some ELLs may find fractions unfamiliar or difficult to understand.

- *Measurement*: Unlike the United States, most countries use the metric system exclusively. Consequently, some ELLs may find adapting to the U.S. customary system (of feet, pounds, quarts, etc.) difficult because the relationship between units seems to be arbitrary, compared to the regularity of a system based on powers of 10.

In other cases, ELLs may experience difficulty making sense of concepts that do not have a representation in their native language. Some cultures do not have representations for concepts studied in the U.S. mathematics curriculum including the following:

- *line*—some Native American languages (Lovett, 1980);
- *fractions*—Hmong (Kimball, 1990);
- *multiplication*—a Shona language and culture of Zimbabwe (Cleghorn, Mtetwa, Dube, & Munetsi, 1998);
- *shape, size, area*—Roma (i.e. Gypsies) (Stathopoulou & Kalabasis, 2006).

The lack of an equivalent term for a concept in the native language makes it difficult for students to translate new ideas from one language to another. Although such instances are potential stumbling blocks for ELL students, they are also opportunities for teachable moments. ELLs might share how particular problems are done in their own culture, and mainstream students can develop alternative approaches. Highlighting differences can also help students realize that mathematics is not a discipline that is done in a single way set down by the ancients.

Other challenges might be associated with the methods used to present information.

> In some countries, the native language is written from right to left or bottom to top. It is not uncommon to see responses from ELL students where English words or symbols are written accordingly. Sometimes, print or symbols are found written in a circular fashion or outer to inner rings or the reverse. (Kopriva & Saez, 1997: 18)

Students in these cases must adapt to new methods of receiving and conveying information.

Some ELLs may be accustomed to algorithms (i.e. procedures for accomplishing specific tasks) that are different from the algorithms typically taught in the U.S. mathematics curriculum. For example, three different approaches to the long division algorithm are shown in Figure 2.1.

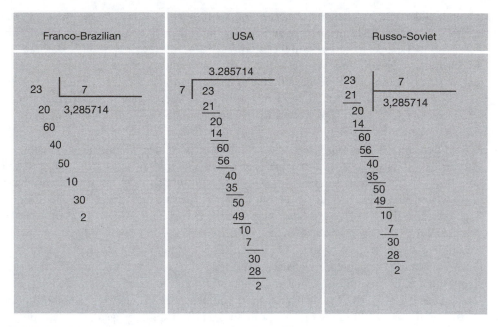

FIGURE 2.1. Division algorithm as represented by different cultures.
Reprinted with permission from Daniel Orey, Project Investigator of The Algorithm Collection Project (http://www.csus.edu/indiv/o/oreyd/ACP.htm_files/Alg.html).

It is essential that teachers do not interpret the use of alternative approaches as a lack of mathematics ability. Rather, students should be encouraged to explain or illustrate procedures they use to the teacher, and, if appropriate, to the entire class. Such sharing helps ensure that a variety of methods are valued in the classroom. Likewise, when students make errors that the teacher cannot decipher, it may be prudent to talk with the student; the student may have made a minor numerical error and be generally quite competent with the procedure. In addition, mathematics teachers in the United States often require students to show work by writing the steps for solving a problem, but in many other cultures students are encouraged to use mental mathematics. As a result, some ELLs may not be accustomed to producing written work and may find that requirement challenging.

In sum, it is important to recognize that the subject matter and its representation may provide challenges that are linked to students' prior cultural or schooling experiences. The various approaches available for teaching and learning mathematics can cause potential confusion for students, particularly during their early encounters in mathematics classrooms. Teachers and students are able to adapt to each other if various approaches are valued, shared, and made explicit.

Cultural Links to Mathematics Learning

The literature that examines culture and mathematics education focuses on two primary areas—cultural views on learning mathematics and culturally relevant teaching of mathematics. Regarding the former, several writings from the late 1980s discuss the influence of students' cultural background on their views about mathematics learning. More recently, because of the diversity of the student population, research has focused on the need to provide culturally responsive or relevant instruction to students, as discussed in Part 1. In this chapter, we highlight findings on both of these major areas.

Classroom Interactions

Several studies document a relationship between students' cultural backgrounds and their mathematical attainment. These studies suggest that students' culture not only provides a lens through which to examine their experiences with mathematics, but also provides insights about their experiences in the mathematics classroom. A student's culture affects his or her values, interpersonal communications, and interactions with the teacher and other students in the classroom. Gorgorió and Planas (2001) illustrate how a student's cultural values played a role in her classroom interactions:

> Through the interview with Ramira, we conclude that she never told her teacher that she could not understand her because that would have conflicted with her cultural pattern of behavior. According to her values, it is not good manners to tell the teacher that one cannot understand her, nor to talk with her friends while the teacher is talking. She preferred to "become lost" than to behave improperly according to her values. (p. 18)

In addition to cultural influences, an ELL's prior mathematics schooling experience may influence behaviors in the mathematics classroom. A classroom that emphasizes student-to-student discourse as envisioned by the NCTM standards may be foreign to students whose prior experiences consisted primarily of listening to the teacher and the teacher listening to them.

Learning Style Preferences

Park (1997a, b, 2002) has studied the learning styles of secondary school ELLs from various cultures, including Armenian, Chinese, Filipino, Hmong, Korean, Mexican, and Vietnamese. She found that Filipino, Hmong, Mexican, and Vietnamese students preferred group learning whereas Armenian and Korean students did not. In addition, she found that ELLs from certain groups showed higher preferences for visual learning, although to different extents, with Korean, Chinese, and Filipino students being more visual than their Anglo counterparts. Park concluded that ELLs' preferences indicate their prior educational or cultural experiences. She found that Korean, Chinese, and Anglo students had a negative preference for group learning whereas Vietnamese students showed a major preference and Filipino students showed a minor preference for group learning. Korean and Armenian students may never have experienced small-group learning or interactive learning activities because their cultures tend to focus on individualism and competitiveness. In contrast, Hmong students may prefer group learning to individualized learning because their culture tends to emphasize mutual support and assistance. Park (1997a, b) also reported that learning style preferences were correlated to the length of residence in the United States. That is, learning style preference can change if students experience success with new or alternative approaches. Similar findings have been found for other cultural groups. Reid (1987) examined the learning styles of Arabic, Spanish, Japanese, Malay, Chinese, Korean, Thai, Indonesian, and English speaking college students in the United States. She found that most ELLs preferred kinesthetic and tactile modes of learning. Other researchers (Rhodes, 1990; Swisher & Dehle, 1987; Wauters, Bruce, Black, & Hocker, 1989) found similar results when examining the learning styles of Native Americans and Alaskan Natives.

Community and Family Views of Mathematics

The importance that the community and the family place on mathematics also influences students' learning experiences by providing additional motivation (Tsang, 1988) or limiting students'

(Cocking & Chipman, 1988) and parents' (Leap, 1988; MacCorquodale, 1988) involvement with education. Hispanic women and Native Americans often have negative images of mathematics because they perceive mathematicians "as remote, sloppy, obsessive, and (no pun intended) calculating" (Cocking & Chipman, 1988: 32). Such perceptions impact the motivation for learning mathematics. Native Americans tend to view education as a reflective, visual, and holistic/global activity, so they often learn better when they work in a cooperative small-group setting (Ezeife, 2002; Reyhner, Lee, & Gabbard, 1993).

Collectively, the results from research suggest that understanding students' cultural perspectives and backgrounds might provide insights about behaviors and reactions to instructional approaches. For example, a teacher who is not familiar with Native American learning preferences and culture may not realize that an instructional style focusing on competition, reception of auditory information, and teacher-centered instruction may result in underachievement. To provide all students access and opportunities to learn, teachers need to recognize how culture influences their students' engagement with mathematics and in mathematics classrooms.

As with all research about cultural groups, it is important to recognize that research findings provide insights about the predominant preferences of a group, which may or may not be true for any particular individual member of that group. That is, we should not make assumptions about a particular student based solely on insights from learning styles research. Instead, research findings should be used as a springboard for learning more about each student in the classroom. In addition, we cannot be expected to learn about the culture of each and every group that is represented in the school community. In some communities this would be an overwhelming and daunting task. For example, over 100 different languages are spoken by students in Miami–Dade County public schools in Florida. However, it is important to learn about groups from which a large portion of the student population emanates and those who are directly under our charge.

Our goal in this section has been to raise a level of awareness that commonly used practices are not perceived the same by every group. ELLs may need some transition as they learn to function in their new environment. It is important for teachers to recognize the possible influence of learning style differences so that approaches can be incorporated to support students' preferred strategies as they learn to function in a new environment. It is also important to recognize not all ELLs have the same needs. Strategies that work for Hispanic students may not be effective for others, such as Hmong students. Further, strategies that are effective for ELLs with prior schooling experiences may be less effective with ELLs with no formal schooling experience. In addition, students' level of language proficiency and length of time in their new environment may dictate their comfort level with various instructional approaches.

Culturally Responsive Pedagogy

According to Gay (2000), culturally responsive teaching acknowledges and honors students' cultural backgrounds and ways of learning, builds links between home and school, uses a variety of instructional strategies to embrace different learning styles, and incorporates multicultural materials. To provide culturally responsive instruction, teachers need to understand how students' culture (i.e. values, beliefs, customs, social norms, and language) influences their expectations for learning, their preferred learning styles (e.g. independent vs. collaborative), and their preferred communication and problem-solving style. Children experience success in classrooms in which their language and cultural background are taken into consideration and are valued. Culturally responsive instruction has been encouraged as a means to address the needs of a diverse student population in the mathematics classroom, including ELLs (Cahnmann & Remillard, 2002; Gustein, Lipman, Hernandez, & de los Reyes, 1997).

Cahnmann and Remillard (2002) studied the issues and challenges two teachers experienced while teaching mathematics in culturally, linguistically, and socioeconomically diverse classrooms. They examined the teachers' role in providing equitable mathematical experiences to all students while providing culturally relevant instruction. Even though both teachers were deeply committed to fostering mathematics understanding in their students, they implemented the ideas of culturally relevant teaching in different ways. The teachers had different interpretations of reform ideas (i.e. standards-based practices), received different types of support and professional development in their educational communities, and had different comfort levels with and knowledge of mathematics. Although it may be beneficial if the cultural and linguistic background of the teacher is similar to that of the students, such similarity is not sufficient to ensure that the teacher is able to connect to his or her students. All mathematics teachers can learn from the available research to incorporate culturally responsive mathematics instruction that serves a diverse population.

Summary

Academic performance is influenced by many factors, including language, culture, and learning styles. As a result, it is not sufficient to focus solely on ELLs' content-area performance. Teachers need to learn about students, their experiences, and their culture, consider how these factors work collectively to mediate students' experiences in mathematics, and use that information to design their instructional programs. Teachers are encouraged to learn about cultures represented by groups of ELLs in their local setting and find ways to include information about them as part of classroom instruction. In particular, instruction should be provided that incorporates information from students' background whenever possible and honors diverse learning styles and preferences.

2.6
Assessment Results, Practices, and Procedures

Assessments are used to gather and interpret information about students' knowledge, achievement, and accomplishments in relation to meeting established educational expectations or goals. Typically, assessments are used by educational leaders and teachers to improve instructional programs. Assessments are also often used for purposes of accountability linked to rewards or sanctions for teachers, schools, or school systems. As noted earlier, ELLs take longer to develop their academic language skills than their social language skills. However, most assessments are written in academic language and use mainstream cultural contexts. Therefore, ELLs' academic accomplishments may be underestimated if they are assessed in the same way as their English speaking peers. Because assessments often inform decisions about students' placement in mathematics curricular tracks, inappropriate assessments or inappropriate interpretations of assessment results can have a lifelong impact on ELLs' opportunity to learn mathematics, particularly if they are incorrectly placed into lower-level curricular tracks. In this chapter, we examine assessment issues that influence ELLs' ability to demonstrate what they know and are able to do in mathematics.

Language Proficiency and Mathematics Achievement

Over the years, researchers have provided evidence that language influences student performance on mathematics assessments (see for example Abedi & Lord, 2001; Aiken, 1971, 1972; Bradby, 1992; Cocking and Chipman, 1988; De Corte, Verschaffel, & DeWin, 1985). Overall, research indicates a positive correlation between English proficiency and achievement in mathematics. That is, the mathematics performance of students who are in the process of learning English as a second language is lower than that of their English speaking peers.

Although language proficiency has been identified as having a strong link to students' performance, some research suggests that students' socioeconomic status (SES) might also influence student achievement (Bradby, 1992; Brown, 2005; Krashen & Brown, 2005). In particular, for Asian students, Bradby (1992) found that SES influenced achievement more than English language proficiency. Brown (2005) found that low-SES ELLs and non-ELLs performed similarly. Nevertheless, the continued achievement gap between ELLs and their non-ELL peers is an area of concern.

Researchers have also examined the influence of the assessment structure on ELLs' achievement in mathematics. Several studies suggest that standardized tests are usually based on an English speaking population and are inherently biased against ELLs (Gronna, Chin-Chance, & Abedi, 2000; Liu, Anderson, & Thurlow, 2000). For example, Gronna, Chin-Chance, and Abedi investigated the performance of a large third, fifth, and seventh grade Hawaii public school population on the Stanford Achievement Test (ninth edition) administered during the 1998–1999 school year in order to study the relationship between ELLs' achievement and their English language proficiency. They found that performance varied significantly between ELLs and English speakers. ELLs had higher achievement in mathematics than in reading. Further, ELLs tended to do better on calculation problems than word problems.

In contrast to multiple-choice items, performance items require students not only to read questions but to explain how they solved the problems in writing. These items typically require higher literacy skills, expect students to use multiple mathematics concepts and steps to find solutions, and have students express their knowledge using words. Some advantages associated with use of such items are that they measure student progress over time, provide students opportunities to show what they know and can do, and require students to use their knowledge in authentic contexts (Moya & O'Malley, 1994). However, the literacy-based or language-rich nature of performance assessments may put ELLs at a disadvantage. Research reveals that ELLs are likely to score worse on performance assessments than their non-ELL counterparts (Brown 2005). Specifically, ELLs may not be successful at solving word problems and may be challenged by the academic language used in such assessments (Abedi, 2004; Abedi & Lord, 2001; Abedi, Hofstetter, & Lord, 2004; Brenner, 1998; Kopriva & Saez, 1997; Olivares, 1996; Solano-Flores & Trumbull, 2003). In addition, the inclusion of extraneous information or distractors negatively influenced students' performance (Leon, 1994). Overall, Abedi and colleagues (e.g. Abedi, 2004; Abedi, Leon, & Mirocha, 2003) report that performance differences between ELLs and non-ELLs was greater on tests of analytical mathematics containing linguistically complex items than on tests focusing on mathematics computation. However, higher scores were reported on assessments that had word problems written in ELLs' native language (Bernardo, 2002).

Cultural Influences of Language Used in Test Items

One's culture and experiences influence how assessment items are interpreted and what responses are provided (Solano-Flores & Trumbull, 2003; Stanley & Spafford, 2002). In particular, first-hand home or community experiences may color and shape approaches used to make sense of the contexts of test items. Solano-Flores and Trumbull used item microanalysis to examine how students' linguistic, cultural, and socioeconomic backgrounds shape the ways students make sense of test items. They used this process to analyze the following lunch money item from the 1996 National Assessment of Educational Progress:

Sam can purchase his lunch at school. Each day he wants to have juice that costs $.50, a sandwich that costs $.90, and fruit that costs $.35. His mother has only $1.00 bills. What is the least number of $1.00 bills that his mother should give him so he will have enough money to buy lunch for 5 days?

The microanalysis focused on three types of item properties: formal, empirical and differential. First, they identified *formal* properties by examining the problems' linguistic features (language and words). Based on this analysis they determined that the phrase "$1.00 bill" might be problematic. Normally, students think of $1.00 as a noun or an object with which to work. In this context, however, $1.00 is an adjective that describes the type of bills with which students work, and this is an unusual language structure. The answer will not be a monetary amount; rather, it will be a number that describes the money in terms of how many dollar bills are needed. In addition, the authors determined that the use of the word *least* in the phrase "least number of $1.00 bills" to be somewhat outdated, particularly because it is not often used to modify nouns, as in this problem, but is used to modify adjectives (e.g. least expensive). Also, the first two sentences might lead students to believe that they will be provided with a dollar amount that either Sam has or his mother has given him. Further, they asserted that the last sentence is complex.

> It contains a main independent clause in the form of a question ("What is the least number") with a prepositional phrase ("of $1.00 bills") followed by the dependent clause that modifies the first clause ("so he will have enough money") followed by the infinitive phrase ("to buy lunch") with the prepositional phrase at the end ("for 5 days"). (Solano-Flores & Trumbull, 2003: 10)

Next, they identified *empirical* properties by examining student think-aloud protocols and interviews with students to determine how they made sense of the problem. They focused on problems students had reading and making appropriate interpretations from read information. Students found the words *purchase, enough, least,* and *only* problematic. Many students were not familiar with the word *purchase*, but were able to determine its meaning in context. Students found the word *enough* difficult to read. Students did not appear to understand the meaning of the word *least* in the given context. Students misinterpreted the use of the word *only* in the phrase "has only $1.00 bills." That is, they assumed that the word *only* restricted the number of dollar bills, rather than the number of dollar denominations.

Last, the researchers identified *differential* properties by "examining how observed and formal properties operate in combination with students' linguistic and cultural backgrounds to shape their interpretation of items" (Solano-Flores & Trumbull, 2003: 4). Low-income students responded differently to the items:

- They tended to misinterpret the word *only* more often than did high-income students.
- When they read the problem, they modified the story by adding phrases that did not appear in the original problem, such as "His mother has given him only one dollar" (p. 10).
- They were more likely to provide the restrictive interpretation of the word *only*.
- When asked to interpret the story, they provided responses like the following: "it's about Sam, trying to get her lunch, but her mom only has one dollar, and she needs more for five days, so I think she should give her a dollar ninety-five" (p. 10).

Overall, their findings indicate that students from different socioeconomic backgrounds tended to interpret words and test items differently. Low-income students tended to project their own experiences and concerns into the context provided by the problems. The study also reported that teachers from low-income schools found the context of the problem inappropriate for their students because many of them participated in free-lunch programs and so did not purchase lunch at school. This analysis shows that assessment items cannot separate language from cultural context or socioeconomic issues because many ELL and minority students filter information based on their lived experiences. In addition, ELLs may not be able to solve some word problems if they are unfamiliar with the cultural context of the mainstream society and cultural knowledge is taken for granted in the word problem. For instance, students in rural settings may not be familiar with contexts related to public transportation (e.g. subways) that are familiar to students in some urban settings. This research suggests teachers need to be sensitive to the experiences of their students when designing or using contextual problems.

Test Accommodations and the ELL

To determine methods for making mathematics assessments equitable, researchers have investigated the effect of various accommodations on ELLs' performance. In this case, *equity* refers to creating tests or testing situations that permit ELLs opportunities to show what they know and can do in mathematics. Specifically, *accommodations* refers to either changes in the test format or changes in the test procedures meant to remove disadvantages to ELLs based on their lower English proficiency that do not advantage those receiving the accommodations over those not receiving the accommodations. Changes in mathematics test formats include translations and adaptations of texts, for example:

- a translation of the assessment into the student's home language;
- a bilingual version of the test (items in English and in the home language);
- modifications to the linguistic complexity in the test; or
- incorporation of home language and/or English glossaries into the test. (Abedi, Courtney, and Leon, 2003: 11)

Modifications that involve students' home language assume that ELLs are literate in their native language. It is important to recognize there are many ELLs who do not read or write in their native spoken language.

Tests can also be linguistically modified or adjusted so that language does not become an impediment to understanding the nature and intent of the item. Linguistic modifications can be incorporated that do not change the complexity of the item (Abedi, 1995). Below we list approaches that were used to modify items in research (Abedi, Lord, & Plummer, 1997).

- Replace unfamiliar or infrequently used words with words that are either more familiar or are ones that students are likely to encounter frequently. Such a change recognizes that the vocabulary of students, including ELLs, at various stages differs. In other words, the vocabulary of a typical eighth grade student is likely different from that of a college educated adult.

  Original: Sally purchased a smock for $75.

  Revision: Sally paid $75 for a coat.

- Replace passive verbs with active verbs.

  Original: A sample of 85 batteries was selected for closer examination.

  Revision: He selected a sample of 85 batteries to examine.

- Reduce or limit the number of nominals (a word or group of words that function as a noun) that are used. In particular, reduce the use of complex compound phrases that include modifiers.

Original: The Company's former chief executive officer decided to . . .

Revision: Peter decided to . . .

Original: The man on the boat from Colorado purchased a book.

Revision: The man purchased a book.

- Replace or change the order of conditional clauses (e.g. if–then)

Original: If two toys in the sample were found to be broken . . .

Revision: He found two broken toys in the sample.

- Remove or recast relative clauses (i.e. a phrase that refers to and provides additional information that usually begins with words such as *who*, *which*, or *that*). The revision simplifies the sentence by taking pertinent information from the relative clause.

Original: Find the total number of books that James sold in 10 days.

Revision: How many books did James sell in 10 days?

- Revise complex question structures to simplify them.

Original: "At which of the following times"

Revison: "When . . ." (Abedi, 1995: 29)

Original: "Which is the best approximation of the number"

Revision: " Approximately how many" (Abedi & Lord, 2001: 221).

- Make abstract or impersonal presentations more concrete.

Original: "The weights of three objects were compared using a pan balance.

Two comparisons were made."

Revision: "Sandra compared the weights of three objects using a pan balance.

She made two comparisons" (Abedi, 1995: 29).

Another type of assessment accommodation focuses on changes to the test administration. That is, students take the same test, but in a different test setting or with additional supports. Methods for adjusting testing procedures include:

- allowing English language learners to have extended time to take the test on the same day;
- multiple testing sessions, small group or separate room administration, or individual administration;
- administration by a familiar test administrator;
- availability of published dictionaries or bilingual glossaries;
- simplified directions;
- repeated instructions;

- translating the directions; or
- reading the directions or questions aloud. (Abedi, Courtney, & Leon, 2003: 11–12)

These adjustments are intended to limit negative influences of language on students' ability to perform on the assessment.

Researchers have investigated the effect of using modified assessments for both ELLs and non-ELLs. The research results indicate the following:

- Both ELLs and non-ELLs benefit from test accommodations (Abedi, Lord, Hofstetter, & Baker, 2000).
- There is a high correlation between mathematics and reading scores (Brown, 2005).
- ELLs typically found the linguistically modified items (i.e. those employing simpler language and less complex language structures) easier to comprehend (Abedi & Lord, 2001).
- ELLs who took a modified version of a test performed better and achieved higher test scores than those who took an original version (Abedi & Lord, 2001; Abedi, Lord, Hofstetter & Baker, 2000; Kiplinger, Haug, & Abedi, 2000).
- The percentage improvement on the modified assessment was higher for ELLs than for non-ELLs (Abedi & Lord, 2001).
- ELLs' performance on mathematics tests with a high number of word problems was strongly related to their reading abilities in English (Kiplinger, Haug, & Abedi, 2000).
- The performance of ELLs and non-ELLs improved when they were permitted to use a glossary that explained unfamiliar or difficult words and were given extra time (Abedi, Lord, Hofstetter, & Baker, 2000).
- The higher the level of linguistic complexity in a test item, the higher was the performance gap between ELLs and non-ELLs (Abedi & Hejri, 2004).

Collectively, these findings suggest that it may be important to provide ELLs with test accommodations, particularly in high-stakes settings, in order to gain an enhanced understanding of their mathematical knowledge and ability. It is not sufficient simply to require ELLs to take the tests administered to their English-proficient peers in the same set of circumstances. Accommodations acknowledge the developmental level of ELLs and recognize that language may hinder their ability to demonstrate mathematics knowledge and competence.

Summary

This chapter discussed the need to use assessment practices that are equitable for ELL students. It is not just language that poses difficulties on assessment tasks. Often, cultural referents contain implied assumptions that must be understood in order to make sense of the mathematics embedded in the task. Research findings suggest that providing test accommodations can be an effective means to provide ELLs opportunities to show what they know and are able to do.

2.7
Recommendations for Improving the Mathematics Preparation of English Language Learners

The chapters in Part 2 thus far have included discussions about influences on ELLs' mathematical experiences and found that their achievement and performance are dependent on a variety of premises woven into the dynamics of classroom interactions. Many of the studies suggest that the underachievement in mathematics of ELLs should not be attributed solely to their lack of language proficiency, in isolation from classroom practices that are shaped by a wide spectrum of psychological, pedagogical, social, cultural, economical, and political factors. Factors that influence ELLs' experiences in the mathematics classroom include the adjustment period in the new school, community, and social environment (which could be very different with respect to their native culture), as well as teaching and assessment methods. Further, teachers' awareness of issues related to ELLs, teachers' expectations, and their curriculum, instruction, and assessment practices all play a role in the mathematics education of ELLs. Several recommendations have been made to support the mathematical education of ELLs based on research findings. These are provided in the sections that follow.

Curriculum and Instruction

Despite the fact that mathematics is often referred to as a "universal language," this language (specific content-area vocabulary, symbols, and syntax) and how it is interpreted must be clarified and made explicit in a mathematics classroom. That is, the meaning inherent in mathematics and its symbols are developed through communication. Additionally, there is a need to recognize that the approaches used for teaching and learning mathematics differ among countries and cultures. For example, recent reports of international assessments reveal that there is variation in mathematics instruction and expectations for students in different countries (Gonzales et al., 2004). Although international assessments tell us that teachers in the academically advanced countries lead students to invent, reason, and think, this is not always observed in U.S. classrooms, particularly in classes that include ELLs. The improvement of ELLs' mathematical understanding depends on the abilities of teachers, teacher educators, curriculum developers, and policymakers to implement the instructional strategies recommended for ELLs.

Researchers interested in the mathematics achievement of ELLs have provided some suggestions for improving instruction for them. For example, Cahnmann and Hornberger (2000) recommend three ways to address language while teaching mathematics: "1) clarify mathematics/ language objectives; 2) focus on process over product; and 3) contextualize instruction in ways that recognize students' language, culture, and worldview" (p. 45). This suggests a need to create an environment in the mathematics classroom in which students discuss questions and work in supportive groups to solve problems. This type of environment would provide ELLs opportunities to grapple with vocabulary they need to learn while also dealing with challenging mathematics. In a similar vein, Secada and de la Cruz (1996) suggest that teachers can promote a thorough understanding of mathematics when guided by the following principles: (a) the choice of the mathematical concepts taught should be determined by taking into account students' interests and abilities; (b) teachers should use frequent assessment to encourage the development of conceptual understanding, in addition to the development of procedural or computational skills; (c) instructions should be based on students' educational, cultural, and linguistic backgrounds; and (d) the mathematical terminology should be embedded within the context.

There are other recommendations for instruction that can be drawn from research to enhance the mathematical experiences of ELLs. For example, teachers should use a language-based approach to the teaching of mathematics. That is, teachers should place an emphasis on helping students understand mathematics vocabulary, symbols, and syntax that are important when studying various concepts. This approach would help students with the transition needed for problem solving by explaining linguistic items through visuals, manipulatives, graphic organizers, and other methods of communication.

Recent research illuminates the positive effect of the implementation of a culturally relevant curriculum and instruction in mathematics. Cahnmann and Remillard (2002) suggest innovative ideas for teachers to incorporate word problems and activities that relate ELL students' experiences and their families' "funds of knowledge." For example, students may ask their parents for help writing their own mathematics word problems. As another idea, journal writing in mathematics can be used as a technique for ELLs to share experiences and, at the same time, develop better writing skills in English using mathematics subject-specific terminology. Thus, ELL students might learn to verbalize better what they know and to explain their solutions. They may also begin to enjoy mathematics more and appreciate its relevance to their lives.

It is essential that ELLs be presented with challenging mathematics, as recommended in the NCTM (2000) standards. That is, ELLs should be exposed to the full range of mathematics topics and courses provided by the secondary school mathematics curriculum. As part of classroom instruction, ELLs should experience the full range of practices recommended for teaching and learning mathematics. Key to this is the NCTM communcation standard, which plays an important role in every aspect of the mathematics classroom. Although the presence of ELLs might alter the dynamics of the classroom and ELLs may require additional support and strategies, their presence should not result in the use of a "watered-down" curriculum that limits what mathematics they learn and how they learn it. The goal for instruction should be to determine approaches that help ELLs develop a robust understanding of the content. To achieve this goal, teachers, as professionals, must seek and implement appropriate instructional strategies that recognize and acknowledge the mathematical understanding that these students possess, engage them in all classroom activities, and provide them opportunities to learn important and challenging mathematics.

Assessment Practices

Another area in need of improvement is the assessment practices applied in mathematics education. In its *Assessment Standards for School Mathematics* (1995), NCTM, in accordance with its vision that "all students are capable of learning mathematics" (p. 1), recommends the use of assessment strategies that reflect ELLs' development in mathematics as well as students' proficiency in English. Although quizzes and tests that measure students' procedural fluency in mathematics are still appropriate, alternative assessments may enable teachers to better evaluate the understanding of mathematical concepts that individual students possess, independent of proficiency in the language of instruction. In addition, teachers will gain tools with which to expand their understanding of students' learning processes and thus become able to help them improve.

It is crucial that assessment developers and teachers adjust assessment methods to accommodate potential language deficiencies that students may have. Making such accommodations has the potential not only to assist ELLs, but to be helpful for English speakers with limited reading abilities as well. For example, students at different levels of proficiency could be asked to illustrate through the use of pictures or diagrams what they understand about particular topics. They can also be asked to create word problems using a combination of words and pictures or to compose a journal describing approaches for solving a mathematics problem. In addition, such alternatives would give ELLs opportunities to use learned mathematics vocabulary. That is, assessments can be designed to allow students to reveal their level of understanding based on their ability to communicate what they know about particular mathematics concepts. Another strategy would be to improve students' use of mathematical terminology by posing essay-type questions on exams. This would provide additional opportunities for students to share what they understand about mathematics topics.

Teacher Education and Professional Development

It is pertinent that those upon whom reform relies see the importance of improving teachers' understanding of ELLs in order to provide effective instruction to students from diverse backgrounds. The education of pre- and in-service teachers should provide them with the knowledge to reach *all* students and improve instructional practices so "that all students have the opportunity to develop their mathematical potential, regardless of a lack of proficiency in the language of instruction" (NCTM, 1989: 142). However, research findings indicate that there is reason for concern regarding the preparation of preservice and in-service mathematics teachers to effectively teach ELLs (Meskill, 2005; Watson, Miller, Driver, Rutledge, & McAllister, 2005). This suggests that teachers could benefit from programs developed to help them learn methods that provide greater access to ELLs' reasoning and conceptual understanding processes when they are learning mathematics while simultaneously acquiring English as a second language. Additionally, teacher preparation and in-service professional development programs should ensure that teachers are able to "move beyond the comforts of their own experiences" and learn "about mathematics and cultural issues that complement one another" (Cahnmann & Remillard, 2002: 201). Generic programs for all teachers may not be appropriate given the specialized nature of mathematics, its words, and its symbols. Reyhner, Lee, and Gabbard (1993) also argue that "there is not one type of training needed for all teachers, but rather a need for culturally appropriate approaches for different groups" (p. 26). They further suggest that, "wherever a specific ethnic minority is concentrated (whether that minority be Native, Black, Hispanic, or Asian), nearby teacher education programs need to give extra attention to the culture and needs of that group" (p. 32). The current reform effort demands "that reasonable and appropriate accommodations be made as needed to promote access and attainment for all students" (NCTM, 2000: 12). But in order for teachers to be able to provide such reasonable and appropriate accommodations, they need to possess not only vast mathematical knowledge, but also an understanding of findings from anthropology, sociology, and history. Thus, it is crucial that scholars from different domains collaborate and add to the knowledge base that can provide educational communities with tools for successful reform.

Summary

Kersaint (2007) encouraged teachers to use active engagement to support students' learning. Similar practices are being advocated here. Teachers are encouraged to maintain awareness of issues related to ELLs, changes in mathematics education, and changes in school and school district policies that may affect them. Further, teachers are encouraged to share information and address issues that may impede or limit students' access to opportunities to learn mathematics. It is our professional obligation to find ways to address the needs of all students in our classrooms. We do not select our students and we cannot change them. Rather, we have to consider the influence of our own practices and change these practices if they do not adequately meet students' needs. In Part 3, we share instructional practices that may be used to realize the vision for teaching ELLs in ways that are accessible and that build on findings from research.

Part 3
Best Practices to Support English Language Learners in the Mathematics Classroom

3.1
Overview
Classroom Environments that Support English Language Learners

The research evidence in Part 2 presents clear evidence that teachers play a significant role in the creation of learning environments that influence the experiences and engagement of English language learners (ELLs) in mathematics. What can you do to help facilitate their transition to their new environment and help them build the vocabulary needed to communicate basic needs and begin the process of learning mathematics? In addition to teaching mathematics, you will have to teach these students to function in your learning environment. When making choices about instructional approaches and activities, emphasis should be placed on methods tailored to meet students' needs, including direct instruction, guided discovery, cooperative learning, and technology-assisted learning (August & Pease-Alvarez, 1996). Which methods are selected depends on lesson goals and objectives, learner characteristics, English language proficiency, and available resources. Teachers modify instruction to support student learning no matter what type of instruction is provided. However, teaching mathematics to ELLs is not just "good teaching." It is "good" and "strategic" teaching that acknowledges and takes into account the specific needs of ELLs by incorporating strategies that directly address those needs. For example, orchestrating classroom discourse in classes with ELLs requires more than knowledge of mathematics and the language of mathematics; it demands the creation of learning environments that support and promote language development as well as conceptual development. That is, teachers must attend not only to ELLs' cognitive development, but also to the linguistic demands of mathematics language presented in oral and written discourse.

The National Council of Teachers of Mathematics (NCTM) (2000) identifies problem solving as central to the mathematics endeavor. Because of this, it is generally accepted that focusing solely on mastery of basic computational skills prior to exposing students to challenging mathematics topics is not the best approach to mathematics instruction because it limits the quality of students' mathematics experiences. Teachers are encouraged to engage all students, including ELLs, in mathematics tasks and activities that require them to use critical thinking and problem-solving strategies. Mathematics teachers pose questions and design (or select) tasks that engage students in thinking and that require them to clarify understandings and justify their reasoning. Such learning environments inherently have a focus on language because students are required to describe, explain, hypothesize, clarify, elaborate, and share findings. Clearly, students will need language to express their thoughts and points of confusions, as well as to debate areas of disagreement and communicate what they know. In general, communication and authentic discourse occurs within the context of mathematical problem solving or inquiry.

With the increased emphasis placed on problem solving, command of mathematical language plays an important role in the development of mathematical ability. The language demands in such classrooms are significant, yet they provide important experiences for ELLs. By combining mathematics and language instruction, ELLs are afforded opportunities to build their mathematics understanding while concurrently improving their ability to learn English. In fact, such environments allow ELLs to engage the entire spectrum of literacy skills (e.g. listening, speaking, reading, and writing) (Thompson, Kersaint, Richards, Hunsader, & Rubenstein, 2008).

In the chapters that follow, we provide strategies that may be used to support ELLs as they transition to mathematics classrooms that focus on communication and problem solving. As mentioned in Part 1, different communities have to address different types of needs given the type of ELL population that they serve (e.g. ELLs who speak the same language versus ELLs with a variety of linguistic backgrounds). The chapters in Part 3 provide strategies that mathematics teachers can use to interact with and instruct ELLs so that they are provided access to a high-quality mathematics education. Chapter 3.2 provides strategies teachers can use to ensure that the information provided in the classroom is comprehensible to students. In particular, it highlights ways to orchestrate classroom discourse to support student learning. Chapter 3.3 offers strategies for explicitly teaching the language of mathematics. Chapter 3.4 discusses the importance of engaging ELLs in solving problems and provides strategies to support and encourage success as ELLs engage in problem solving. Chapter 3.5 describes methods for providing assessment accommodations for ELLs. Chapter 3.6 discusses strategies for culturally relevant instruction. Finally, Chapter 3.7 discusses special issues that relate to teachers of mathematics who are themselves English language learners.

Middle school and high school teachers may have at least two different preps on a daily basis. If they have several ELLs in their classroom, perhaps speaking different languages, it is not reasonable to expect that they can develop separate lesson plans for these students on a daily basis. Rather, they need to develop instructional strategies that are sensitive to helping all ELLs comprehend classroom communication and internalize mathematics language. The strategies presented in the chapters that follow are intended to be used in conjunction with currently used instructional approaches. They highlight ways that teachers can provide accommodations for ELLs and scaffold instruction to ensure that all students are provided equitable access and opportunities to learn mathematics.

3.2
Orchestrating Classroom Discourse to Support Mathematics Concept and Language Development

The role of language is ubiquitous. It is the medium by which teachers introduce and convey concepts and procedures, through which text and problems are read and solved, by which mathematics achievement is measured. Language skills—particularly reading skills are required to understand and follow an instructor's representation of a problem's solution—are vehicles through which students learn and apply math concepts and skills.

(Crandall, Dale, Rhodes, & Spanos, 1985: 130)

Teachers must orchestrate classroom discourse in ways that ensure English language learners (ELLs) have access to discussions, including whole-class and small-group interactions. Like others (Goldenberg, 1991; Waxman & Tellez, 2002), we advocate the use of instructional conversation or conversational language to facilitate classroom discourse because it encourages student participation. Unlike a typical lecture, instructional conversations are conversational in nature; that is, they appear to be natural and spontaneous rather than a scripted "lecture" to be delivered. These conversations leave students with the impression that they are participating in a discussion as they would in a social environment. However, the discussion focuses on mathematics, key concepts, and related topics. Teachers must facilitate these conversations in ways that lead students to greater and deeper understanding of mathematics. Instructional conversations allow students to appreciate and build upon each others' experiences, knowledge, and understandings. While engaged in instructional conversations, the teacher and students are actively engaged in hermeneutic listening (Davis, 1994; 1996), listening that focuses on the intent of the speaker and not on the assumption of the speaker's intent made by the hearer. The listener does not anticipate or make assumptions about what is being said. Instead, instructional conversations require each party to be responsive to the other by paying close attention to what is said, building upon or extending presented ideas, and challenging areas of disagreement. In sum, both the teacher and students are required to present ideas and respond to presented ideas.

To facilitate discourse when ELLs are present, teachers can make the language of mathematics more comprehensible to ELLs by modifying the ways in which they speak and interact with students. Below we present several strategies you can use to modify classroom conversation as you engage ELLs in instructional conversations.

Speak and Enunciate Clearly to Make Language Comprehensible

There are many differences in how individuals pronounce words or use words in combinations; individuals also speak at different speeds. When ELLs are part of the instructional setting, it is important to ensure that they are given every opportunity to make sense of presented information. This might require adjusting the way in which we speak to allow ELLs to process information. Remember, ELLs are interpreting and learning information based on what they hear during classroom discourse. When ELLs are unfamiliar with vocabulary, they might not recognize whether differences in pronunciations represent different accents or two different words with different meanings. To illustrate this, consider the following conversation between a teacher and an ELL.

Ms. Jones:	How else can we say divide? [She calls on an ELL.]
Pilar:	Guzinta is divide.
Ms. Jones:	[confused by this statement] Is that how you say divide in your home language?
Pilar:	[with a perplexed expression] No, in English? You say "7 guzinta 28 four times," so guzinta is divide. No?

It was at that moment that Ms. Jones realized that the ELL heard "guzinta" when she had said *goes into* quickly. Apparently, she had said this phrase often enough that the ELL associated the word she thought she heard, "guzinta," with *divide*. To aid the student's understanding, the teacher then wrote on the board: "7 goes into 28 four times," clarifying that she had meant to say *goes into*. The ELL could then learn the intended phrase, even though what she heard sounded different.

In addition to the pronunciation of words encountered as part of mathematics discourse, ELLs may have difficulty pronouncing written text, including both words and symbols. In English, the correct pronunciation of some words may not be readily obvious and, at times, may not be strictly discernable from the way they are spelled (e.g. *Pythagorean*; *arithmetic* as pronounced for computation versus in describing a sequence). Symbols, even simple ones such as $\leq$, need to be pronounced for students (*is less than or equal to*). To help students make the connection between words and symbols and their pronunciations, teachers can write potentially difficult words on the board when they are used as part of oral discourse; in fact, mathematics words, even simple ones, should be written to help ELLs, particularly those at levels 1 and 2 (preproduction and early production). In addition, all students can be taught how to articulate words in order to facilitate their ability to speak mathematically. For example, a teacher can ask students to pronounce new words they encounter (e.g. "Let me hear you say 'per-pen-di-cu-lar'."). In addition to accepting a choral response, the teacher can ask individual students, not just ELLs, to say the word. It is important that all students recognize the value being placed on speaking mathematically.

Simplify and Elaborate Language

As part of orchestrating mathematics lessons, teachers should take care to teach the language of mathematics explicitly. Lack of redundancy in mathematics discourse has been identified as a major cause of difficulty for ELLs, so it is important that teachers find ways to restate presented information so that ELLs are provided ample opportunities to make sense of what they read or hear. Richard-Amato and Snow (1992) recommend that teachers use simplification, expansions of ideas, direct definitions, and comparisons to build in redundancy. They illustrated the use of these approaches as part of a lesson on sales tax and discount:

Simplification: "She will receive a *discount*. She will pay less for the dress."

Expansion of ideas: "She will receive a discount. The dress will cost less than the original price. She will save money because she will not pay the full price for the dress."

Direct definition: "She received a discount. The discount is the amount taken from the original price." (p. 151)

Comparisons can be made by connecting ideas to familiar notions (e.g. "a discount is like paying for something that is 'on sale'.") Using this approach the teacher does not limit the vocabulary that students experience by always using simpler terms. Rather, students are provided opportunities to learn rich vocabulary as they connect ideas that allow them to improve their academic skills in the new language. Language simplification, elaboration, and paraphrasing provide ELLs a variety of entry points to understanding of discussions and access to the mathematics inherent in tasks while they maintain the essence of the original context and problem. Although learning tasks for ELLs can be adjusted in terms of linguistic complexity, the mathematics should not be made simpler than it is for other students. Without compromising the mathematical integrity of the item, avoid unnecessary linguistic complexity and provide definitions of non-mathematics terms (Abedi, Hofstetter, Baker, & Lord, 1998).

Express Information in Multiple Ways

Teachers need to be cognizant of the multiple ways in which we express information, both formally and informally. Consider, for example, the various ways in which we can verbalize the algebraic expression $n - 3$. ELLs may not recognize a particular instance of its verbalization (e.g. "the difference of n and 3") and we as teachers may conclude that they lack mathematical understanding. However, the ELLs might have fully understood if a different interpretation had been used (e.g. "n take away 3"). To ensure that ELLs have access to learning opportunities, it is important to say and write information in multiple ways to allow students to make connections between new and familiar phrases, thereby expanding their language skills. As part of instructional conversations, teachers can invite students to share other ways of stating the same information (e.g. "What's another way to say that?"). Both English speaking students and ELLs can be encouraged to provide suggestions. Depending on the ELLs' English proficiency, it might be appropriate in some circumstances to provide an opportunity for ELLs to share their ideas first so that they are permitted to use their limited language skills, ensuring participation. Other students can then build upon or expand their suggestions.

Use Controlled Vocabulary

Mathematics teachers can reinforce vocabulary development by purposefully selecting a few words to emphasize during a particular class session and finding multiple and varied ways to help students understand those words. Limiting the number of words introduced during a class session provides time for ELLs to grapple with and make sense of the selected words without being overloaded with a lot of new words. During a lesson, teachers can find many ways to revisit a learned word. As part of whole-class and teacher-to-student discussions, a teacher can use prompts to connect students' understanding to the intended word (e.g. "We used that word earlier; would someone remind us of what it means?" or "Please use the word we learned earlier in that sentence."). The goal is to maximize every opportunity to help students connect a few essential words with their intended meaning. ELLs improve their receptive vocabulary as they hear words multiple times. They expand their expressive vocabulary as they are provided opportunities to use the words. Murray (2004) notes that students need to use a new word at least 30 times in order to own it. Therefore we need to incorporate methods that allow students to hear, say, and use mathematics vocabulary if they are to engage in mathematics communication.

Limit the Use of Pronouns and Adjectives

In everyday language, pronouns and adjectives are often used to vary language patterns and add insight and interest. However in mathematics, the use of pronouns and adjectives may be challenging to ELLs, particularly when the referent is unclear. Imagine viewing the image in Figure 3.1 on a board, when a teacher says "They are corresponding angles." Would it be possible to determine what was being referred to without clarification?

Of course, mathematics teachers would label the angles and refer to the angles using their labels. However, this illustration shows the importance of being able to discern the referent. When ELLs are members of the class, it is important to recognize that the use of pronouns or adjectives might make it difficult for them to make sense of the conversation. Although speech that limits the use of pronouns and adjectives may appear to be stylistically uninteresting, it provides a level of clarity that allows ELLs access to mathematical understandings. Being careful with our use of pronouns is similar to the care we would use if we had a visually impaired student in our class who had to understand our instruction through the visual images created through our words; we would limit our use of *this* and *here* with such students. The same needs to be true when we have ELL students.

Limit the Use of and Explain Idiomatic Expressions or Culturally Based Terms

Many idiomatic expressions that are commonly used may be unfamiliar to ELLs and other culturally or experientially diverse students. Many of the phrases used in everyday language are grounded in cultural experiences. In the classroom, no assumptions should be made about what is "taken-as-shared." Even within the United States, there are regional differences related to communication and experience that require "negotiation of meaning." As a result, it is important to

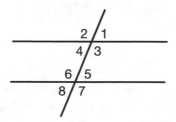

FIGURE 3.1. Parallel lines.

clarify phrases that may be unfamiliar to the intended audience because of cultural, economical, or experiential diversity. Consider the examples below:

Example 1

> Mr. Jones wants to purchase sod for his lawn. Sod is sold in pallets that cover 400 square feet. Each pallet costs $129.99. How many pallets would he need to cover his lawn that is 20 yards × 20 yards? How much would he pay for the sod?

Example 2

> The State Youth Fair features giant statues of comic strip characters. The ratio of the character's height to the statue's height is approximately 1 to 4. If the height of the statue is 96 feet, what is the approximate height of the character?

Related to example 1, students, including ELLs, who live in a densely populated urban environment may not have any experience with sod or may not even know what it is. As a result they may have difficulty understanding the intent of the problem, making it difficult for them to determine what mathematics is needed to solve the problem. ELLs, in particular, may not understand the meaning of the words *pallet* and *cover*. Although some ELLs might be familiar with the social use of the word *cover*, they might be challenged with its use in this context because of their lack of familiarity with other words used in the problem.

The second example also makes assumptions about common life experiences. For example, a student from another country may not be familiar with events such as state youth fairs or with literary forms such as the comic strip. Although it is possible to solve the problem without this information, the context humanizes the mathematics, exposes students to other information that will help them relate to their new cultural environment, and provides motivation for solving the problem. To avoid such challenges, a teacher might attempt to sanitize mathematics so that it is devoid of real-life experiences or contexts. Although such action will place the focus on the mathematics concepts or skills to be learned, it will also diminish students' interest and not allow them to see how mathematics might be used or its usefulness. Instead, in both of these cases a teacher can simply explain the meaning of the words by providing examples so that students can connect the words with their intended meaning.

Limit "Asides" or Conversations that Are Not Linked to the Lesson at Hand

ELLs may have difficulty distinguishing between the pertinent components of the lesson and conversations that are unrelated to the topic being discussed. As teachers, we recognize that it is not difficult for a lesson to move in a direction other than intended as students engage in classroom discourse. Although typically acceptable, these "side conversations" may be distracting or even confusing to ELLs as they attempt to connect ideas. When the class is engaged in "side conversations," it is important that ELLs recognize them as such. A direct approach is to make a point of clarifying the intent of these conversations when ELLs are present.

Pause Frequently and Increase Wait Time

ELLs require additional time to process information in their new language. ELLs must listen to information in English, translate it into their native language to make sense of it, and possibly determine an appropriate response, and then must consider how to communicate that response in English. Clearly, each stage of this process requires some time. It is important to embed time for ELLs to process information, reflect on presented information, and grapple with mathematics ideas. So, it is important to increase the amount of wait time based on the language proficiency of ELLs; more wait time is likely needed for level 1 students than for level 3 students (see Part 1).

Use Drawings and Illustrations to Support Communication

During classroom discussions, we can assist ELLs by drawing diagrams and other illustrations to help them make sense of information they hear. Although teachers can find and use actual images (the internet is an excellent source for these), illustrations used to support classroom discourse need not be sophisticated. Consider the images used to distinguish the men's and women's bathrooms in public places. Illustrations to support conversations only need to be clear enough for a nonnative speaker to understand their intent. ELLs, particularly those at the early stages of their language development, can also be encouraged to illustrate their mathematics knowledge using pictures. For example, they can illustrate the method they use to solve problems using a combination of words, pictures, and symbols. These visual aids provide students a means to participate in classroom discourse and demonstrate knowledge on classroom assessments. In addition, they provide us a means for assessing what they know. Using and allowing students to use visuals to support communication sends the message that all students and their contributions are valued and encourages student engagement in learning activities. An extension of this idea is to write key terms, phrases, and concepts on the board so that students can visualize words they hear to expand their written, as well as verbal, literacy.

In addition, teachers can use illustrations to help students connect pieces of information that are presented. Because ELLs may not understand the language that we use to connect ideas, other forms of communicating connections may be necessary. As one teacher noted, "Arrows become your friend" (R. Peregoy, personal communication, September 2007). Arrows can be drawn from a word to a picture to a symbol to help students in early stages of language development (i.e. preproduction and early production). The diagram in Figure 3.2 is meant to help students think about evaluating the expression $4n + 5$ for multiple values of n. Does the diagram make clear what it means to evaluate $4n + 5$?

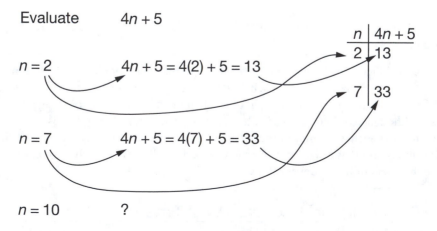

FIGURE 3.2. Use arrows to connect ideas and language.

Use Dramatic Gestures, Actions, and Verbal Intonations

ELLs require cues to make sense of information that they hear. As mentioned earlier, visual representations are one means for providing such cues. However teachers can provide cues by the way they interact with students during instruction. Monotone communication styles do not allow students, particularly ELLs, to understand what is important to note or understand. Teachers can use intonations (voice quality) to engage students and to help them differentiate between types of information provided. However, it is not necessary, and is generally counterproductive, to talk in a louder voice. ELLs can hear; they just may not know the meaning of the English words being used in instruction.

In addition, gestures (e.g. hand motions) can be used to help students relate to words. For example, consider how you might illustrate the concepts *greater than* (>) and *less than* (<) using hand and arm motions. The aim here is to use a variety of nonverbal as well as verbal means to communicate with ELLs.

Engage ELLs in Classroom Discourse

While orchestrating classroom discussions, teachers must engage and incorporate ELLs and their knowledge in all learning activities. We should invite ELLs to participate by asking them to contribute to the conversations. This helps ELLs recognize that they are valued and included as part of the learning community. However, it is not appropriate to force ELLs to speak in a whole-class setting if they are not ready. Linguistically, level 1 (preproduction) students in our class may be in the silent period and so are really only absorbing all the linguistic input; they do not have the facility to express themselves whether the teacher wants them to or not. Other students might be disillusioned by their new cultural experiences and as a result not want to talk. To make good judgments about how to engage students, teachers must be mindful of learner characteristics and the stages of language acquisition (preproduction, early production, speech emergence, and intermediate fluency) discussed in Part 1. In addition, teachers must recognize that the expectation to speak as part of a mathematics class might be foreign to students from different cultural backgrounds. Because of this, it will be important to help students understand classroom expectations and norms related to talking as part of mathematics class, as well as the need to explain and justify their thinking.

Initially, teachers can engage ELLs in individualized conversations (e.g. student–teacher, student–student) to provide opportunities for ELLs to take risks on a small scale and build confidence prior to asking them to share their ideas with the whole class. Teachers can make statements like "Tell a partner what you think the answer is and why." This would provide every child, including ELLs, an opportunity to participate, not just those who raise their hands. As a teacher listens to students' statements and responses, she may provide additional encouragement to individual students by making statements such as "That is an excellent explanation. Would you be willing to share your strategy with the class?" In addition, during these private conversations, teachers can prepare ELLs for success by correcting their attempts at communication (e.g. "You said . . . but I think you meant to say . . ." and "Can you say that again using this word?") prior to asking that they share information with the class.

To facilitate participation, ELLs should be permitted to use a variety of options for communication. Depending on their level of English proficiency, some students may opt to use their second language, English, as a means of communicating. In such cases, teachers can use *revoicing*, a technique in which the teacher repeats what a student says with elaboration (Coggins, Kravin, Coates, & Carroll, 2007). This helps students make connections and develop a deeper understanding of the terms. For instance,

Kashif: Parallelogram has four sides and sides parallel.

Ms. Smith: Right. A parallelogram is a quadrilateral, meaning it has four sides and opposite sides are parallel (pointing to the opposite sides). So there are two pairs of parallel sides (pointing to the pair of parallel sides).

In revoicing the ELL's statement, the teacher validates the student's response, provides additional information to clarify the intended message, and allows the ELL to hear an appropriate means for conveying the intended message. To clarify communication, the teacher points to the figure as she speaks to ensure that students connect the concept of four sides to the term *quadrilateral* and to show that it is the opposite sides that are parallel.

In the example below, the teacher recognizes the need for students to see and hear a word multiple times for it to "click." She therefore builds redundancy into their language instruction as she elaborates a student's response.

Hassan: Do same to both sides of equation.

Ms. Smith: Right. When we solve an equation, we have to use the same operations on both sides. So we have to add the same expression to both sides, or multiply both sides by the same amount.

In her revoicing, the teacher expanded the meaning of the student's statement, "Do same to both sides of equation," to explain the process for solving equations.

As indicated in Chapter 2.4 on discourse, redundancy and revoicing are essential ingredients of classroom instruction because they give ELL students multiple opportunities to engage with the concepts. We need to recognize that redundancy and revoicing are also important for building vocabulary knowledge so that students broaden their limited descriptions of a term, as indicated by the ELL student's definition, to be able to include important characteristics and features of the term.

In contrast, an ELL might find it easier if he or she were permitted to supply the answer in his or her native language. This would allow the student to address the cognitive complexity of the task without the interference of language. To support the student, teachers might try to follow the student's reasoning based on what he or she writes or by asking another student to translate, if possible. (That is, teachers engage in the same practice that ELLs are expected to use.) When teachers encourage students to use their own language to communicate with each other or with the class, they demonstrate that they value the students' backgrounds, abilities, and identities (Gutierrez, 2002). This type of classroom interaction is possible in classroom environments in which different languages and variations in language proficiency are accepted as part of the discourse community.

Below are several strategies to ensure that ELLs have equitable access to classroom participation:

- *Numbered heads*—When students are working in a cooperative group setting, each student is assigned a number (e.g. 1 through 4). A problem or question is presented. The group discusses the problem or question for a set amount of time. During the whole-class discussion segment of the lesson, the teacher calls on students to speak by randomly selecting a number, using a spinner or other method for randomization. This process ensures that all students have an equally likely chance of being selected. This also lets students know that everyone is expected to contribute, not just a select few (Kagan, 1994).

- *Talking chips*—Each member of the discourse community receives the same number of chips, or comparable items. Each time a member wishes to speak, he or she places the chip on the center table (or other specified location). Once an individual uses all of his or her chips, that individual is no longer permitted to speak. The discussion proceeds until all the members have exhausted all of their chips. This allows students to regulate their contributions by determining when they want to contribute and recognize that they cannot dominate the conversation (Kagan, 1994).
- *Response sticks*—Each student's name is placed on a popsicle stick or tongue depressor. When asking questions, the teacher selects the student to speak by randomly pulling one of the sticks. The stick can then be returned or placed to the side to ensure that the student is not called again.
- *Thumbs up/thumbs down*—The teacher poses a question or a problem that can be answered yes or no. At the teacher's signal the entire class responds by showing thumbs up or down. This allows the teacher to obtain feedback from all students by viewing their responses simultaneously and privately.

As a transitional step to using these strategies, students can be forewarned about the types of questions that might be asked so that they are provided time to prepare and rehearse possible responses, particularly in cases where students will be called upon randomly. This would give ELLs time to consider and rehearse how they might respond to intended questions.

Regardless of the methods used, the teacher controls the pace, direction, and topic of the discourse and also determines who gets to talk, to whom, and for how long. During these instructional conversations, teachers may vary question prompts in ways that take into account ELLs' mathematics backgrounds and language proficiency. Table 3.1 provides a list of sample prompts that may be used with ELLs at various stages of language development in the mathematics classroom.

TABLE 3.1. Questions to engage ELLs at various stages of language development

Preproduction (level 1)	Early production (level 2)
Point to the _____	Can you describe _____?
Is the answer positive or negative?	How are _____ and _____ different?
What is this called?	What do you think comes next?
Which one is larger/smaller?	What can you tell me about _____?
Show me an example of a(n) _____	Where would you place this on the chart?
Do you agree or disagree?	What is the problem about?
	Distinguish between _____ and _____ .
	Do you agree with what _____ said? Why?

Speech emergence (level 3)	Intermediate fluency (level 4)
What did you try?	What do you think will happen when _____?
Explain that in your own words.	Why is this true?
What do you know about this part?	Show and explain how you solved this problem.
How did you classify _____?	What would you change in order to _____?
Provide a definition for or an example of	Why did _____ changes occur?
_____.	Compare your approach with the one _____
How was this similar to what we have done	presented.
before?	What changes would you recommend?
Why does that make sense?	How did you reach that conclusion?

Overall the goal is to engage ELLs in every aspect of the mathematics discourse by providing multiple and varied opportunities to listen to, speak, read, and write mathematics. However, it is important that teachers do not confuse a student's fluency in conversational or social language with other aspects of communication (Valdez-Pierce, 2003). As mentioned earlier in this book, ELLs will develop their basic interpersonal communication skills (BICS; i.e. conversational language) before they develop the cognitive academic language proficiency (CALP) that is needed to be successful in academic environments.

When our instruction moves from the use of concrete tools (i.e. manipulatives, or real objects) to pictures to more abstract discussion of concepts, we are sequencing instruction so that we begin in Cummins' Quadrant I and end in Cummins' Quadrant IV (Cummins, 1992) (see Part 1).

Summary

In this chapter, we have recommended specific techniques for teachers to use as they orchestrate discourse in a classroom with ELLs. In order for ELLs to develop facility with language, both English and the language of mathematics, they need to participate in a language-rich classroom environment. The recommendations provided in this chapter can help teachers engage in discourse in ways that can support ELLs' ability to participate as full members of the class community.

3.3
Strategies to Help English Language Learners Understand Mathematics Language

As indicated in Chapter 2.3, the language of mathematics contains many challenges embedded within it in terms of vocabulary, symbols, syntax, and semantic structure. These issues of language are often challenges for all mathematics students, and even more so for English language learners. In fact, Thompson, Kersaint, Richards, Hunsader, and Rubenstein (2008) suggest that teachers consider all students to be *mathematics language learners*. In this view, strategies that help native English speakers become conversant in the language of mathematics will benefit English language learners (ELLs) as well. Teachers may just need additional sensitivity to incorporate certain of the strategies on a more regular basis.

As Ron (1999) notes, and as referenced in Chapter 2.2, the current curricular movements in mathematics education

> put a great deal of emphasis on having children explore, explain, reflect, reason, and communicate. The goal is to have children become proficient at analytical reasoning, not just at calculation. All this exploring, explaining, reflecting, and reasoning is communicated through language. (p. 24)

Although some may believe that a language-free classroom provides access to ELL students, nothing is further from the truth. We build understanding of and meaning in life experiences, as well as mathematics, through language. When teachers fail to provide ELL students with experiences that enable them to internalize mathematics language, they hinder ELLs' ability to think about mathematics concepts and develop understanding. These students have no means to talk about the concepts, and their achievement and learning are stifled. Their situation is not much different from hearing-impaired students who sometimes have difficulty with specific content areas, such as geometry, that are highly language-dependent and require more fluency with language for understanding (Usiskin, 1996).

In this chapter, we describe a number of strategies that teachers can use to help students gain fluency with mathematics language. Depending on students' educational background, they may or may not have technical vocabulary for mathematics terms in the first language. Some immigrants to the United States have had very little schooling in their native country; these students need to learn mathematics concepts as well as the language to describe them. Others have had high levels of education in their native country; they know the mathematics concepts and simply need to learn the English labels for them. At some point, however, even these students may encounter mathematics concepts they have not previously studied.

Some educators (e.g. Garrison & Mora, 1999) suggest that ELLs benefit when learning new concepts if instruction occurs in the first language. In some parts of the country there may be many home-language resources to help students struggling with English (e.g. Miami–Dade County and towns along the southern U.S. border for Spanish, or Minneapolis for Somali). But in other parts of the country there may be few or no resources. As a teacher, what do you do if you have just one student who speaks Japanese, or there are no aides who speak the first languages spoken by several of your students? You still have a professional obligation to help students develop academic content knowledge as well as academic content language. The strategies we describe in this chapter are designed to help all students in the classroom, including native English speakers, ELLs at the first two levels of language fluency, and ELLs who are quite fluent in English as their second or third language.

Strategies for Students at the Preproduction Stage of Language Development

When students enter your mathematics class and speak very little English, what are some strategies you can use to jump start their learning of mathematics in English? What are some essential academic basics that students need to know to communicate mathematically in English? Certainly, students need to know the names for numbers and how they are written, as well as some basic shapes. The strategies provided below are intended to introduce ELLs with limited or no English language skills to some initial vocabulary on which they can build additional learning. These become the basic building blocks for mathematics study.

Children's Picture Books

One strategy is to have some children's books that emphasize basic concepts, such as numbers or shapes, visually and with minimal language. The key is to find resources that are not so elementary as to be offensive to young adolescents. For instance, look for books in which the pictures are based on real life and are not stylized pictures of young children. Some resources that can be used to connect basic concepts with the appropriate words in a context that can be appealing to middle and high school students are listed below:

Number. The following books can be used to introduce ELLs to vocabulary for numbers. They show how to represent numbers symbolically as well as in written form.

- Crosbie, Michael J. *Architecture Counts*. New York: John Wiley & Sons, 1993. The numbers from 1 to 10 are counted using wonderful architectural pictures and features.
- McGrath, Barbara Barbieri. *The M&M's Counting Book*. Watertown, MA: Charlesbridge Publishing, 1994. M&M's are counted and a set of 12 candies is sorted into sets of different sizes. In addition, basic colors are introduced to describe the M&M's. Three shapes (circle, triangle, square) are also introduced.

- McMillan, Bruce. *Counting Wildflowers*. New York: Mulberry Books, 1986. Wildflowers are used as a theme to count from 1 to 20.

Fractions. ELLs from other countries may not have had experience with fractions if their prior mathematics education focused primarily on decimals. As a result, some ELLs might need to be introduced to fraction concepts regardless of their current grade-level assignment. Books such as the ones identified below enable ELLs to gain perspective on fraction concepts pictorially, in symbols, and in words. They help students to visualize relationships among fractions and wholes, as well as equivalent fractions.

- Adler, David A. *Fraction Fun*. New York: Holiday House, 1996. Aspects of fractions are introduced in a lively fashion with many diagrams and real-world contexts.
- Mathews, Louise. *Gator Pie*. Littleton, MA: Sundance Publishing, 1979. Students are presented with a visual perspective of fraction concepts. The pictures illustrate that fractions are based on pieces of the same size and shape.
- McMillan, Bruce. *Eating Fractions*. New York: Scholastic, 1991. Pictures show food cut into various fractional parts. Real-life contexts help students make connections to fractions in the real world. Students also learn English words for some basic foods.
- Pallotta, Jerry. *Apple Fractions*. New York: Scholastic, 2002. Different types of apples are used to introduce fractions. Basic computations with fractions that have the same denominator are also illustrated.
- Pallotta, Jerry. *The Hershey's Milk Chocolate Fractions Book*. New York: Scholastic, 1999. Hershey bars are used to introduce fraction ideas.

Shapes. Using books such as the ones listed below, ELLs learn the English words for basic geometric shapes (e.g. circles, triangles, and squares) in a variety of contexts.

- Bulloch, Ivan. *Shapes*. New York: Thomson Learning, 1994. This book considers all kinds of shapes in the world and looks at different objects that can be made from each shape.
- Crosbie, Michael J. *Architecture Shapes*. New York: John Wiley & Sons, 1993. ELLs are introduced to geometrical shapes through architectural pictures and features.
- Ehlert, Lois. *Color Zoo*. New York: HarperCollins Publishers, 1990. Shapes are introduced through nested cut-out pages. In addition, ELLs learn names of familiar animals.
- Hoban, Tana. *circles, triangles, and squares*. New York: Simon & Schuster, 1974. Photographs of real-world objects are used to introduce these shapes.
- Hoban, Tana. *Shapes, Shapes, Shapes*. New York: Mulberry Paperbacks, 1986. Photographs of real-world objects introduce students to a wide variety of shapes.
- *Secret Shapes: A Changing Picture Book*. New York: Dorling Kindersley Publishing, 1995. Pull-down tabs reveal examples of a given shape.

Measurement. Books such as the ones listed below introduce ELLs to words they can use to describe measurement concepts (e.g. relative size and measures). Visual connections enable students to understand the meanings of words.

- Hoban, Tana. *Is It Larger? Is It Smaller?* New York: Mulberry Paperbacks, 1985. Relative sizes are explored through photographs of real-world objects. Students are introduced to words indicating comparative relationships in real-life contexts.
- Pallotta, Jerry. *The Hershey's Milk Chocolate Weights and Measures*. New York: Scholastic, 1992. Weights and measures related to Hershey bars are illustrated.

Many of these resources use limited vocabulary beyond the words needed to introduce the concept. ELL students at the preproduction stage can therefore use these books as starting points for learning the essential academic language needed to progress in mathematics.

Teachers can use these literature resources in several ways. At the beginning of class when other students are completing a warmup exercise, the teacher might work through a few pages of the book one-on-one or with a small group of level 1 ELL students. The pages in the book become the warmup exercises for these preproduction stage students to help them build language that will let them participate successfully in class.

Teachers can audiotape the books so that students can listen to the book and follow along. Many schools now require community service hours from students, or clubs such as honor societies complete service projects; proficient English speakers could audiotape these books as part of their service hours. Then, during warmups or when students have independent work time, ELLs can listen to the book.

Alternatively, students might take the books and audiotapes home as part of their homework. Teachers can modify homework assignments by replacing some problems from the text with problems based on a few pages of the book. For instance, if students are using the book *Architecture Shapes*, the teacher might give students several pictures and have them identify the shape using the book as a resource.

These books can serve as a foundation for a student to build his or her own personalized dictionary of important concepts; for students literate in their own language, the books can serve as the basis for an English-first language glossary. For students not literate in their own language, they can focus on basic language and the ways that numbers and shapes are written. The sample resources we list are all very visual. (If books are not available, teachers can create flashcards for basic numbers and shapes. Stickers appropriate for adolescents can be used to serve as a motivating factor.)

Teachers can make these books available in a consistent location in the classroom. Any time that ELL students want to check on a word or concept or review language related to these basics, they can go to the location and retrieve the book. Making these books consistently available is important because these words and concepts are not necessarily ones that would be introduced in the class as a whole nor are they ones that would be found on a class word wall.

Take Advantage of Elementary Reading Programs

Many companies offer programs combining written and audiotaped materials to help students learn to read, and school districts often purchase these for elementary students. Many of these programs contain mathematics books as well. Schools can purchase a site license and students can listen to these resources read aloud. Middle school and high school students will likely progress through these resources rapidly, because typically they will know the basic mathematics concepts from schooling in their first language. They simply need to make the connections to relabel the concepts with appropriate English words.

Teachers can use these resources in several ways to help their ELL students at level 1. Students can listen for 10 to 15 minutes during class or can take the materials home and listen to a given portion of the text for homework. For students who do not have the English skills to work through a middle or high school mathematics text on their own or do not have support at home for deciphering text, such a resource can enable students to engage in mathematics and extend their academic mathematics language. Materials that require more language support can be explored in the classroom.

Summary

The strategies suggested above—using picture books or using audiotape recordings of elementary mathematics texts—are designed to help ELL students make relatively rapid progress on some basic vocabulary and concepts so that they have some background on which to build instruction during their regular class. These resources can continue to be available for support as students engage in their mathematics classes, along with the regular support that teachers provide for ELL students.

Make Vocabulary Learning a Natural Part of Instruction

In Chapter 2.3, we highlighted some of the difficulties that are inherent in mathematics technical vocabulary. Because of these difficulties, teachers need to make the learning of vocabulary a natural part of their instruction. This does not mean that teachers devote special days to the learning of vocabulary, but rather that teachers make a conscious decision to engage students in learning vocabulary as it occurs in lessons. In addition to the mathematics objectives that teachers have for their lessons, they need to think about language objectives that they want students to master. Students need to use words regularly in order to internalize them and make them a natural part of their mathematics language (Murray, 2004). So teachers need to find ways to help students use mathematics vocabulary if they are going to be able to produce mathematics communication. If students fail to master mathematics vocabulary, they have no way to talk about or think about mathematics concepts, and their learning is stifled.

Build Important Vocabulary from the Concepts

In disciplines such as English, unfamiliar words can impact students' ability to focus on the underlying meaning in a piece of literature. However, the situation is somewhat different in mathematics (Coggins, Kravin, Coates, & Carroll, 2007; Thompson *et al.*, 2008); students can explore a mathematics concept and then attach related language to it. That is, the vocabulary arises from the experiences and the investigations. Consider the following vignette:

Ms. Smith had prepared a lesson on graphing linear equations. Over the course of the year, she has found that her ELL students can engage with the concepts if she builds activities that actively engage them in mathematics. In addition to her mathematics objectives, she regularly has language objectives as part of her lesson plans. She intended to have students explore multiple linear equations with a graphing calculator and to determine the effects of m and b on graphs of equations of the form $y = mx + b$. By the end of the lesson, she wanted students to be able to use the words *slope*, *y-intercept*, and *x-intercept*. Rather than starting with vocabulary, she had students work in small groups with graphing calculators. Each group was expected to graph all four sets of equations (see Figure 3.3) and to look for how the graphs were alike and different within each set and among the sets. As students worked, she circulated around the room to ensure that the groups were on task and making notes of their observations.

After time to work, the class came together to discuss the results with different groups sharing their results.

Set 1	Set 2	Set 3	Set 4
$y = x + 3$	$y = x + 4$	$y = -x + 1$	$y = 2x + 1$
$y = 2x + 3$	$y = x + 1$	$y = -2x + 1$	$y = -2x + 1$
$y = 3x + 3$	$y = x - 5$	$y = -4x + 1$	$y = 3x + 5$
$y = 5x + 3$	$y = x - 2$	$y = -6x + 1$	$y = -3x + 5$

FIGURE 3.3. Four sets of linear equations to look for patterns in slope and y-intercept.

Set 1: "The lines cross the y-axis at the same place. The lines slant more as the number in front of x gets larger."

Set 2: "The lines all slant the same. They cross the y-axis at different places."

Set 3: "The lines all cross the y-axis at the same place. They slant the opposite way from the lines in sets 1 and 2."

Set 4: "The first two cross the y-axis at 1 and slant in opposite directions. The second two cross the y-axis at 5 and slant in opposite directions."

After the groups shared their observations using informal language (e.g. "slant," "cross the y-axis"), Ms. Smith introduced formal language. She drew two lines on the board and labeled the meaning of the *x-intercept* and *y-intercept* on each; she carefully pronounced the word *intercept* and had her students repeat the word. She also introduced the word *intersect* (e.g. "cross the axis") and had students listen for the difference between *intercept* and *intersect*. She then wrote the words *slope* and *steepness of the line*, helping students connect those two ideas, indicating the line on the left has a positive slope and the one on the right has a negative slope (see Figure 3.4); she also connected students' use of the word *slant* to the concept of *slope*. She is always careful to print the words on the board, rather than use cursive writing, so that it is easier for students to interpret the letters.

She then had students review their observations for the first set of equations. She asked the students to restate their observation orally, using the words *slope* and *y-intercept*, and to indicate whether the lines had a positive or negative slope. Then students wrote the observations as sentences. Ms. Smith gave a transparency to one group of students and

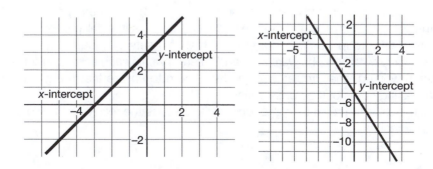

FIGURE 3.4. Two lines with x- and y-intercepts labeled.

had the sentences placed on an overhead for all to see. For homework, students were directed to write two to three sentences for each of sets 2, 3, and 4 to describe the lines. Students were expected to use the words *slope*, *positive* or *negative*, *x-intercept*, and *y-intercept* in their descriptions for each set.

There are several aspects of Ms. Smith's instruction that support the learning of all of her students, and particularly of her English language learners. She consciously planned a language objective as well as a mathematics objective. She built vocabulary from students' mathematics experiences so that *language followed concept development*. She wrote the vocabulary on the board, so that students could see each new word and hear it said. She had the students use the words in their own descriptions. *See, hear, and say* is one strategy to help students make mathematics vocabulary their own (Thompson *et al.*, 2008).

However, for ELL students, having vocabulary arise from concepts means that students gain concrete experiences to which to connect their new vocabulary. They can attach vocabulary to what they have already experienced and described in an informal manner. This teacher had students practice the words orally and then use repetition when they wrote those same observations. She used visuals to help make sense of the vocabulary (e.g. her graphs with their *x*-intercepts and *y*-intercepts labeled and students' graphs from their calculators). She gave students specific words that needed to be included in their observations to guide their use of language.

If teachers are building new concepts using vocabulary that students have previously studied, previewing that vocabulary prior to beginning the lesson ensures that the vocabulary is brought to the fore for students. However, when new vocabulary is being introduced, build the concept first and then attach the vocabulary (or the label for the concept).

Connect Mathematics Language to Social Language

As we have indicated several times throughout this text, ELL students first develop fluency with social language, and fluency with academic language often takes several additional years. So, when introducing mathematics vocabulary, try to build on students' social vocabulary, when possible, to help provide meaning for new terms. In this way, we scaffold new knowledge by providing supports for connecting new knowledge to existing knowledge. For instance, students are familiar with line markings on a road; this context can be used to help students think about *parallel lines*. Clip art can be found to highlight these real-world connections (see Figure 3.5).

FIGURE 3.5. An example of *parallel lines.*

Likewise, the *median* of a divided highway can help students think about the median as being in the middle (see Figure 3.6). For ELL students, making these connections between social language and the academic meaning of words not only builds on their life experiences but helps them build mental images of the mathematics terms. Students are able to draw on the similarities between the meanings to make sense of the term in a new context.

Use Concrete Objects to Introduce Vocabulary

To the extent possible, teachers should bring in concrete objects to illustrate vocabulary. For example, physical models of geometric solids should be shown in the classroom when introducing terms such as *sphere*, *cylinder*, *prism*, or *pyramid*. Students need to touch the objects, not just look at pictures in a book. When they touch, they can feel the *edges* and *vertices* in *polyhedra*; they can cover the *base* or the *faces* and think about surface area. The physical touch combined with the use of language can help students internalize the meanings of terms.

Students need multiple experiences with objects, both observing during teacher explanations and manipulating the objects themselves. Consider the following scenario.

When Ms. Smith wanted to help students make sense of the words *base*, *face*, *edge*, and *vertex* of a *rectangular prism*, she brought in multiple cereal boxes and small raisin boxes. As she discussed the vocabulary related to the prism, she continuously pointed to the appropriate portion of the prism and had students do the same. Throughout, she built in comprehension checks, asking students to trace their fingers along the edges, or to point to the vertices. To determine if students understood the essential characteristics of these terms, she brought a hexagonal prism from her relational solids kit into the class. Different students were asked to come to the front of the class and identify the appropriate parts of the prism. As she prepared to focus on surface area, she used the cereal and raisin boxes so that students could flatten them out to determine the area of each face.

Ms. Smith recognized that students need redundancy when introduced to new terms. Not only did she have the terms written on the board for her students, but as she said the terms, she constantly pointed to their location on the prism and on the board. Her students could see the term in writing, hear it pronounced, and see a concrete manifestation of the term.

FIGURE 3.6. An example of *median* in the real world.

As Ms. Smith demonstrated with the prism, she had questions in mind to use with students at different levels of language proficiency. Some questions or prompts were factual in nature and appropriate for students at the first two levels of language fluency: trace an edge of the prism; touch a vertex; point to a face. She also had higher-level prompts for students able to make inferences: What is the difference between an edge and a vertex? By consciously thinking about questions at difference language levels, she ensured that her ELL students could feel included in the lesson.

Draw Comparisons and Contrasts between Vocabulary Terms

As we indicated in Chapter 2.3, mathematics shares many words with ordinary English and with other disciplines. Teachers need to help students draw comparisons and contrasts between these uses of the word, especially if it is likely that the word's usage in a new context might cause difficulty for students. How can teachers help students make these comparisons and contrasts?

One way is to use drawings or other illustrations to highlight differences. Consider the word *solution*, which is used in both science and mathematics with different meanings. (Notice that *solution* is used in language arts to mean the answer to a problem or dilemma; in this sense, its meaning is similar to that in mathematics.) For ELL students at lower levels of language proficiency, a visual model would be helpful to highlight a solution in mathematics (i.e. an answer) and a solution in science (i.e. a liquid used in experiments). See Figure 3.7.

As students' language proficiency increases (to speech emergence or fluency), written comparisons can be used to enhance a visual comparison/contrast. For instance, students can be instructed to respond to one of the following journal prompts as part of their homework assignment:

Complete the following sentence. In math, a solution is _____.

In science, a solution is _____.

Explain how the word *solution* means different things in math and science.

The first prompt provides a structure for the type of written response that is expected. Some educators (e.g. Bouchard, 2005) indicate that such framing sentences are helpful for ELL students who need more guidance in appropriate sentence structure for making comparisons and contrasts.

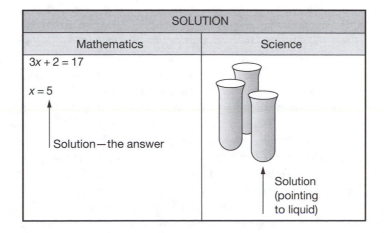

FIGURE 3.7. Illustrating two different meanings of *solution*.

Give Explicit Attention to Reading Symbols

Just as vocabulary presents challenges for ELL and indeed all students, attention must be given to helping students read symbols. Symbols have their own challenges for ELL students, who may be accustomed to using different symbols for mathematics concepts than those used in the United States. For instance, in Chapter 2.5 we noted that commas and periods are often used differently in the United States than in Latin America or Europe.

There are other potential differences in symbols. As Perkins and Flores (2002) note, some Mexican textbooks represent angles as ABC rather than $\angle ABC$. Therefore teachers must make explicit for students how to write a symbol for a particular concept as well as how to verbalize it. As with vocabulary we advocate *write the symbol, verbalize it, write the verbalization*, and have students *practice verbalizing* the symbol.

It is important to remember that students need to deal with the vocabulary and symbols of mathematics in order to make sense of mathematics text. So we cannot ignore helping students develop fluency with symbols. One way to help students learn to verbalize symbols is to create opportunities for them to read mathematics sentences containing symbols aloud. Students can do this in small groups. To ensure that students read and interpret verbalizations correctly, have students work in pairs. One student can read a sentence aloud while a second student tries to write down what the first student said. When finished, they can see whether the written statement agrees with the statement the first student was reading. Any discrepancies can be discussed. Students should then reverse roles so that both students have opportunities to read as well as hear verbalizations of symbols. Keeping the activity in a small-group setting may encourage ELL students to participate who would be reluctant to talk in a whole-class setting.

Simple activities like this one can take just a few minutes in class, and could be used as part of a warmup activity or a closing activity. As an alternative to working in small groups, one student can read a sentence for the rest of the class to translate into written form. Although such activities are beneficial for all students, they are particularly beneficial for ELL students because they provide opportunities for students to engage in language—oral and aural.

Teachers need to be cognizant of the multiple ways that we express concepts (Rubenstein & Thompson, 2001). Consider, for example, the algebraic expression $n - 3$. If teachers always verbalize this expression as *n take away three* or *n minus three*, then they fail to help students connect such expressions to other common verbalizations in algebra, such as the *difference of n and three, n less three*, or *three less than n*. It might not be prudent to use all these various verbalizations in the same class period. However, during the time that we are investigating such expressions, we need to ensure that students have the opportunity to understand that all five verbalizations mean the same thing. Once all of the variations of the symbols are introduced, they should be revisited often as part of classroom discourse (e.g. "What is another way to say . . .").

There are several ways that teachers can help students become accustomed to multiple verbalizations. Teachers can create card decks with a symbol and various verbalizations, one per card. Students can play games with the cards, such as Concentration (looking for pairs) or a variant of other games in which students try to make sets of three to four cards that have the same meaning. The more sets the student makes, the more points. These card games can be available in a center in the classroom for students to work on when they have time, before or after school, or during lunch. They can also be packaged, so that students can check them out and take them home. ELL students can be encouraged to complete a home pack once a week, with adjustments to other homework assignments on nights when students are engaged in a home pack. Two or three questions that can serve as written assessments and comprehension checks can be included in the home pack to encourage accountability on the part of students. For example, after the students have studied various ways to express $n - 3$, they can be given the following problem for homework: "Write $10 - t$ in three different ways."

Construct Word Walls and Personal Dictionaries

Elementary school teachers have often used word walls as part of their language arts or mathematics instruction. This strategy consists of words and their definitions placed on large newsprint or posters and hung around the room so that they are readily visible for all students to see. Mathematics teachers in middle and high school can use the same technique so that ELL students have the mathematics terms to reference when needed. Many of the companies that publish supplementary materials often sell ready-made posters. However, we think it is just as effective, and perhaps more so, for students to generate their own entries for a word wall. The left column of Figure 3.8 shows a possible entry for a word wall. Students can also write a personal dictionary entry that contains the same information; the entry shown in the right column contains the class definition of the term as well as a definition in the student's own words. ELL students who are literate in their first language can be encouraged to write a definition in their own words in their first language if desired. Even literate students may not know the technical mathematics word in their first language; using an appropriate dictionary, students can look up the technical term and include it in the personal dictionary entry, to help build their literacy in both languages. Even without the use of native language, the entry will convey the meaning of the term. The personal dictionary entry should contain a definition in words, an example of what it is and an example of what it is not, and a visual representation of the term. The personal dictionary is a resource available to the students at home when working on homework and is a resource that parents can use to help make language connections as well.

Personal electronic dictionaries can help students translate from their native language to English and vice versa. In addition, there are sites, such as *Free Translations Online* at

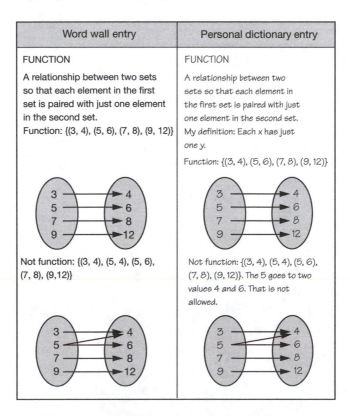

FIGURE 3.8. Word wall and personal dictionary entries for *function*.

http://translation2.paralink.com, that offer the free use of translation software. Although such sites may not provide perfect translations, they can be a resource for teachers when there are no other resources for the languages of the students in the class. These word walls, personal dictionaries, and electronic dictionaries should be available to students at all times, including on classroom assessments. Word walls and personal dictionaries provide opportunities for students to put concepts in their own words and to make connections to their own experiences.

There are many ways that teachers can facilitate the use of these ideas with their ELL students.

- Generate a basic template for a personal dictionary so that students need only to complete a copy of the template. Keep multiple blank copies on hand for students to use (see Figure 3.9).
- At the beginning of a unit, provide students with index cards cut in half. Students list the words that will be studied over the course of the unit, one word per card. As the words are introduced throughout the unit, students complete a dictionary entry for the card. Cards can have one hole punched in them and then hooked together with a small ring. Students are encouraged to use their cards whenever needed.
- Use flashcards on a regular basis, perhaps twice a week. One side of the flashcard can have a picture of a term or symbol; the other side can have the word or verbalization of the symbol.

Term: _____

Math Definition:

My Definition:

Example:

Non-example:

Picture:

FIGURE 3.9. Template for personal dictionary entry.

Students can work in pairs to check the comprehension of their partner by showing the term or symbol and determining if the partner can verbalize it appropriately. Although this activity is also good for English speaking students, it is particularly helpful for ELL students who may not have opportunities to use English outside the class. Students need to become fluent with the vocabulary of mathematics if they are going to be able to use it to discuss mathematics. Work with flashcards can take place for five to ten minutes at the beginning or end of a class period. Flashcards can be easily made on a computer and reproduced on card stock to focus on concepts and terminology most applicable to the class. Work with flashcards should be supplemented with exercises in which students are expected to use the vocabulary in meaningful contexts.

Model with Graphic Organizers and Concept Maps

Graphic organizers are visual models that help students make sense of the relationships between words and concepts. A concept map helps students understand and show relationships. Consider the concept map for a polyhedron in Figure 3.10. Students see the features of a polyhedron (faces, vertices, faces as polygons), examples, and non-examples.

When students generate concept maps, they might begin by working in a small group so that ELL students have an opportunity to engage in oral and written use of language. Teachers might give students newsprint on which to create their concept map. Groups should have an opportunity to share their concept maps with other groups and then to revise them as needed. Sharing and revising suggests to students that their efforts to build concept maps are important and that groups work together to improve their work to enhance learning. For ELL students, including pictures on the concept map is important to provide visual support for language.

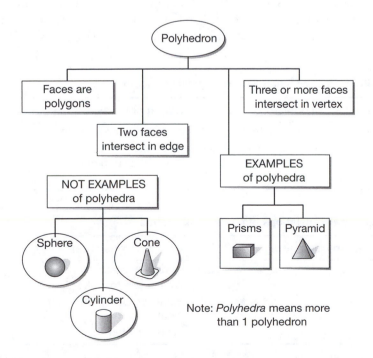

FIGURE 3.10. Concept map for *polyhedron*.

Model Vocabulary Physically

Some vocabulary terms can be modeled kinesthetically with one's body. Students can be asked to lie down on the floor to illustrate the meaning of *horizontal*, or stand up to illustrate the meaning of *vertical*. Students can use their arms to illustrate *acute*, *obtuse*, *right*, and *straight* angles. Students can trace a line through the air with a *positive slope*, *negative slope*, or *zero slope*. Although all students can benefit from these activities, such mathematics aerobics are particularly beneficial for ELL students. Students can hear and see the term and model with their body. The physical actions help connect words with images and enable students to generate their own meanings for important concepts.

Translate Logical Connectors

Logical connectors are used in mathematics to show relationships. For instance, *if* ____, *then* _____ highlights a relationship between the hypothesis (the *if* part) and the conclusion (the *then* part), so that if the hypothesis is true the conclusion is also true. Such sentence structures are often difficult for native English speaking students, and even more so for ELLs. Teachers need to help students rewrite such sentences using direct language (see Table 3.2).

Simplify Mathematics Instructions

As mathematics teachers, we are typically cognizant of the mathematics terms in the lesson and we build our instruction in such a way that students become aware of those terms. But mathematics texts contain instructions in the problem sets that signal students to certain actions, at least on problems that emphasize procedural fluency. Words such as *solve*, *simplify*, *evaluate*, *compute*, and *draw* suggest certain actions on the part of students. We need to ensure that students are aware of the meanings of these words so that they are able to engage with the problems that help them develop proficiency in mathematics. We can demonstrate the meanings of these terms by working through problems as well as by translating the terms into informal language (see Table 3.3).

TABLE 3.2. Statements with and without logical connectors

Statement with logical connector	Statement reworded in direct language
If a figure is a square, *then* it is a rectangle.	A square is a rectangle.
If one value in a data set is much larger than the others, *then* the median should be used instead of the mean.	One value is much larger than the others. Use the median and not the mean.

TABLE 3.3. Informal translations of mathematics terms

Mathematics instruction term	Informal translation
Solve	Find an answer.
Simplify	Write again to make simpler.
Evaluate	Put a number for the *x* (or *y* or variable). Work it out.
Draw	Make a picture.

Reading Mathematics: Extending Strategies for Use with ELLs

In addition to learning vocabulary and symbols, all mathematics students need to learn to read mathematics, including reading their textbook. Current mathematics textbooks are much more language-intensive than mathematics textbooks of just a couple of decades ago. At first glance, textbooks might be intimidating to ELLs. But a few carefully introduced strategies can help students learn to get meaning from their textbook.

Identify Important Features of the Text

Students need to learn to use the features of their text that provide insight into language and conceptual development. Is there a glossary? How are important words identified (e.g. bold, color, put in a box)? Is there a list of important vocabulary for each chapter that identifies the lesson in which the vocabulary was introduced? Are the objectives or main points of a lesson shared with students? Each of these features helps students focus on the important concepts of a lesson. All textbooks contain some non-essential language, that is, language that could be omitted without any loss of meaning. Boldface, boxes, and color help students distinguish essential from non-essential language.

For ELL students, teachers might provide reading guides (Bouchard, 2005) to identify those portions of a lesson on which students need to focus. Helping ELL students focus is important; the cognitive load of reading text in English is great even without the added complexity of technical mathematics text. We want students to use their cognitive energy on critical portions of the text that are essential for understanding. With their normal teaching responsibilities, it may not be feasible for teachers to create reading guides for every lesson in a text. So help ELL students recognize that sentences with bold words (usually definitions) are important; boxed or highlighted explanations, examples, and summaries are essential. If the objective or main idea of a lesson is written at the beginning of the lesson, this can help students focus on what they are expected to learn. Giving ELL students explicit guidance early in the year on which features of the text should be their focus helps build metacognitive skills that are important for overall learning.

Preread to Set the Stage for Learning

Many native English speaking students have not developed the skills to read technical text, such as that in their mathematics textbooks. Spending some instructional time to help all students learn to read their book can help all students move forward, including ELLs. First, start with some prereading strategies. Have students skim the subheadings in the lesson. Based on these subheadings, students should be able to draft a question they should be able to answer by the end of the lesson. Skimming the subheadings can also activate prior knowledge by having students brainstorm what they already know about the concept. Students can perhaps bring experiences from their culture to bear on the concept.

How might looking at subheads specifically benefit ELL students? A discussion of the subheads gives an opportunity to preview vocabulary or concepts that students have already studied that are essential to the current lesson. Subheads help focus students' interaction with the text. They provide an opportunity for students to hear and say a word that might be seen again in the context of the text, perhaps a word that students are expected to define through engagement with the text. Although all of these results are important for native English speaking students as well, they help

ELL students narrow the cognitive demand of working in their non-native language so that they don't spend energy and effort on aspects of the text that are not going to move their mathematics learning forward.

Use Explicit Reading Strategies

There are several ways to engage students in reading text. At the beginning of the year, the teacher might read aloud with students following along in the textbook. The teacher can stop to give further explanations, create visuals, or write or label words on the board. In essence, the teacher is engaging in modeled talk (Herrell & Jordan, 2008). The teacher models for students the kinds of actions in which they should engage as they read a portion of text. Teachers can help students answer the questions they generated from skimming the subheads.

As students progress through the year, they should engage in reading with partners or in small groups. One strategy useful here is called *say something* (Siegel, Borasi, Fonzi, Sanridge, & Smith, 1996), in which students read a small portion of a text and then tell one thing about what they read to their partner. Depending on their level of language proficiency, ELL students could share their understanding via a picture or diagram.

An alternative strategy that encourages all students, including ELLs, to use mathematics language is reciprocal teaching (Bouchard, 2005; Hill & Flynn, 2006). Hill and Flynn indicate that reciprocal teaching involves four components: summarizing the main points, generating questions to ask of the partner to assess their understanding, clarifying any confusing parts of what was read, and predicting what might occur next. Students can read a small portion of a lesson and then apply reciprocal teaching to that segment. In a small-group setting, ELLs are able to determine their comprehension of the text and learn to generate good questions. As students work in groups on reciprocal teaching, the teacher can circulate around the room but focus specifically on groups with ELL students to assess how they are proceeding with the concepts.

Some might consider reciprocal teaching to be appropriate only for non-mathematics classes because mathematics students are not expected to read their textbook. We do not agree with this view. Students need to be able to read their text to learn on their own and to enhance the instruction that occurs as part of class. Students need to construct their knowledge through carefully crafted tasks and activities that teachers orchestrate. Teachers cannot just dispense knowledge through lecture and expect students, English speaking or ELL, to comprehend.

Reciprocal teaching can also be used after an instructional segment in class. Students can be paired to reteach to their partners what was discussed in a whole-class setting. Such an activity provides the redundancy that is essential to give ELL students multiple exposures to essential language and concepts.

Summarize after Reading

After reading, it is important to summarize what was read. Graphic organizers, described earlier, are one means to help students make connections between important parts of a lesson. Another strategy is to have students retell the lesson to a partner, with a particular list of words that need to be used during retelling (Bouchard, 2005). The teller checks off words as they are used; the listener also checks off words as they are heard. This strategy enables students to use social language while also strengthening academic language because there is a specific list of mathematics terms that need to be used in context.

If the lesson is one that involves procedures, such as constructing a triangle, creating a box-and-whiskers plot, or solving a quadratic equation, students can generate a list of the steps needed to complete the procedure in the proper sequence. These lists can be posted on newsprint throughout the room and could become part of students' personal dictionaries.

Use Strategies that Combine all Stages of Reading: SQ3R

Some common reading strategies are useful in mathematics. SQ3R (Robinson, 1970) involves several stages. Students *survey* the lesson by looking at headings, boldface text, or titles in order to get a sense of the lesson. Students generate *questions* to be answered based on their survey. Then they *read* the lesson to answer the questions, *recite* what they learned, and *review* by summarizing the information. For ELLs, SQ3R provides a structure to guide them in using their text. If the teacher has also generated a guide to help students know which portions of the lesson need to be read, then SQ3R can help students focus on obtaining meaning from those portions of the text identified by the teacher.

Preview and Summarize with Anticipation Guides

Anticipation guides (Herber, 1978) enable students to connect their preknowledge of a concept with post-knowledge. The teacher creates a series of statements, some true and some false, related to a lesson or unit (e.g. "A cone is a polyhedron"; "A cylinder has circles for bases"). Prior to beginning study, students read the statement and decide whether they believe it is true or false. After studying, students revisit the statements and determine whether they are true or false based on the information that was learned. For ELLs, anticipation guides help activate prior knowledge. They alert students to the concepts on which they need to focus as they go through the lesson; that is, they help structure the content for students by distinguishing what is essential from what is not.

Incorporate Writing in Mathematics: Extending Strategies for Use with ELLs

Part of helping ELLs develop understanding of mathematics concepts is helping them develop the ability to express their understanding orally and in writing. When students express themselves, they make their understanding visible. Peers can help them clarify thinking and the teacher can determine what further instruction to plan to move academic language and mathematics understanding forward. Oral and written language are productive actions on the part of the student, in contrast to reading or listening, which are receptive actions. Although students at the early levels of language often function in the receptive mode while listening, we want them to produce language. Khisty (1995) indicates that when students do not "have the means of expressing mathematical ideas, they . . . are curtailed from participating in those activities that develop and enhance mathematical meanings and comprehension" (p. 282). When students write, they can indicate what they know about a concept, explain their methods, justify their reasoning, and reflect on their learning experiences.

Use Link Sheets to Encourage Connections

We have already discussed some strategies that teachers can use to bring writing into the classroom, such as personal dictionaries or sentences that use particular words. Another strategy that integrates writing with visual perspectives is a link sheet (Shield & Swinson, 1996), with which students represent a given concept through a mathematics example, a real-life example, words describing it in their own language, and a formal explanation. In some respects, a link sheet is similar to a Frayer Model (www.justreadnow.com/strategies/frayer.htm), which many literacy experts advocate to help students make connections among different aspects of a term. Consider the following link sheet for obtuse angle (see Figure 3.11).

The link sheet can be completed not only by students whose native language is English but by ELLs at any of the four levels of language proficiency. Students at any of the language levels, but particularly at the preproduction or early production levels, might complete much of the sheet with diagrams and use minimal entries in English; for the real-life example, students could draw a picture of a stop sign and point to the angle, as indicated in the figure, or paste pictures cut from magazines. Teachers can help students write appropriate additions to the sheet in English to support them in moving language forward. If students are literate in their native language, they can be encouraged to research the term in that language to aid in building their mathematics fluency in both languages. Link sheets can become part of a personal dictionary and used as references throughout the year. When teachers permit students to use these resources during assessments, they send a signal that these writings are important learning tools for students and that they provide support for ELLs to show what they know. Teachers can also monitor students' ability to expand their work on such sheets throughout the year.

Facilitate Note-Taking with Guided Notes

Many students, including ELLs, benefit from guided notes during instruction (Thompson *et al.*, 2008). Taking notes during instruction requires a certain cognitive load. It is too much to expect students who are concentrating on understanding English as it relates to mathematics to be able to attend to language, understand the concepts, record information in a second language, and keep up with the pace of instruction. Yet failure at any of these tasks creates barriers to learning. One way to help students bridge the language difficulties is to prepare a set of guided notes. In essence, teachers prepare an outline of the major points in the lesson, leaving opportunities throughout the notes for students to provide entries, which might be examples, vocabulary, or a description. However, the amount the students need to record is limited, so they are left able to focus on understanding the concepts being discussed. Guided notes can provide as much or as little scaffolding as needed based on students' experiences and language proficiency.

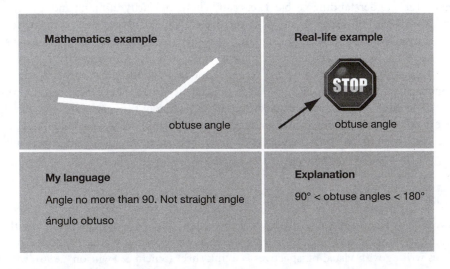

FIGURE 3.11. Link sheet for *obtuse angle*.

As teachers discuss the lesson, they can display a template of the guided notes on a transparency so that they can model for students what should be recorded, including words, numerical examples, pictures, and any other symbolic or pictorial descriptions (e.g. arrows) that will enhance learning.

Use Multiple Representations

One of the keys to success for ELLs in learning language is to use multiple representations. Students need to use words, pictures, symbols, gestures, and physical actions to develop understanding of mathematics concepts. One aspect of multiple representations is the use of concrete materials to highlight concepts and help students make sense of mathematics. Consider the following lesson that incorporated the use of manipulatives for teaching integer addition and subtraction:

Ms. Smith had attended several professional development sessions related to providing effective instruction to ELLs. She learned that teachers could use various strategies to engage their students, including the use of manipulatives and word walls. Ms. Smith's fifth period eighth grade class includes 7 of 23 students who are ELLs, of whom only two speak the same language, Spanish. Because of the range of language proficiencies in her class, she decided to use two-color counters to help students make sense of integer operations. In addition, she recognized the need to include a word wall to help students make sense of the vocabulary that she was using. She planned carefully for her lesson and considered possible pitfalls that her ELLs might experience. She wanted the students to work together, but had to think strategically about how she would arrange her students. Prior to her class session, she considered her students' mathematics background, their English language proficiency, and with whom they would work during the lesson.

During class she asked students to sit with their predetermined partner. Because the ELLs did not understand her, she motioned to them to come to the desired location in the room.

Ms. Smith: Today we are going to use counters to learn some math. I would like you to work with your partner as we do this today. Some of you are paired with someone who doesn't speak a lot of English, so I need your help. Together, we are going to make sure that they understand what we are doing in class. If you haven't done so already, take a minute to introduce yourselves.

She gave students some time to introduce themselves by stating their names.

Ms. Smith: We are going to use two-color counters to learn to add and subtract integers. To do this, we have to agree on what each color represents. So let's use red to represent negative one. Why does it make sense to let *red* represent negative one?
Jill: When you are "in the red" that means you owe money.
Ms. Smith: That's a good example.

She drew a red circle on the whiteboard and wrote next to it "represents −1 'owe money' or 'you have to pay'." Then she repeated the statement while pointing to the red side of the counter and to the appropriate sentence on the board. As she did this, she made eye contact with each of her ELLs to make sure they understood what she was trying to communicate.

She noticed that several ELLs were not paying attention, so she tapped at the screen and signaled that students should have "eyes forward." She repeated the above statement and asked each ELL what the red chip represented to ensure that they were paying attention. She wanted the ELLs to know that she expected them to be engaged.

Ms. Smith: Kashif, what does this [pointing to the red side of the chip] represent?
Kashif: Negative one.
Ms. Smith: So the yellow side will represent a positive one.

She drew a yellow circle on the whiteboard and wrote beside it "represents +1 'get money'." She repeated the statement while pointing to the yellow side of the counter and pointing to what she wrote on the board to ensure that once again the students were following. She pointed to the yellow side of the chip and asked another ELL to identify what it represents. Deepak responded: "Positive one."

Ms. Smith: We are going to leave this key on the board so that we can refer to it. So, what do you think will happen if we group a negative one and a positive one? What operation are we talking about if we group things together?
John: Adding.
Ms. Smith: You are absolutely correct. I am going to add that to our word wall. Can anyone think of another way to say "add"?

On a sheet of chart paper, she drew the symbol for addition "+" then wrote the word *add* underneath. The students began to identify other words, including *sum* and *plus*. As students called out the words, she added them to the list. She was surprised that some of the ELLs volunteered words to be added to the list.

Ms. Smith: So, we are going to *add* integers or find the *sum* of two integers. [She emphasized the words and pointed to them as she said them to ensure that the students would make connection to the words.] What do you think would happen if we added a negative one and a positive one?

She wrote "(−1) + (+1) = ___ or (+1) + (−1) = ___".

Ms. Smith: Can someone think of a way to help us make sense of what that means? Think about what we said about negative and positive numbers yesterday. Talk to your partner and see what you get.

She provided time for students to talk. A male student volunteered that it would be zero.

Tim: Well, it's like what we did on the number line. If I move forward one in the positive direction and move back one in the negative direction, I will be at zero.
Ms. Smith: Would you come up and draw a number line so that we can *see* what you mean? [Tim drew a number line and restated his claim.] What do you think? Does that make sense? [Students responded affirmatively by nodding their heads.] Can someone think of another example?
Jody: How about money?
Ms. Smith: What do you mean?

Jody: If you owe a dollar and then get a dollar then you really don't have any money because you have to give it to the person that you owe.

Ms. Smith wrote the on the board "–$1 + $1 = 0", while restating the student's comment. She pointed to "–$1" when she said "owe one dollar" and pointed to "+$1" when she said "got a dollar." She allowed other students to share a few more examples.

Ms. Smith: Excellent! So are we okay with the fact that negative and positive one will give us zero? [The students responded affirmatively.] Okay, so I would like you to show me the following using your counters: negative three plus two. [Then she wrote "–3 + 2" on the overhead projector.] We have a negative three so we will need three red counters and we have two so we have two positive counters.

When she was done, she made sure that each student had the same information shown on their desk. She also asked students to make sure that their partner had the right information. She continued the lesson by asking students if they had any zeros. Students were able to determine that they had two zeros. As she walked around the room she asked an ELL the meaning of the combination of a yellow and red chip. The student was able to say "zero."

Ms. Smith: So, if we have two zeros, what is the value of the chips on your desk? What do we have left?
Pilar: Negative one.
Ms. Smith: Excellent.

She continued the lesson by asking students to use their chips to solve other problems in pairs. As the students worked with their partners, she observed each ELL to ensure that he or she had built some understanding. As she observed pairs of students, she noticed that some of the English speaking students were mimicking her approaches for working with ELLs by pointing and saying words. When she pulled the class together, she asked for volunteers to explain their thinking. She was encouraged when an ELL volunteered to share his work.

Ms. Smith's overall goal was to use a variety of tools to communicate ideas in mathematics and to allow students to see the connections among the ideas. Even though several students were ELLs, they were able to follow the physical actions on the materials to generate their own meaning and develop conceptual understanding for adding and subtracting integers. Rather than assuming that ELLs could not participate, she used strategies to ensure their engagement.

Summary

Today's mathematics classroom is one in which language plays a vital role. Students need to attach language to concepts and symbols in order to be able to think about them. As students talk about mathematics, they internalize concepts and build connections that enhance learning.

Explicit instruction with vocabulary and language must be part of our mathematics lessons. We can build on social language that students have to grow their academic language. Multiple representations—visual models, symbols, verbalizations, gestures—are all part of language development in the mathematics class.

3.4
Emphasizing and Supporting Problem Solving

Effectively teaching mathematics content to English language learners (ELLs) requires instructional settings and situations in which students are engaged in solving interesting problems that encourage critical thinking along with basic skills development and practice. ELLs learn language and content best when they are involved in authentic and interactive environments. Instruction that emphasizes inquiry, problem solving, and communication provides ELLs a venue for enhancing their understandings, receiving input, and practicing "comprehensible language." Such classrooms focus on language-rich activities that require students to question, describe, explain, hypothesize, debate, clarify, elaborate, verify, and evaluate. Teachers must recognize that ELLs are able to develop inquiry-based and problem-solving strategies before they are language-proficient (Jarret, 1999). ELLs can enhance their language development as they move from concrete to more abstract content while solving problems. However, this is possible only when such activities are relevant to students' experiences and provide them opportunities to solve problems as they engage in various literacy-related aspects of mathematics.

Although advanced mathematical ability is likely to be revealed when students are engaged in tasks that require computational or algorithmic procedures, ELLs may experience difficulty when confronted with language-intensive problems or complicated directions that require some level of proficiency with the English language. Indeed, students who usually excel in mathematics might be frustrated by their inability to address problems that utilize lots of words. Clearly, this is an area where it is important for teachers to provide accommodations, such as translating problems into a student's first language, helping students role-play a problem to understand what is being asked, helping students distinguish essential from non-essential language in a problem, rewriting the word problem in English using shorter sentences with simplified language, or reading a problem out loud for the students. It is not appropriate to deny these students opportunities to solve such problems. By engaging with problems set in context, ELLs are provided additional situations in which they can build language knowledge. Word problems can also serve as a bridge from social language to academic language, because the social language used in many word problems can provide the context in which students are then able to use academic mathematics language.

Word problems are a ubiquitous part of mathematics content. Because of the specialized nature of mathematics language, many students, not just ELLs, find word problems challenging. However, the language used in word problems can be particularly challenging to ELLs because word problems often integrate the use of social language and academic mathematics language (Abedi & Lord, 2001; Solano-Flores & Trumbull, 2003). In addition, students may have difficulty with word problems if they are not familiar with the mainstream cultural context of the problem. Informed mathematics teachers recognize that in addition to teaching mathematics we are required to teach students to read, write, and speak mathematically because all students are *mathematics language learners* (Thompson, Kersaint, Richards, Hunsader, & Rubenstein, 2008). Strategies to help ELLs will likely benefit other students as well.

Connect Mathematics to Life Occurrences

It is important to provide ELLs ample opportunity to see how mathematics might be used in various contexts. Instructional activities can be designed that not only address important mathematics topics, but also help ELLs make connections to their new environments. For example, middle grades students could be asked to work in groups to plan meals for a family of four for a week, and given a budget and local market newspaper advertisements. Alternatively, an activity could involve students in planning a dinner event for 150 people for which they must order food. At the high school level, students could be asked to design a packaging container that will minimize the amount of wasted space used to ship a particular product. These activities provide students opportunities for problem solving while interacting with their peers. As part of this interaction, students will learn and use words related to the context of the problem to communicate their ideas and respond to ideas presented by others. There are resources available to help teachers engage students in the examination of mathematics while solving or explaining real-world problems and issues (see, for example, Topical Application of Mathematics at www.cimt. plymouth.ac.uk/resources/topical/).

Elaborate the Meaning of Words Provided in Real-World Problem-Solving Contexts

When addressing word problems, it is important to recognize that, in addition to the mathematics terminology, ELLs may have difficulty understanding the context of the problem. Consider the following word problems. What words might need to be explained in order to help ELLs make sense of the context? Why might students, particularly ELLs, find these questions challenging?

1. Ramie makes his own pottery vases. It costs him $2.25 in materials for each vase. He sells them for $10 each. How many vases does he need to sell in order to make a profit of $93?
2. In a school kitchen during lunch, the timer for pizza buzzes every 14 minutes; the timer for hamburger buns buzzes every 6 minutes. The two timers just buzzed together. In how many minutes will they buzz again at the same time?
3. Satisfied customers often acknowledge good service by leaving a tip of about $0.20 for each dollar spent. If a bill is $50.23, how much tip should a satisfied customer leave?
4. The cost to ride the subway train from zone A to zone B is $2.15. A 10-ride pass costs $20. How much would Alisa save by buying a 10-ride pass instead of 10 one-way tickets from zone A to zone B?

The mathematics needed to solve these problems is not considered difficult if students have basic understandings of mathematics computation. However, knowledge of computation is useful only if one is able to discern which operation to use. In addition, a question makes sense only to the extent that you understand the context of the given problem. Words that an ELL might find problematic include the use of the word *profit* in question 1, the use of the colloquial word *buzzes* in question 2, and the use of the words *bill* and *tip* in question 3. A basic understanding of these words is needed to understand the context of the problem and to determine what mathematics is needed to solve the problem. In fact, some of these words might be challenging to students whose native language is English. In these cases, teachers could help students by helping them understand the social words that appear in mathematics word problems. Teachers can engage students in a brief discussion about the problem to help them relate these words to their prior experiences. Real-world contexts are culturally laden (Solano-Flores & Trumbull, 2003; Stanley & Spafford, 2002) and may assume common experiences that ELLs do not have. For that reason teachers must be mindful of the potential influence of the problem context on students' understandings and clarify them when possible. In question 1, a teacher could ask "What does it mean to make a profit?" This allows her to assess students' knowledge of this specific word and provides students with opportunities to share information that others can use to help them solve the problem. In question 4, students from a rural setting may not understand the notion that fares vary from one zone of a city to another.

It is important to recognize that the recommendation is not to limit the type of problems that are introduced to students. That would limit ELLs' opportunity to learn about new situations and to learn new vocabulary. Exposing students to new contexts can provide a rich opportunity for expanding their social and content knowledge base. However, teachers must be aware of possible challenges related to the use of real-world contexts so that they can devise plans for facilitating classroom discussions and making links to students' experiences. Discussion about the contexts will enable students to make sense of the provided scenario, help them notice how other related information could be used to further understanding, and provide an entry to solving the problem. Overall, such discussions will help develop the mathematics literacy of all mathematics language learners.

Use Representations to Translate and Visualize Problems

Concrete and visual representations or dramatizations can be used to help students understand what is occurring in a problem. Because ELLs may not understand the language that is used in a problem, it is important to incorporate other means for communicating when possible, particularly for those who are at the beginning level of their English language development, as discussed in previous chapters. Consider the following problem:

> Movie tickets cost $5.95. Three friends regularly go to the movies together. How much will the three spend together for four movies?

How might this problem be visualized to help ELLs make sense of the context?

Explicitly Teach and Model Problem-Solving Processes and Strategies

Many mathematics textbooks include a section that describes the problem-solving process for students to use when solving mathematics problems. Although the steps listed vary among books, the four basic steps shown in Table 3.4 are always included.

When working with ELLs it is particularly important to focus on the first step. As mentioned earlier, their ability to comprehend a problem is dependent on their familiarity with the context of the problem and their proficiency with the language used to present the information. Often, this first step is bypassed in order to focus on the mathematics needed to solve the problem. If ELLs are provided opportunities to make sense of the context of the problem, many of them are able to determine appropriate approaches for addressing the mathematics.

Problem-solving strategies are actions or thought processes that may be used to accomplish particular tasks. It is not sufficient to tell students that they are able to use a variety of strategies to solve problems. They must be taught various strategies and be taught how to use them effectively. Because different tasks lend themselves to different strategies, students must be taught the decision-making skills to assist them in deciding which strategy is most effective for the task at hand. Table 3.5 lists the most commonly used strategies for solving a variety of mathematics problems.

Students should be provided ample and varied opportunities to practice using the various strategies. While solving problems, students learn when certain strategies will or will not work. To scaffold student learning, allow ELLs to move from relatively simple linguistic requirements to more complex ones. These strategies can be revisited whenever students are engaged in problem-solving activities.

For example, for students at the first two stages of language proficiency in particular, strategies that involve drawing a picture or making a table should be encouraged, as they provide concrete means to begin solving a problem. Such strategies are good for all students but particularly for students with limited English. As students gain greater language fluency, they can be encouraged to expand their approaches to consider strategies that are more abstract.

Teachers can use informal language when demonstrating the processes and steps used to solve a problem. This overt *modeling of thought processes* provides ELLs and other students an opportunity to understand the various experiences, including false starts, that are inherent in solving problems. Teachers can *think aloud* as they demonstrate methods used for solving particular

TABLE 3.4. Polya's problem-solving process

1. Understand the problem	Recognize the nature of the context, what is assumed, and what is required
2. Devise a plan	Make a decision about an approach to solving the problem
3. Carry out the plan	Implement the selected approach
4. Look back	Check the results against the context and other information provided in the problem

Source: Polya (1957).

TABLE 3.5. Problem-solving strategies

Guess and check	Simplify the problem	Find a pattern and generalize
Make a table	Make an organized list	Work backwards
Act it out	Make a drawing or model	Write a number (algebraic) sentence
	Use logical reasoning	

problems and ask students to do the same. This prepares students for sharing their thinking with others. Students often emulate the behaviors of teachers as they solve problems and interact with peers. Overt modeling of this type of behavior also prepares ELLs and their English speaking peers to work together.

Embed Clarity Checks

Teachers reinforce the first step in the problem-solving process by checking to see if students, particularly ELLs, understand the task or problem prior to allowing them to work independently or with peers. These checks can be used to clarify vocabulary that students may not understand or contextual settings that may not be familiar to students but of which understanding is necessary to interpret the problem or task. It is not enough to ask, "Do you understand?" Too many students are likely to answer "yes" to avoid embarrassment or because of cultural expectations that limit their willingness to acknowledge to a teacher that they did not understand. Rather, to check for student understanding, teachers should use specific prompts, such as "Please restate the problem in your own words" or "What does _____ mean in the problem?" Another strategy is to have students draw a picture or diagram to illustrate what is happening in the problem; the picture or diagram helps teachers determine whether students understand the basics of the problem and can help students translate the words into an equation or computation that leads to a solution. Another strategy is to have students identify the steps needed to solve the problem without actually solving the problem. This gives ELLs an opportunity to practice their language skills by reading and interpreting the problem and provides an initial basis for obtaining a solution.

Provide Opportunities to Work with Peers to Solve Problems

When they are working with peers, ELLs can discuss and listen to interpretations of a problem, identify steps for obtaining a solution, compare and contrast various approaches, and check and validate solution strategies. As students verbalize alternative solutions to the problem, they have an opportunity to inspect the problem-solving approaches advocated by other students and compare them to the approaches developed on their own (Chamot & O'Malley, 1994). In addition, students obtain feedback on preliminary attempts to represent the problem and are led to examine their own strategies based on feedback from peers. Peer group work can also encourage and support ELLs in their efforts to verbalize their problem-solving process. Cooperative learning experiences expand the number of strategies students may encounter and use, and encourage them to be flexible when they solve a problem. "Students who verbalize problem-solving steps and strategies associated with them are more likely to transfer problem-solving procedures to subsequent problems" (Chamot & O'Malley, 1994: 237). Strategies for engaging ELLs in cooperative learning are discussed in greater detail in Chapter 3.2.

Limit the Number of Problems Assigned

Although it is important to keep high expectations for learning, the quantity of assigned work may need to be carefully monitored and adjusted. As with oral discourse, ELLs must interpret written information presented in an unfamiliar language, translate it into their native language to make sense of it, possibly consider the mathematics needed to solve it in their native language, and then present their solution by writing or speaking in English. Because of this, consideration must be given to the number of problems a student really needs to complete in order to demonstrate mastery of a concept. Is it important to complete 20 problems, when students' knowledge can be assessed with five carefully selected problems? Modification of prepared worksheets or assignments from the textbooks may also be needed. For example, the number of problems assigned may be adjusted or the amount of time allowed for completion of work may be altered. The goal is to focus on fewer problems that address the essential concepts and skills being emphasized and that allow students to demonstrate knowledge and misconceptions.

Avoid a Focus on Key Words

An approach often used to assist students with solving word problems is to teach them to identify and translate key words found in the problem. Although this has the potential to provide students with a mechanism for addressing the problem, it also has the potential to cause confusion. Consider the following list of key words used to signal mathematics operations (see Table 3.6).

Because of the variations that are possible, using *key words* or rules to teach mathematics problem solving can limit students' ability to solve problems. Students might focus on the key words without considering the context that results in a different interpretation of the word. For example, consider the use of the phrase *increased by a factor of* in each of the following problems.

The length of the ribbon was increased by a factor of 2. It is now 12 inches long. What was its original length?

The length of a square garden was increased by a factor of 3. The area of the original garden was 16 square feet. What is the area of the new garden?

This year's profit from the sale of televisions represents an increase by a factor of 4 over last year's profit. Last year's profit was $10,000. What is this year's profit?

TABLE 3.6. Key words commonly used to signal mathematics operations

Addition		Subtraction	
altogether	total of	difference	decrease
both	added to	fewer/fewer than	reduce
in all	together	how many more	subtract
sum	combined	how much more	remains
more	and	less/less than	exceed
			left

Multiplication		Division	
times	of	each	per
multiplied by	product	ratio of	out of
at this rate	area	quotient	share
every (e.g. $5 *every* day for 5 days)		distribute	average
at (e.g. *at* $3 a yard)		a (e.g. $3 *a* gallon)	half (divide by 2)
and (e.g. combinations of shirts *and* pants)			
twice (i.e. 2 times some number)			

Students who are taught to focus on key words might assume that *by a factor of* means to multiply and as a result multiply the numbers represented in the problem. Unfortunately, that would lead to a correct response only for the third question. In the other two cases, the student must interpret the use of that phrase in context in order to determine the best approach to find a solution to the posed question.

ELLs need assistance to interpret the context of each of the problems. Key words, and many rules for that matter, have limited applications; using them can prove to be detrimental as students transition to more advanced mathematics. If students make sense of mathematics and other vocabulary within the provided context, they will be in a better position to recognize, make sense of, and use their understandings in subsequent mathematical experiences.

Address the Use of Extraneous Information in Word Problems

Extraneous information, or distracters, is information included in word problems that, if used, will produce an incorrect response. Typically, this is information about the problem context that is not directly linked to the posed problem. As part of an assessment, a distracter is used to discern whether students are able to identify key features needed to solve a problem. Consider the following problem:

> Anja earned $70 on her part-time job working at the movie theater. She spent $25 on a dress and $16 for a shirt. After buying a magazine for $4, she saved the rest. What is the ratio of the amount of money Anja spent on the shirt and the magazine to the amount that she earned?

The distracters ("she spent $25 on a dress" and "she saved the rest") are not pertinent to providing a response to this item, but provide more details about the context of the problem. To provide a response to this question, students are expected to distinguish important from unimportant information. In addition they are expected to recognize that the question posed does not require subtraction although the context involves spending money.

Teachers should be mindful of the added burden that distracters within a word problem might cause ELLs. Depending on the language proficiency level of students, it might be appropriate to eliminate the use of distracters that may negatively affect student performance, particularly for level 1 and level 2 ELLs. This would allow students to focus on the fundamental mathematics, without the added burden of making sense of distracters provided in a different language. However, as students become more proficient with the English language, it becomes important to teach ELLs to analyze problems to determine whether they include extraneous information and how to deal with it.

Be Sensitive When Using Cultural References

Teachers need to be sensitive when they use cultural referents in the classroom. All problems in mathematics, even the ones provided in textbooks, should be carefully considered for whether they could be offensive or demeaning to certain individuals or groups. To be inclusive, it is often recommended that teachers relate subject matter to the lived experiences of students. However, teachers often do not have similar experiences or backgrounds to their students. Teachers may make assumptions about students based on their English language proficiency or their perceived socioeconomic status. As we stated earlier, labels we use for students do not adequately capture the many variations that exist within groups. In addition, many assumptions are based on stereotypes that can denigrate a group. Because of this, we must use care when we generate problems in the classroom, particularly as we attempt to use multicultural examples or examples that we believe represent the experiences of students. In addition, teachers need to ensure that the examples used are age-appropriate as well as appropriate in the larger school context. Some teachers have caused outcries when they incorporated mentions of experiences they wrongly believed reflected the lives of their students, such as gang life or easy access to guns. Teacher-generated problems can be culturally charged and laden with "hidden" attitudes toward race, gender, identity, or political power. Care must be taken not to send unintended messages about the status of individuals or groups through examples that are used in the mathematics classroom. Consider the following contexts a teacher might use to embed mathematics topics:

> For the school's cultural festival night, 6 girls were cleaning the tables in the cafeteria, while 4 boys were setting up cables for music equipment. Three more boys came . . .

> In the local youth correctional facility there are 25 Black students . . .

> Betty wanted to lose weight . . .

> Terrorists in Iraq were found to . . .

One can easily see how each problem raises a politically or socially charged issue in modern-day society. Each context may leave students with an impression about the status and perceptions of a certain group, particularly examples 2 and 4. Example 3 may cause problems because many adolescents are weight-sensitive. Example 1 might be useable; we certainly do not want to imply that teachers cannot ever use contexts in which males and females have somewhat typical roles. However, females should not always be placed in service roles and males in technical roles, or vice versa. The recommendation is not to eliminate the use of controversial topics. Some researchers have identified the value of such engagement by teaching mathematics for social justice (Gutstein, 2000; Gutstein, Lipman, Hernandez, & de los Reyes, 1997). Instead, the intent is to raise awareness and encourage teachers to discuss the implied messages and address concerns that might be raised by them. In fact, carefully crafted problems can help ELLs (and all students for that matter) develop an appreciation and understanding of the cultures of others while they examine mathematics and its applications in the real world. As mentioned previously, this is only possible in classroom environments that encourage the development of respect and mutual appreciation of all cultures, backgrounds, and experiences.

Encourage Students to Write Original Problems

Asking students to generate their own problems can motivate them to engage in the problem-solving process. This task allows students, including ELLs, to write problems that are directly linked to their social or cultural experiences. In addition, as ELLs write problems they are pushed to use everyday and mathematics words that they are learning. The generated problems can be shared with peers and used as part of classroom learning activities.

Summary

In sum, ELLs benefit from mathematics classes that are highly interactive, emphasize communication, and incorporate problem-solving and inquiry activities. Such classes provide meaningful contexts in which ELLs can learn mathematics while also developing their language skills. Language- or acquisition-rich mathematics classes that focus on solving authentic problems provide ELLs opportunities to learn and practice English while learning the precise and technical language of mathematics.

3.5
Assessing English Language Learners in Equitable Ways

Assessing ELLs in an equitable manner poses interesting challenges for mathematics teachers. We want to assess in a way that enables ELLs to share what they know and are able to do, rather than administer an assessment that simply determines what they are not able to do. Too often, assessment seems to emphasize a deficiency model that leads to erroneous conclusions that students not yet proficient in English are not able to function in mathematics.

Yet, as we have discussed in previous chapters, focusing only on skills is not an option. We want students to have a deep conceptual understanding of mathematics. As a result, we have advocated a language-rich classroom in which students are encouraged and expected to talk about mathematics and represent their understanding in a variety of ways—with words, pictures, and symbols. Consequently, our assessment needs to align with our instructional expectations.

So, given these constraints, what are some strategies that we can use during our regular classroom assessments?

Provide Access to Learning Tools during Assessments

Allow Use of Personal Dictionaries and Word Walls

What tools and supports might we consider making available to ELLs as well as to other students in our classes? We should permit students to use their personal mathematics dictionaries (see Chapter 3.3) as well as conventional English–other language dictionaries during assessments. Obviously, the use of other dictionaries is possible only when students are literate in their own language; for those who are not, their personal dictionaries, perhaps with many pictures, are more realistic. When students are regularly permitted and encouraged to use their personal mathematics dictionary, we send a message that this is an essential tool in learning mathematics. We emphasize the importance of keeping the dictionary up to date and that it is a useful tool to enable success in mathematics.

We should encourage students to use the word walls that we have compiled and put on display for all students. Obviously, when students have access to such resources, we need to move beyond simply asking students to provide a definition of a term as part of the assessment.

Audiotape Assessments

We might consider audiotaping the assessment (Williams, 2007). An audiotape enables students to listen to questions as they read them. Students can rewind and listen multiple times. So many of our students have personal music players, and a recording of an assessment can easily be downloaded for students to listen to throughout the test. Williams, who taught in a school with many international students, found that students' scores increased and anxiety levels lessened when students were able to listen to an assessment while completing it. For students who are still struggling with reading English, listening to the test may reduce some of the cognitive demand in English and let students focus on the mathematics.

Create Personalized Test Notes

A beneficial assessment strategy for all students and one that might be particularly helpful to ELLs is to have students create their own personalized notes for use during a test. We do not usually allow students to use all of their notes; when students have access to all of their notes they often fail to study and spend too much test time flipping through their notes. Rather, we prefer to give students the option of having one page of notes that they have created for use on the test. Students must write the notes by hand in ink, so that they are personalized; we don't want one student to create notes on a computer and share with everyone else. We want students to review the mathematics being studied and determine what concepts are thoroughly understood, what concepts might require a brief hint, and what concepts might still need some major support. When students create their notes based on their review of the content, they must self-monitor their learning to determine where they need support. Often, by the time students have completed such notes, they no longer need to use them on the test. For ELLs, we would allow students to complete the entire set of notes in their first language or to use a combination of first language and English, depending on their own comfort level. ELL students could use these personalized test notes in addition to appropriate language dictionaries (Thompson, Kersaint, Richards, Hunsader, & Rubenstein, 2008).

Provide Access to Concrete Materials When Appropriate

If students have regularly used concrete materials as part of instruction, those materials should be available to students during assessment. For instance, if teachers have used two-color chips when exploring integer operations, or pattern blocks when exploring fractions, or algebra tiles when multiplying and factoring binomials, then students should have the opportunity to use those materials during assessments if they so desire. This strategy is good for all students, but may be particularly helpful for ELL students who are still struggling with language. The concrete materials give students a means to interact with the concepts, even when they lack the English language fluency needed for discussing the concepts. In addition, the concrete materials may help students draw representations of the concepts to demonstrate understanding.

Avoid Linguistic Complexities

In designing assessments, there are a number of issues to consider to ensure that the assessment does not contain roadblocks that impede access by ELLs.

Use Caution with the Use of Proper Names

One non-mathematical issue that needs to be considered is the names used in word problems. Names, such as Pat or Mark or June, that have ordinary English meanings can get in the way of students making sense of the problem (J. Hickman, personal communication). Even though a name is generally a non-essential piece of information in the problem, students may be applying the English meaning of the word and trying to determine how that relates to other aspects of the problem. There is no reason for students to face this difficulty when a simple change in the name would prevent confusion.

Avoid Using Synonyms in Problems

Another practice that can create difficulties is use of synonyms in the problem. Consider the following variants of the same problem:

Version 1

> Janet plants *lilies* in her garden. She plants them 6 inches apart. How many *flowers* will she plant if her garden is 9 feet long?

Version 2

> Janet plants *lilies* in her garden. She plants them 6 inches apart. How many *lilies* will she plant if her garden is 9 feet long?

Although only one word is different in version 2 (*flowers* was changed to *lilies*), that one word can influence students' ability to understand the problem and to be successful. In the first version, students must recognize that flowers is used as a synonym for lilies; if students don't make this connection, then they may not be able to determine how to proceed. In contrast, in the second version, the question relates directly to the initial statement of the problem. With such alterations, the student's focus can remain on the mathematics needed to solve the problem, and undue barriers related to the English language can be avoided.

Provide Test Accommodations

Depending on the English language proficiency of your ELL students, you may need to provide various accommodations.

Reduce the Number of Questions

We need to realize that thinking in English takes more time for many of our ELL students, who often translate from English into their first language and then back again to English to respond. So, it may be necessary to adjust the number of questions to which ELL students are expected to respond in order to give them the same amount of time for thinking about mathematics as our English speaking students. The extent to which the number of questions should be adjusted will likely vary based on the course and the ELLs' level of language proficiency.

Adjust the Amount of Time

ELL students may need more time to complete an assessment because they need time to process English as well as think about mathematics. How can this be accomplished in a class situation? One might give ELL students a test in parts, with students taking different parts on different days. Students might be permitted to complete a test during a study hall or after school, although teachers would need to be sensitive to transportation issues for any after school adjustments. If students have time with an ESL teacher, then it might be possible to arrange for them to complete a mathematics test during that time.

Give Part of the Test Orally

Teachers might consider administering all or part of a test orally to their ELL students. One advantage of such an accommodation is that the teacher can probe students' understanding of mathematics by asking questions to ensure that difficulties are the result of a lack of mathematics knowledge rather than language difficulties. Such an approach is feasible if there are only one or two ELL students in a class because the teacher can administer some questions to ELL students in the back of the room while the rest of the class is taking the test. If the number of ELL students is large, the teacher might use an audiotape of the test or read the questions on the test aloud, one at a time, giving students an opportunity to respond before reading the next question. With these adjustments, the teacher loses the opportunity to probe for understanding but still ensures that language proficiency is not a barrier to demonstrating mathematics knowledge. One disadvantage of reading questions aloud one at a time is that students must proceed at the same speed, instead of at their individual pace. Nevertheless, these may be viable alternatives depending on the makeup of a class.

Consider Alternatives to Traditional Individual Tests

Depending on the composition of a class, it may be feasible to consider some alternative arrangements to administering tests. For instance, students might take all or part of a test with a partner. Teachers could administer some procedural questions individually and enable students to work with partners on problem-solving questions that require more language skills. However, teachers will need to ensure that both students contribute equally to the exam.

Alternatively, teachers might give pairs time to discuss questions together, but with no writing utensils on the desks. After the allotted time for discussion, students must then complete the test on their own. An advantage to this arrangement is that students must quickly skim the test and determine which items they might like to discuss; that is, we are helping them learn to self-assess and monitor their own learning. However, students must then complete the test on their own so that there is individual accountability.

Modify Questions to Reduce Language Complexity

At times, teachers may need to reduce the complexity of the language in problems. For example, for students at the very earliest stages of language proficiency (particularly preproduction), problems

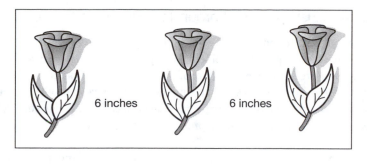

FIGURE 3.12. Version 3: Simplified version of the lilies problem.

might be rewritten in a visual form. Consider the lilies problem from earlier in this chapter. We might express this problem in a third version with minimal English (see Figure 3.12).

At other times, it may not be necessary to minimize English as much as in version 3. But we may still need to consider simplifying a word problem. Consider the following:

Problem A

> The department store was having its annual Fall Clearance. Everything was marked 50% off. John wanted to buy a shirt that originally cost $25 and a pair of pants that cost $30. How much would he pay on sale, without sales tax?

Problem B

> John is buying a shirt that costs $25 and a pair of pants that cost $30. They are on sale for 50% off. What is the cost without tax?

Problem B does not lessen the cognitive demand of the problem or the mathematics that is required. The first sentence in problem A, albeit interesting, was not essential. Also, the question in problem B is in present tense rather than the tense used in problem A. There is now less language that students need to address in order to solve the problem. Problem B could be made even more accessible by including a picture of the shirt and pants with the cost attached and a sales tag reading "50% off." The picture would then support the language in the problem.

Daily Assessments

Secondary mathematics teachers regularly assign homework or other types of daily assessments to students, even if they do not collect the assessments and grade them. But several of these daily assessments provide opportunities for teachers to monitor the progress of ELL students.

Ensure Students Have the Background for Homework

If our daily classroom instruction is language-rich, then our assessments also need to be language-rich. If students have been engaged in problem solving as part of class instruction, then students need to be engaged in problem solving as part of their out of class practice. However, we need to be sensitive to challenges for our ELLs. When students work on word problems during class, they have an opportunity to interact with their peers and get needed language support. How can we provide comparable support for homework problems? Here are two possible strategies.

- Spend a few minutes in class ensuring that students understand the contexts embedded within word problems that are in the homework. If the problem mentions an archeologist, then discuss in class what an archeologist does so that the word and/or context are not stumbling blocks.
- Make a transparency of the word problems. Spend a few minutes in class reading through the problems and helping students sort essential from non-essential information. Cross out sentences and words that are included in the problem but are not really needed to understand the problem. Think back to problem A earlier; by striking through the non-essential parts of the problem, we lower the language demands on our ELL students and make it easier for them to focus on the essential mathematics:

  ~~The department store was having its annual Fall Clearance~~. Everything was ~~marked~~ 50% off. John wanted to buy a shirt that ~~originally~~ cost $25 and a pair of pants that cost $30. How much would he pay on sale, without sales tax?

- Take time to read through word problems with students. Help them create a mental image of the action in the problem to ensure understanding. A mental image of the problem can help ELLs, and all students for that matter, transfer action into a solution. Obviously, this strategy requires that teachers plan their class time to permit time for such reading and mental imagery to occur.

Modify Homework Assignments for ELLs

Just as teachers often need to provide accommodations for ELL students during tests, teachers may need to modify homework assignments. Modifications should not eliminate all contextual or language-embedded problems. But if the typical assignment has 10 word problems, for instance, modifications might reduce the number of word problems to five to seven for ELL students, depending on their level of language proficiency. Such modifications acknowledge that ELLs need more time on each problem because of the language demands; modifying the number of problems helps keep the time commitment for ELLs comparable to that for their English speaking peers.

Establish Routines for Making Homework Assignments Known

Many secondary teachers provide homework assignments to students in advance so that students are able to plan ahead or keep abreast of class even when they are absent. For instance, teachers might distribute the homework assignments and schedule for an entire chapter when the class first begins the chapter. All students can benefit from this advance notice. For ELLs, advance notice can provide an opportunity to work with an ESL teacher to complete the homework, if they have time scheduled during the day with that teacher. In addition, it allows them to avoid struggling at the end of a class period to record an assignment mentioned hastily in class; they have a structure that lets them know what to expect, which can lower anxiety. If the schedule is provided in addition to the homework assignment, students can look ahead to the lesson so that there is some foundation prior to class instruction, or students can look ahead to determine if there are words or contexts in problems that they do not understand. They then have a chance to ask for help before working alone at home.

Use Journals for Students to Dialogue with Teachers

Journals, used once or twice a week, provide an opportunity for teachers to communicate one-on-one with students. For ELLs who may be reluctant to speak up in class or to ask questions face-to-face, a journal provides an opportunity for dialogue. Even students who are struggling with English can communicate via pictures. Students can receive credit for completing a journal entry rather than having a specific grade attached. In addition, a journal provides a record of progress over the course of a year so that teachers and students can measure the extent to which academic-content language and mathematics learning improve throughout the school year. Here are a few sample prompts, with possible language proficiency levels at which they might be used.

[Given a picture of a prism] Label *base*, *face*, and *edge*. Name a real object that is a prism. (*level 1*)

An example of a prism is _____. It is a prism because _____. (*level 2*)

A cylinder is like a prism because it _____. It is not a prism because _____. (*level 3*)

Compare cylinders and cones to prisms and pyramids. Describe how they are alike and how they are different. (*level 4*)

I need help with _____. (*levels 1 and 2*)

In class today we studied _____. I have questions about _____. (*levels 3 and 4*)

Projects as Assessments

Alternative assessments provide opportunities for students to demonstrate what they know without the pressure of a timed, on-demand test. In addition, alternative assessments provide a venue for teachers to include students' culture into the classroom in a natural way.

Projects provide outlets for students to demonstrate their mathematical understanding of a concept in a manner that often is less language intense. Students can be expected to build a model or design a poster that illustrates a mathematical concept; students could research information on the internet, such as finding pictures with particular types of symmetry. When students are engaged in such projects, we want to make them as open as possible, so that students can draw on their own experiences. Depending on the nature of the project, students can be encouraged to use their own cultural background as the basis for the project. Consider the following two project ideas.

- As part of a geometry unit that included study of transformations, the teacher built a summative assessment in which students were to create a geometric design that included at least two types of symmetry. In addition, students were to find at least one example of a piece of art or a building or a sculpture that incorporated symmetry (e.g. lines of symmetry or rotational symmetry). Students were to write a few sentences to indicate the nature of the symmetry. Cultural examples were provided to illustrate the types of designs that might be possible, such as a Navajo rug, an Aztec warrior shield, and African kente cloth. Students were encouraged to create a design representative of their culture if they so desired. Although the teacher encouraged students to use cultural examples, she did not force students to bring their culture into the classroom if they were reluctant to do so. The concrete example of building a design is helpful to ELLs who benefit from visual perspectives tied to life experiences; expecting students to write a few sentences to describe the symmetry in their designs helps build a bridge from the concrete to the use of academic content language.

- Throughout a marking period, students studied numerous concepts: ratios, proportions, scale factors, surface area, volume, and patterns of change in area and volume when scaling dimensions up or down. Rather than give a traditional marking period exam, the teacher decided to assign a cooperative group project that integrated all of these concepts. Students were to work in small groups to build a scale model of a portion of a village or town with the following restrictions: a picture of the real village or town must be provided (and students were encouraged to choose a village based on their cultural background); there must be at least 10 buildings; the scale factor between the original and the model had to be determined and reasonable; and the surface area and volume of the buildings in the models had to be provided. The teacher provided materials (e.g. small pieces of cardboard, tape, string, and glue) and assigned a cost amount to each; groups had a budget of $30 to build their model. Throughout the time that groups worked on the project in class, the teacher circulated among them to assess students' contributions and to ask questions about their understanding of the concepts. She was able to adjust questions to students' level of language proficiency (e.g. preproduction: Which is the smallest building in the village? Which areas are common?; early production: Which scale factor would you choose? Why? You want to build the buildings in their real-life size. What scale factor do you need to use for the model?; speech emergence: To create a village of your choice, what materials would you need?; intermediate fluency: What do the original model and all models that you build have in common? What do you think is different in each model?). All students were able to participate in the project; her ELLs were actively engaged because of the use of hands-on materials and she was able to probe with questions to ascertain their levels of understanding.

The use of projects is helpful for all students because projects help make abstract concepts more concrete. For ELLs, projects involve hands-on materials that help them build on prior experiences while learning new vocabulary and concepts. Students can potentially work with others who provide language support. The teacher is able to modify questions in a one-on-one setting while students are working and to probe for understanding. This type of interaction is often difficult to orchestrate during an independent timed assessment.

Summary

Teachers need to be sensitive to ensure that their assessments provide equitable access to ELLs. If we work to modify classroom instruction to build a supportive environment, modify our instruction to use visuals and provide language support, but then continue to administer the same assessments as always, we undermine our efforts to make our classrooms more inclusive. Nothing is more discouraging than to have worked on the concepts and then to perform poorly on a graded assessment because of language barriers and not understanding what is being asked. Accommodations provided as part of assessments provide teachers with appropriate measures of what ELLs know and are able to do.

3.6
Teaching Mathematics in Ways that are Culturally Responsive

Prior sections of this book have discussed the importance of culturally responsive or relevant pedagogy as a means of engaging ELLs in mathematics. How do we, as teachers, provide such instructions in a mathematics classroom? Specifically, how do teachers attend to the mathematical learning needs of ELLs in ways that are both challenging and accessible to them? How can mathematics teachers be sensitive to ELLs' experiences and cultural backgrounds? Some strategies that have been used to respond to the cultural needs of students have been using personal names from various cultural backgrounds, such as Maria and Ahmed, in word problems and using images of individuals from various backgrounds in textbooks and classroom posters. Although important, these strategies are at best superficial means of integrating students' cultures. Mathematics instruction needs to be sensitive to students' prior experiences and backgrounds, incorporate cultural perspectives, and allow students to use their own culturally based approaches as they engage in mathematics. That is, a learning environment would be established that exposes students to various points of view about mathematics, mathematics learning, and approaches to solving problems in mathematics. Beyond the mathematics classroom, this approach has a more significant societal value. In addition to enhancing the self-image of culturally and linguistically diverse students, it will also help *all* children learn to negotiate more effectively in a multicultural environment (Nelson, Joseph, & Williams, 1993).

"There are relatively few examples of what it means to teach meaningful mathematics in ways that build on diverse students' cultural and linguistic knowledge" (Remillard & Cahnmann 2005: 169). In this chapter, we identify ways that mathematics teachers can be culturally responsive as they teach mathematics. As part of this discussion, we highlight issues and challenges inherent in providing culturally responsive instruction. We begin by clarifying that providing culturally responsive instruction is not limited to actions that relate directly towards teaching mathematics content. Instead it is multifaceted: "It involves curriculum content, classroom management ('ability' grouping and cooperative learning groups), assessment practices, the involvement of families and the community, teacher expectations, and professional development" (Zaslavsky, 1996: 14). In particular, culturally relevant mathematics refers to the creation of the space or environment that enables *all* students to learn.

Teacher Critical Self-Examination and Self-Reflection

Prior to considering what it means to provide culturally responsive instruction, teachers must engage in critical self-examination (Howard, 2003) to determine the extent to which current beliefs and practices might influence the learning of students. In particular, teachers might ask themselves the following questions:

- What types of interactions do I personally have with individuals of backgrounds different from my own? Do they occur within a professional or social context? Are there implications related to this?
- How connected am I to the cultural experiences of my students?
- What assumptions do I make about the student population that I am teaching? What prejudices do I have?
- Am I aware of the variety of ways in which individuals learn? Am I aware of how individuals that I teach prefer to learn? Do I incorporate these various approaches as part of my classroom instruction?
- What about my classroom environment or instruction may adversely affect the learning opportunities that I provide to students from different cultural or linguistic backgrounds?
- Am I honest about how I relate to individuals from different backgrounds? Do I expect them to be more like "me" or am I accepting of their ways of relating to the world?
- What are my personal beliefs about teaching ELLs and teaching mathematics to ELLs? Are they inclusive?

Earnest answers to these questions are essential. We need to be mindful of our own biases in order to address them in the learning environment. In fact, we need to recognize that everyone has some biases regardless of his or her attempts to be accepting and tolerant. These biases are related to our own background, experiences, and interactions with others or what we know about others from external sources (e.g. the media). It is imperative that teachers "own up" to their biases to minimize the extent to which they can negatively influence students' learning experiences. Answers to questions like those presented previously provide the baseline from which to grow professionally and to enable us to consider the ways in which we can establish an inclusive learning environment, provide equitable access to learning, and address the needs and concerns of students from different cultural and linguistic backgrounds. Research (Ladson-Billings, 1995; Nelson, Joseph, & Williams, 1993) suggests that teachers who provide culturally responsive instruction share the following characteristics. They

- hold high expectations;
- teach challenging materials in a student-centered environment;
- use "bridges" and "scaffolding" to increase students' interest and knowledge;
- ensure that students experience success;
- develop and maintain cultural competence;
- foster a community of learners; and
- commit to the collective, not just individual empowerment.

Critical self-reflection and self-examination are necessary to determine whether we provide instruction in ways that are accessible and supportive and the extent to which we do. Clearly, Ms. Smith, who has been referred to throughout this book, has high expectations for students and uses strategies to communicate those expectations.

Provide a Welcoming Environment for ELLs

Teaching mathematics to students who speak no or very limited English can be extremely challenging. What can you do to help facilitate their transition in their new environment and help them build the vocabulary needed to communicate basic needs and begin the process of learning mathematics? In addition to teaching mathematics, we will have to teach ELLs how to function in their new learning environment. Throughout earlier chapters, we have focused on the need to develop a supportive learning environment. Learning to say *hello, please,* or *thank you* in the student's language can go a long way to help students feel welcome in your class. In addition, learning some of the basic phrases that are part of classroom management, such as *Please pass your papers forward* or *Take out paper and pencil,* in a student's native language can help students begin to understand the expectations of the classroom environment. You do not have to speak the language to do these simple things. There are many resources available to support your efforts, not just within your local community. For example, there are many online translation dictionaries that can be used to translate words and phrases. (See, for example, www.freetranslation.com or http://translation.langenberg.com.) If resources are available locally, you can have someone write down the phonetic way to say these words or phrases. Otherwise, "talking" dictionaries are available to help with word pronunciation. Such little gestures can help make the classroom much less frightening for your ELL students. Your willingness to learn a few words sends the message that you are committed to their learning and provides encouragement for them to learn to communicate with you in English.

Attend to Individualized Cultural Characteristics and Experiences

ELLs should be treated as individuals rather than a homogenous group that can be effectively characterized by one label. Within each cultural group, there are many variances. Teachers should be guided by the fact that many students who speak the same language do not share the same cultural experiences. For example, discussing the use of labels for Spanish speaking individuals, Moschkovich (1999) notes:

> The labels *Latino, Hispanic,* and *Spanish-speaking* may be used as general descriptors for a population of students. However, these labels can obscure critical distinctions. . . For example, students labeled as Latino can differ in length of residence in the United States, language proficiency in English, language proficiency in Spanish, prior school experience, and socioeconomic status. (p. 5)

For example, the mathematics experience of a Spanish speaking ELL from a small village in a rural region of Latin America with limited or no access to school will differ from that of an ELL from a city in Argentina who had been in school. It is important that we recognize these distinctions in order to provide appropriate accommodations to meet individualized student needs within the mathematics context.

Teachers can use a variety of means to gather information about students, both formally and informally. If resources are available, ELLs can be asked to provide a brief mathematics autobiography (oral or written). This will allow teachers to learn about students' prior schooling and mathematics experiences directly. Questions that may be asked include:

- Are you new to the area (country)?
- What language(s) do you speak at home? Do your parents speak English?
- What math courses have you taken? Have you been in school?
- How do you feel about math and why?
- How can I help you in math class?

Teachers can also ask questions to garner insights about particular aspects of students' experiences (e.g. "Have you ever worked with others when learning mathematics?"). The knowledge gained from these autobiographies can be used to organize instruction in mathematics in order to address these students' needs more directly. Students who are literate and yet not proficient in English could be given the option to write in their native language. This information can then be translated if resources are available to do so. Oral presentation could be permitted if bilingual assistance is available. Teachers can seek external resources to translate the questions into the students' native language and have the findings reported to them in English. There may be organizations that are in place to support new arrivals, particularly refugees during their transition to the United States (e.g. Arriba Juntos in San Francisco, which offers programs to assist individuals who speak Cantonese, Mandarin, Russian, and Spanish; the International Center in New York; and national consulates in the local area). Making connections with such organizations demonstrates your and the school's commitment to providing the best education to these students.

Create a Culturally Respectful Learning Environment

As previously mentioned, ELLs face the challenging task of learning mathematics in a language and culture that may be unfamiliar to them. As a result, ELLs might feel out of place or may not initially participate because they are unfamiliar with certain classroom norms. They might also believe that they do not have much to contribute to the classroom discourse and so limit their engagement in classroom activities. It is our responsibility to assist students with their transition.

Teachers' attitudes and behaviors play an essential role in and send a clear message about expected standards of student behavior. Teacher behaviors help ELLs understand how to interact and respond in their new learning environment. Teachers communicate these messages through their interactions with ELLs (e.g. engagement or lack thereof), instructional strategies, and the actions they initiate and facilitate. Because of this, it is important to demonstrate enthusiasm and a belief that each ELL is able to learn mathematics and can contribute to the classroom learning experience and the collective creation of knowledge. ELLs come to school with a wide range of talents and skills that need to be supported and encouraged. It is imperative that we create a learning environment where differences are respected and students learn how to communicate with each other effectively. In order to support ELLs, the teacher could design student-centered mathematics activities that encourage ELLs and their English speaking peers to work and learn together. To make ELLs feel comfortable and encourage their active participation, it is important for teachers to find ways to incorporate ELLs and their culture in their mathematics classrooms. In such an environment, ELLs will more easily interact with peers, share their ideas, and value the contribution of others. All students at the same time will be exposed to a variety of approaches to learning a mathematical concept, and will become accustomed to collaborating with people from different backgrounds.

Use Cooperative Learning to Facilitate Language Acquisition and Mathematics Comprehension

Some former ELLs[1] report that they were often ignored in classrooms and were not given opportunities to practice the new language that they needed to learn. They report being isolated from their English speaking peers. Clearly, this is not an effective means to encourage language development. Language is acquired as we engage in language-rich interactions. Peer interaction between native and non-native speakers of English is one means of promoting language development, or "comprehensible input," as described by Krashen (1985).

English speaking students who are taught to work effectively with peers of diverse backgrounds, including ELLs, can provide a safe environment in which to share and obtain information. Engaging in cooperative learning activities encourages ELLs to interact with peers in a manner that allows them to give and receive instruction related to both content and language. Working in structured and strategically assigned groups (groups assigned to address the specific needs of the students in the class) can increase the variety of ways that information may be processed and shared, and help students relate current and previous knowledge. Indeed, engaging in cooperative learning activities enables ELLs to interact in a language-rich environment that encourages them to practice the use of their newly acquired language. This is not typically possible in traditional mathematics classrooms that focus on teacher-centered instruction and individualized seat work. Whenever cooperative learning is used, teachers should take care to ensure group work does not degenerate into a situation in which the brightest student does all the work. This is likely to have no benefits to ELLs or the other members of the group.

Cooperative learning experiences are encouraged for use with ELLs because they provide students opportunities to:

- interact with peers in a non-threatening and structured learning environment;
- gain comfort to ask questions or seek explanations;
- receive input related to social and academic language;
- generate and refine "comprehensible output" through natural and academic language;
- negotiate meaning through talk;
- validate their thinking; and
- use English speaking peers as a resource to support social and mathematics language development.

However, there are many challenges associated with using cooperative learning strategies when ELLs are present in the classroom. Consider the following situation:

Although Ms. Smith had used cooperative learning successfully with her English speaking students, she was unsure about its use with her ELLs, particularly those in her fifth period class. In this class, 7 of the 23 students were ELLs and only two of them spoke the same language, Spanish. Of the other students, two were from Afghanistan, one was from Pakistan, one was from Iraq, and the other student spoke French. During the professional development sessions, it was recommended that ELLs be paired with bilingual students who speak the same language. Unfortunately, this class did not include a critical mass of students who spoke the same language and could potentially support each other. Given this unique situation, she had the following concerns regarding the use of cooperative learning strategies:

- Is it fair to burden English speaking students with the responsibility of working with ELLs?

- What can she do to prepare her English speaking students to work with the ELLs?

- How does she organize the groups when bilingual students who speak the same language are not available?

- What types of assignments can be provided that will allow ELLs to work cooperatively to accomplish a particular task or assignment?

Often recommendations made for ELLs do not clarify the types of environments in which they may appear. Although engaging students in cooperative learning groups is widely accepted as a means to engage students in classroom discourse, attention must be provided to the nature of the small-group interactions when ELLs are part of the equation. To organize and maintain effective small-group discussions that involve ELLs, teachers must take great care in assigning students to groups in ways that will benefit ELLs, prepare English speaking students to work with ELLs, and facilitate students' social and cognitive skills that focus on communication about mathematics. Teachers can explicitly teach and model behaviors that are expected (e.g. "Jana doesn't speak much English so we need to find other ways to communicate with him. For example, I use pictures and point to what I mean to help him understand me. Would you be willing to work with him to help him understand?"). Teachers can facilitate interaction among students by creating an environment in which different cultures and cultural approaches to mathematics are respected. In addition, teachers can support students as they interact in small groups. English speaking students must recognize the value of working with ELLs. The emphasis must be placed on learning and on tolerance of errors that relate to use of language. All students should recognize that importance is placed on meaningful communication using a variety of means.

Engaging ELLs in cooperative learning activities not only provides opportunities for students of different backgrounds to work together, but also provides ELLs an opportunity to gain a sense of comfort in a new school setting. The small-group setting provides a safe place for ELLs to communicate with English speakers as they learn the content in English. Students feel more comfortable making errors, including language errors in small-group settings. Of significant importance for ELLs, cooperative learning develops communication skills and makes available a range of thoughts, experiences, and help from others that increase comprehension of the content and enhance other necessary skills. The focus on such interaction should be on communication, concepts, processes, and applications of mathematics. In this way, learning mathematics becomes a context for second language acquisition. Although many strategies are available for engaging students in cooperative learning, we recommend the use of the following when ELLs are initially introduced to a new learning environment:

- *Peer tutoring*—ELLs work with another student (e.g. another ELL, a bilingual student, or an English speaking peer) who understands the concepts. In order for this to be successful, teachers must teach English speaking students strategies (e.g. pointing, drawing) for communicating with the ELLs.
- *Think–pair–share*—These activities help students develop their own ideas, in addition to building ideas that originate from their peers (McTighe & Lyman, 1988). For example, the

teacher poses a problem and asks students to think about it alone for a certain amount of time. Then, students form pairs to discuss and revise their ideas. Finally, they share their answers with the class. This helps ELLs filter information and draw conclusions from the materials before they are asked to speak. In addition, they are given an opportunity to rehearse their attempts to communicate their ideas with another student. The other student can also clarify messages that were intended to be conveyed.

Depending on the language proficiency of the ELL, other more sophisticated cooperative learning strategies may be used, as described below:

- *Jigsaw*—This technique requires students to be responsible for the learning of others (Davidson, 1990). Specifically, students are assigned to small groups and are assigned to learn about a particular aspect of a topic that will later be shared. Each student is then responsible for reporting to their group. If students are to be held responsible for the materials learned, teachers must ensure that ELLs who are engaged in such activities have the language and mathematics skills that will enable them to provide instruction to peers. Level 1 (preproduction) or 2 (early production) students may find it difficult to function effectively in this type of cooperative learning environment.
- *Collaborative assignments or projects*—Students work together to accomplish a specific task or goal. To be effective, ELLs must have the language proficiency and mathematics skills to contribute equitably to the assigned task.

In order for any of the cooperative learning strategies discussed above to be effective, time needs to be taken to establish normative classroom practices and behaviors. Cooperative learning practices allow ELLs to use language related to the task while conversing, collaborating, and tutoring one another. By using their second language skills in authentic discourse, students are exposed to complex language structures and have opportunities to refine their communication skills by negotiating meaning through talk and other informal communication methods. When cooperative learning is used, the teacher becomes the facilitator of learning and does not serve as the primary source of information or the main authority on the subject matter. Cooperative learning encourages ELLs to take an active role in and responsibility for their learning, both mathematically and linguistically.

Allow Students to Use First Language as a Resource for Learning Mathematics

Many people erroneously believe that, in order to learn a new language, students must abandon the use of their primary language. As mentioned earlier, that view is not valid. ELLs come to school with prior mathematical knowledge, experiences, cultural beliefs, and attitudes toward education in general and about learning mathematics in particular. All of these serve as a foundation on which to build new understandings. Many ELLs may be good mathematics students but have difficulty communicating their knowledge in English. Because of this, they may need to process information in their native language.

Teachers should not perceive students' native language as a limitation but instead as a resource to support student learning. Students should be permitted to use their first language as a resource in mathematics development. That is, students should be allowed to process information in a language that is familiar to them before they are asked to translate it into English, a less familiar language. This allows the first language to serve as a bridge, rather than a barrier, to concept development and language acquisition. Groups of students with common linguistic backgrounds should be permitted to speak in their native language if evidence indicates that they are addressing the tasks at hand. This allows students to use terminology that they may find difficult to translate into English. In addition, it helps students to understand that (1) their language and culture are valued and (2) learning mathematics is more important than the language in which mathematics is learned.

Enhance ELLs' Self-Awareness as Members of Cultural Groups that Have Contributed to Mathematical Developments

Many students see mathematics as a topic to be mastered by "others." "Others" typically refers to individuals who are not members of their cultural or ancestral backgrounds. Like other students, ELLs must come to believe that they are a part of a larger cultural group that has contributed to the development of mathematics. Such awareness will help students acknowledge that they, too, are capable of doing challenging mathematics. To raise students' awareness, an ethnomathematics approach can be incorporated regularly as part of mathematics instruction.

> Ethnomathematics reveals all mathematics practices of day-to-day life, of preliterate cultures, of professional practitioners, of workers and obviously what has been called multicultural mathematics, but also includes the so-called academic or school mathematics, taking into account their historical evolution, with the recognition of all the natural social and cultural factors that shaped their development. (D'Ambrosio, 1995: 341)

Therefore, if we look at mathematics from an ethnomathematics perspective, and if we approach the teaching of mathematics by linking it to the development of a functioning society, we can help students learn more about the development of thought and reasoning as they are used today. In addition, such an approach will enable students from various cultural backgrounds to recognize and understand that mathematics is not static and is culturally developed over time to address areas of need. Although a full discussion about ethnomathematics is beyond the scope of this book, there are resources available that teachers can readily use to gain more insights into ethnomathematics. For example, the Ethnomathematics Digital Library (available at www.ethnomath.org) provides a wealth of resources that can be searched by topic, geographic area, or cultural group; resources include research, mathematics as studied and learned by other cultures, and educational perspectives. Additional resources are identified in the last part of this book. Incorporating ethnomathematics or multicultural activities allows ELLs and other students to recognize and appreciate alternative approaches toward mathematics, which will validate approaches they may be using and show that you, as the teacher, acknowledge and value different approaches. The overarching goal is to enable students to see themselves in mathematics. As mentioned earlier, this should extend well beyond the occasional integration of culturally associated names or the display of posters of mathematicians from various cultures.

Work with Others to Make Links to Students' Families

ELLs' families can be viewed as sources of ideas that ELLs can bring to the mathematics classroom (Moschkovich, 1999, 2000). ELLs and their families come from a range of backgrounds, experiences, and socioeconomic statuses. Teachers may find that parents of some of their ELLs have received a formal education in their home countries but, because they themselves are ELLs, might not practice their profession in the United States. Other parents may have received little education themselves but recognize the value of an education for their children. Finding ways to involve ELLs' family members, particularly for recent arrivals to the United States, will provide opportunities for the parents to understand the educational system, instructional practices, and expectations of students in this country.

Parents can also be viewed as a resource to help their children learn mathematics. Assignments or tasks can be structured that make parents aware of their child's learning activities or that encourage parents to contribute to the learning process. By giving parents a chance to discuss mathematics with their children in their first language, parents can utilize an opportunity to become involved in their children's education, even if only to supervise their children' completion of assignments. In addition, parents might provide insights that students can use to enhance their experiences in the classroom. For example, a parent might be able to relate mathematics vocabulary to a familiar word in the student's home language that can aid the student's understanding of that topic. By negotiating meaning and by switching between both languages, learning will occur for both parent and child.

Summary

In order to provide culturally responsive instruction that supports the learning of ELLs, teachers examine current practices to determine the extent to which they allow the individualized needs of ELLs to be met. Teachers recognize that they have the responsibility to learn about and learn from ELLs in order to provide instruction in ways that maximize students' learning. In particular, activities are structured that allow ELLs to engage in an acquisition-rich environment that requires them to listen to "comprehensible input" and generate "comprehensible output." Student-centered activities that permit ELLs to work in a supportive learning environment with their English-speaking peers support them in learning both academic language and mathematics.

3.7
Strategies for Mathematics Teachers Who Are Themselves English Language Learners

Ms. Slavcheva, a mathematics teacher of Eastern European descent, received her mathematics education in Europe. Four years after moving to the United States, she met the requirements to become a high school mathematics teacher. Ms. Slavcheva, an English language learner, was hired to teach mathematics in an urban high school with a diverse student population that was very different from her own schooling experiences. Not only did she have challenges associated with her own usage of the English language, but she also had to meet the needs of a diverse student body that included English language learners, students with special needs, and students from diverse cultural backgrounds. She had to address issues such as the following: "How do I ensure that I am understood by students?", "How do I teach students who speak other languages—Spanish, Portuguese, and sign—that I don't know?", "How do I address the various mathematics needs of students?", and "How do I manage a large class of students with diverse backgrounds and experiences?"

She was assigned to teach two Intensive Mathematics courses, two Pre-Algebra courses, and two Algebra 1A courses (the first part of a two-year sequence for first-year algebra). Students were directed to take Intensive Mathematics if they had scored at the lower levels on the state's high-stakes standardized test. Each of Ms. Slavcheva's Intensive Math classes consisted of about 12 to 15 students, who were Hispanic or African-American. Her Pre-Algebra classes consisted of approximately 20 students each, only a couple of whom appeared to be fluent in English; the majority spoke either Spanish or Portuguese. In these classes, she was assigned a teacher-assistant who appeared to have a good understanding of mathematics and was able to translate the lesson into Spanish. However, no assistance was readily available to those students who spoke Portuguese.

The situation in Ms. Slavcheva's Algebra 1A classes was very different. One of the classes consisted of about 36 students and the other had 27 students, with students of diverse backgrounds in both. Because of the large class sizes, Ms. Slavcheva found it difficult to manage the students. Unlike in her other classes, she did not appear to have time to give her full attention to mathematics. In one class, a teacher-assistant was available to provide translations to three Hispanic students. In addition, there was another teacher-assistant to provide translations to two students with hearing and speaking difficulties in her classroom.

To many, Ms. Slavcheva's circumstances might appear to be farfetched or be difficult to imagine. However, as more school districts attempt to address teacher shortages by recruiting and hiring individuals from different countries to teach in content areas that are difficult to staff, such as mathematics, there will likely be more teachers who will experience some of the same challenges as Ms. Slavcheva. For instance, the *Report to the National Education Association on Trends in Foreign Teacher Recruitment* in 2003 indicated that "Public school systems throughout the country are utilizing the services of perhaps as many as 10,000 foreign teachers in primary and secondary schools on 'nonimmigrant' work or cultural exchange visas" (Barber, 2003: 1). A key finding in the report was that

> the use of temporary foreign teachers appears to have been largely driven by efforts to address perceived teacher shortages, particularly in specific disciplines such as math, science, foreign languages, and special education, as well as in "less desirable" poor urban and rural school districts. Some school districts in major cities like New York City, Chicago, Los Angeles and Atlanta have established their own foreign teacher recruitment bureaus, with significant budgets and expansive global networks. (Barber, 2003: 2)

Companies exist that specialize in finding U.S. employment for prospective teachers from specific geographical areas. For example, mathematics teachers are often recruited from India, Australia, Canada, and the United Kingdom, while Spanish and English as Second Language (ESL) teachers are typically recruited from Spain and Latin America. In March 2002, the New Jersey Legislature even adopted an "Act concerning employment of teachers from foreign countries," which gives local school boards the right to hire foreign teachers in areas of critical shortage.

Teachers who are thus hired, and might themselves be English learners, are required to teach in English and to address students who may speak languages other than English and are themselves in the process of learning English. Clearly, this combination of teachers and students, both English language learners, and of potentially different linguistic backgrounds and language proficiencies, adds an additional layer of complexity to mathematics instruction. What assistance should teachers who are English language learners receive? What type of professional development or other experiences are needed to help these individuals address the cultural differences they will experience? How do these teachers provide quality mathematics instruction to students when they are in the process of learning English themselves? How do we help teachers who have difficulty teaching students who are culturally or linguistically diverse?

No one can deny that the United States is diverse and will continue to be a multicultural society. As mentioned in Part 1 of this book, the demographic changes in society will likely continue such that Americans will attend school with, live near, or work with individuals who are culturally, linguistically, or ethnically different from themselves. As a result, the education community in general, and the mathematics education community in particular, must address issues related to the needs of an increasingly multicultural, multilingual, and diverse teacher and student population. Accordingly, it is imperative that mathematics educators develop strategies to assist mathematics teachers who are ELLs as they attempt to function effectively in an environment that might pose additional challenges for them and their students. Such teachers may be not only new to the teaching profession, but also new to the cultural and social environment in which they must teach. It is our collective responsibility to assist and support these teachers as they transition to their new environment. It is not sufficient to recognize challenges if action is not taken to support and encourage the effectiveness of all teachers.

Create a Learning Environment that Is Accepting of Linguistic Differences

Teachers must create a learning environment in which students and the teacher feel comfortable addressing language issues directly. It is important that teachers who are ELLs publicly acknowledge some of the challenges that may result because of linguistic differences. This public acknowledgment reveals the effort they are willing to take to ensure that they are understood by students; such acknowledgement also emphasizes the importance the teacher places on student learning. Students whose teacher is an ELL need to know that the teacher will assist them to learn mathematics and that they can assist the teacher to learn American English. That is, students should feel comfortable asking the teacher to clarify words and intended messages and the teacher should feel comfortable asking for assistance to facilitate language and mathematics comprehension. In such an environment, a culture of trust and interdependence for learning is created.

Alert Students to Areas of Potential Difficulty Related to Language

A direct strategy for teachers who are themselves ELLs is to alert students to areas of potential difficulty or confusion. As teachers do this directly, they encourage students to assume some responsibility in the "negotiation of meaning." For example, a teacher from an Eastern European country who is accustomed to writing decimals with a comma might tell students about the differences and encourage students to clarify their understanding (e.g. "In my country, we write decimals with a comma so I might make mistakes when I write on the board. If you are unsure about what I mean, please ask. I wouldn't want to confuse you.") Also, this teacher might find that some words in his or her home language are phonetically similar to English words. A Bulgarian teacher, for example, might find the English word used for 100—"a hundred" to be similar to the Bulgarian word "hiliada" which means 1,000. Thus, if an English speaker quickly verbalizes 1,200 as "twelve hundreds," a Bulgarian might register this as 12,000, thinking of "twelve hiliadas." Clearly, this can cause confusion if the teacher and the students do not share the meaning of words. The teacher can also alert students to difficulties in this regard by making statements such as, "When you say 'hundred,' I might confuse it with the word 'hiliada' in my native language, which means one thousand. Please keep an eye on me so that I do not misinterpret what you say." Alerting students to possible areas of difficulty lets them know that it is acceptable to ask for clarification when needed; it also makes it easier for the teacher to acknowledge errors that are made publicly. An added benefit is that some ELL students might be encouraged to participate in the classroom discourse as they find that linguistic errors are accepted and not ridiculed.

Review the Mathematics Text for Linguistic and Symbolic Differences

Differences in language and symbols can be determined by reviewing the textbook to identify words or symbols that are unfamiliar. Once they are identified, a teacher who is an ELL can find ways to address them. In particular, he or she can create a personal dictionary that includes a list of words or symbols that might cause confusion, such as terms and symbols expressed differently in the teacher's native language. The dictionary might include the phonetic spelling of words to facilitate pronunciation as well as other information helpful in understanding the meaning. Some examples of differences between U.S. and Eastern European trigonometry terms and symbols are listed in Table 3.7. Although such differences may be small, they are potential sources of confusion for both teacher and students.

Use Various Strategies to Produce Comprehensible Output

Many of the strategies recommended for students who are ELLs are also relevant for teachers who are ELLs. However, teachers for whom English is a second language must also recognize that their linguistic accents sometimes make some words or phrases difficult to comprehend. These teachers must ensure that they produce comprehensible output. Specifically, their accents might hinder student comprehension because

- The words that students believe they are hearing do not make sense (e.g. students hear "We have to use the *bass* example to support our conclusion," when the intended message was "We have use the *best* example . . .").
- The words that students hear seem inappropriate for the context (e.g. students hear "When graphing we have to interpret the information at this *pint* . . .").
- Literal translations of words used by the teacher do not capture the nuances of the correct word or phrase (see, for example, Canonical List of Humorous English Mis-translations, found at www.geocities.com/Area51/Zone/7474/ohsigns.html).
- Pronunciations of words with different linguistic accents make it difficult for students to understand new academic words (e.g. students hear "spatial triangles" when the teacher meant "special triangles").

Although each of the potential problems just outlined might cause some difficulty for English speaking students, the problems are particularly challenging for students who are attempting to learn English themselves. Thus, teachers who are ELLs should be sure to use several strategies that have been discussed in previous chapters, whether or not they have students who are ELLs in their classes (Rubenstein, 1997):

- Write the intended word on the board, especially when evidence is available to suggest that students do not understand what is being said (e.g. they have puzzled looks on their faces).

TABLE 3.7. Trigonometry words and symbols in some Eastern European countries vs. in the United States

Eastern Europe		American English	
Word	**Symbol**	**Word**	**Symbol**
sinus	sin	sine	sin
cosinus	cos	cosine	cos
tangent	tg	tangent	tan
cotangent	cotg	cotangent	cot

- Ask students or English speaking colleagues to pronounce words and practice saying them.
- Use pictures, objects, and gestures to reinforce and support verbal communication and student comprehension.
- Ask students to restate what they heard.
- Restate or paraphrase statements from students ("you said . . . Is that correct?") to ensure that students are interpreted correctly.
- Invite students to correct or translate teacher talk.

Overall, a teacher who is an ELL should use strategies recommended for use with ELL students (e.g. visuals, highlighting information with different colored markers, using manipulatives, organizing data with Venn diagrams or tables or graphs) to ensure that all students understand the messages that are being conveyed.

Collaborate with English Speaking Colleagues

Mathematics teachers who are themselves ELLs can collaborate with English speaking peers who teach the same topic or are willing to provide language and instructional support. For example, a teacher who is an ELL and assigned to teach geometry might try to collaborate with English speaking peers to address vocabulary issues (e.g. pronouncing words appropriately) or difficulties related to adjusting to a new school environment (e.g. lack of familiarity with the student population). Although the teacher who is an ELL should be knowledgeable about the content in his or her native language, the teacher may find some terms unfamiliar, particularly because words such as *congruent*, *complementary*, or *supplementary* as applied to angles are not used in the native language or have different meanings in social communication. In addition, expressions or symbols used to express mathematics ideas are sometimes different (e.g. *tan* vs. *tg* in Table 3.7). Working with a peer is helpful and an important complement to using a translation dictionary; dictionaries are often insufficient because they do not provide linguistic nuances and cultural meanings that are essential to help students comprehend content. Conversations with native English speaking mathematics teachers can provide insights about instructional differences, student expectations, and strategies to overcome challenges.

Further, although mathematics teachers who are ELLs are knowledgeable about the content in their native language, they may find some of the instructional approaches and practices used in American schools unfamiliar (e.g. students might expect to interact as part of their learning experiences) and may have difficulty relating to students who insist on their use. English speaking teachers who serve as mentors can help their ELL colleagues interpret unfamiliar approaches. For example, when teaching students to solve proportion problems, Ms. Chin, a teacher who was an ELL, found that many of her students used the "is over of" method. (That is, they had been taught to solve a proportion by focusing on key words and placing numbers in the appropriate locations.)

$$\frac{is}{of} = \frac{\%}{100}$$

Ms. Chin was not familiar with this approach and was surprised by the facility with which many of the students used it, so she asked a colleague to explain the method, which the students had learned in an earlier grade. Although she was not keen on that method, she found that her students were proficient with it, so she decided to connect this method to the other approaches she intended to introduce.

Mentors can also plan lessons jointly with teachers who are ELLs. During this planning process, opportunities should be taken to address concerns related to language and communication, students, the subject matter, the curriculum, or other school and administrative issues. In addition to mentors, others may also be able to provide insights about students, particularly when problems arise. For example, the guidance counselor may be able to provide information about students that is not readily obtained as part of classroom instruction but is essential to meet the needs of individual students. In particular, a counselor might be able to identify resources to assist students who are ELLs, particularly if the students are from a language group that is less prominent in the school setting.

Keep a Journal of Idioms/Expressions for Use in Teaching Mathematics

Mathematics teachers who are ELLs might find it helpful to keep a journal of language and communication information obtained from students or colleagues. The journal might include new terms or expressions encountered while teaching or engaging in conversations, as well as different approaches for addressing the subject matter. For example, many teachers who are ELLs or who are English speakers from non-U.S. school systems may not readily recognize approaches commonly used in the United States, such as particular mnemonic devices (e.g. "soh", "cah", "toa" to explain sine, cosine, and tangent). This new knowledge can be used to support and improve communication with students.

Engage in Ongoing Professional Development

Teachers who are ELLs should be encouraged to participate in ongoing professional development to help them function in their role as mathematics teachers and as teachers who will teach students who are ELLs. For such teachers, professional development should not only address the subject matter but also provide insights into an unfamiliar educational system and students' cultural and linguistic backgrounds. Professional development can occur in many forms, including reading professional literature about current trends in the field, the student population being served, and the educational setting, or attending professional development sessions provided at the school or school district level.

Observe Others Teaching Mathematics

All teachers, and particularly teachers who are ELLs, can engage in personalized professional development by observing others teach mathematics. These observations can aid in learning about common approaches for teaching (e.g. cooperative learning) or strategies that may be unfamiliar (e.g. classroom management strategies). One teacher who was an ELL shared with one of the authors of this book that he learned from observation that other teachers tended to embed ongoing review as part of their mathematics instruction. He decided that he would incorporate this strategy in his classes. Further, these classroom observations of peers provided him insights into how to create a positive classroom environment, relate to students, and manage the classroom. During these observations, the non-native English speaking teacher can make note of the following:

- *Discourse community of the classroom*—e.g. How do teachers engage students in classroom discourse? What types of questions does the teacher ask?

- *Classroom management*—e.g. What are classroom norms? What expectations are established? How do teachers engage students in ways that encourage appropriate classroom behaviors?
- *Structure of classroom activities*—e.g. What different phases of instruction are used, such as whole class vs. small group?

Share and Receive Cultural Information

Students will likely be curious about their teachers and peers who come from culturally or linguistically different backgrounds. Strategies should be used to incorporate and share differences as a natural part of instruction. Teachers can share information about their culture, language, educational background, and experiences and invite other students to do the same.

The classroom can be used as a display to illustrate the similarities and differences among cultural groups. For example, a different algorithm for approaching a task can be displayed to illustrate that there are different approaches for solving problems or representing solutions. ELL students and their English speaking peers can be encouraged to add information and materials that exemplify mathematical events or individuals who contributed to the field of mathematics from their own culture. Examples and data from teachers' and students' backgrounds can be incorporated as part of instructional activities (e.g. flags, artwork, architecture, coins, stamps). Students might also find it interesting to learn about the educational environment in different countries.

As part of this process, it is important that teachers who are ELLs become familiar with their students and the community in which they will work. This includes learning and pronouncing students' names accurately, learning of individual and collective student interests, and learning about unique characteristics about the local community. For instance, there might be unique aspects about a particular school community that are not representative of the larger community but that need to be understood to connect with students. Understanding the local context is helpful for interpreting interactions and assumptions. Overall, the intent is for teachers who are ELLs to learn as much as possible about their new work environment to make connections that can facilitate teaching in a culturally and linguistically new environment.

Another method for learning about the local and school context is to participate in extracurricular activities and school events. For example, teachers can learn about culturally specific academic or nonacademic activities or events, such as clubs, pep rallies, or other sporting events. Participation in such activities lets students know that their teachers are interested in them and are willing to take time to get to know them better.

Connect with Parents

All teachers must find ways to connect with students' families. Meetings with parents can be initiated so that they learn about their child's progress. Like their children, parents might want to learn about the educational, cultural, and linguistic background of teachers who are also ELLs. Teachers need to be willing to share information about themselves and let parents know they will work to ensure their child receives the best education possible.

Summary

Teachers who are ELLs need to implement for themselves many of the strategies typically used with students who are ELLs. They also need to create a learning community in which both their students and their peers provide support with language while learning mathematics.

Resources

Internet Resources to Support Mathematics Teaching and Learning

In this section we identify internet resources that teachers can use to support mathematics learning in the classroom. Rather than a comprehensive list of the many sites that relate generally to English language learners (ELLs) and offer general strategies for teaching them, this is an annotated list of selected sites that describes how these sites might be useful to mathematics teachers. Some of the sites offer information related to interacting with ELLs in the classroom; others provide resources that can be used to enhance mathematics teaching and learning. Reputable sites were selected that are expected to have longevity. However, keep in mind that information available on the internet is fluid and ever-changing. We have included the title of each site to permit readers to search for the sites in the future even if there is a change in the internet address (URL). Teachers are also encouraged to conduct additional searches on the internet, as new materials are often added.

Resources to Help Teachers Better Understand the ELLs in Their Classroom

So You've Got an English Language Learner in Your Class for the First Time (www.celt.sunysb.edu/ell/first.php)

This site, created by the Center for Excellence in Learning and Teaching at Stony Brook University, offers readers a range of tips on how to accommodate the needs of individual ELLs in the classroom. The site's components include a test of cultural awareness, commonly encountered problems, the importance of maintaining a first language, tips for teaching ELLs, and videos of ELLs describing their schooling experiences. Mathematics teachers can use this site to gauge their preparedness to work with ELLs and to interpret their interactions with ELLs.

Tapestry at the University of South Florida (http://tapestry.usf.edu/)

This site offers a series of free video lectures by experts in the field of teaching English to Speakers of Other Languages (ESOL). Topics addressed in the lectures include legal issues and ESOL, special education and ESOL, content instruction, and dialect diversity.

Mathematics Education Organizations or Projects that Support the Teaching of ELLs

National Council of Teachers of Mathematics (NCTM) (nctm.org and illuminations.nctm.org)

The National Council of Teachers of Mathematics is the largest organization in the United States that focuses on improving mathematics education for grades pre-K–12. The home page of the website provides links to conferences, journals published by NCTM, and various updates related to mathematics education. In addition, NCTM posts research briefs on important issues as the need arises. The website also provides a link to a catalog of books and other resources to support mathematics instruction. Although this site does not address the needs of ELLs specifically, it offers a range of resources that may be used to enhance mathematics instruction.

TODOS: Mathematics for All (todos-math.org)

TODOS is an affiliate group of NCTM with a mission to support equity for all students, and particularly for Hispanic and Latino students. Of particular interest to readers of this book are the resources referenced on the website, including links to quality mathematics resources in Spanish. In addition, the site provides data collected on issues related to the education of Hispanic students, including a major report on strategies for closing the achievement gap in mathematics that affects Hispanic Americans.

International Study Group on Ethnomathematics (ISGEm) (www.rpi.edu/~eglash/isgem.htm)

ISGEm, an affiliate of NCTM, has as its goal the increase of knowledge about culture and diversity when teaching mathematics. This official site of the organization provides links to the *Journal of Mathematics and Culture* as well as to other sites that address ethnomathematics. The main benefit of such a website is to provide background information for teachers who want to bring more culture into their mathematics classroom as a means to engage their ELLs.

The Math Forum (mathforum.org)

The Math Forum is an online resource with the goal of supporting and enhancing the teaching of mathematics. The website includes a variety of features, including regular Problems of the Week as well as Ask Dr. Math. Most of the resources on the site do not relate specifically to ELLs. However, the site does have a mathematics internet library, and a number of resources in the library relate to teaching limited English students, including an annotated bibliography of resources on the connections between language and achievement for ELLs.

Texas State University System: Mathematics for English Language Learners Project (tsusmell.org)

This website was developed as part of a research initiative to provide teachers with resources that support quality mathematics instruction for language-minority students. The site includes a number of important resources for teachers, including an English–Spanish picture dictionary of terms needed by Texas high school students for the state assessment (most of which would be of value in any state). In addition, the site includes documents with lists of resources of use to teachers, including reviews of literature related to ELLs and mathematics at the elementary, middle, and high school levels. The website is expected to be a living resource, updated with new materials and lessons on a regular basis.

Resources to Support Visualizing Mathematics Concepts

Illuminations (illuminations.nctm.org)

This site supports the implementation of the NCTM (2000) standards by providing resources that teachers can use to improve mathematics instruction. It contains interactive online activities, lesson plans, and links to other exemplary resources that have been vetted by an editorial panel for quality. The visual, interactive nature of many of these lessons and activities may be of particular benefit to ELLs as they work to make connections among important concepts.

National Library of Virtual Manipulatives (nlvm.usu.edu/en/nav/vlibrary.html)

This website, developed at Utah State University, is available in English, Spanish, and French. Students can explore mathematics concepts using online manipulatives. Spanish and French speaking students can work on the virtual manipulatives in their first language as well as in English in order to build language fluency. Sites such as this enable teachers who do not speak their students' first language to engage them in challenging mathematics simultaneously with their English speaking peers, because the site provides language support.

Shodor Foundation Mathematics Interactive (English: www.shodor.org/interactivate; Spanish: www.eduteka.org/MI/master/interactivate)

This website offers a collection of interactive online activities that permit students to investigate mathematics. It is available in English and Spanish. The interactive, visual nature of the online tools can support ELLs as they attempt to make connections among mathematical concepts. The site also includes lessons aligned to the NCTM Standards.

Mathematics Dictionaries

A Maths Dictionary for Kids (www.amathsdictionaryforkids.com)

This web site, developed by Jenny Eather, includes explanations of over 500 terms commonly used in mathematics. When users click on a specific word, an explanation in simple language appears together with a visual display of the term, its definition, and an interactive component to allow students to assess their understanding of the meaning. The site could easily be used as a resource to help ELLs understand new mathematics concepts. The ease of the site and the visual illustrations of the terms makes it beneficial for ELLs at all four levels of language fluency, but particularly for those at the lowest two levels.

Multi-Lingual eGlossary (www.glencoe.com/sec/math/mlg)

This site provides a glossary of mathematics terms and their definitions in various languages, including Arabic, Bengali, Brazilian Portuguese, Chinese, Haitian Creole, Hmong, Korean, Russian, Spanish, Tagalog, Urdu, and Vietnamese. In addition to the definitions, some of the entries include a visual representation of the concept.

Culturally Responsive Pedagogy

In prior chapters we discussed the need to foster an environment of culturally responsive or culturally relevant pedagogy. Below are two online resources on multicultural mathematics, ethnomathematics, and culturally responsive pedagogy and some ready-to-use classroom activities or ideas to aid ELLs in learning mathematics while also learning English. These resources focus more on the cultural aspects of mathematics in general and not specifically on how those cultural aspects connect with ELLs.

Ethnomathematics Digital Library (http://ethnomath.org/index.asp)

This digital library can be browsed by subject, geographical area, or cultural group. It is easy to access mathematics topics (e.g. mathematics history, fractions) to obtain information on the development of contemporary mathematics from ideas originating in ancient cultures, such as China, India, Egypt, Greece, or the Roman Empire. Teachers can search for mathematics ideas originating from a specific geographical area (e.g. patterns in Oriental rugs) in order to gather examples from the specific countries or cultures of ELLs in a class.

Ethnomathematics Snap Shots (www.tacomacc.edu/home/jkellerm/Ethnomath/index.htm)

This website provides easily accessed pictorial representations of mathematical ideas from around the world, such as those found in artifacts of the Incas, the Mesopotamians, and Native Americans, which can be used as visuals in mathematics lessons on a range of topics. The site is especially helpful for teachers who may not be aware of mathematics connections from other cultures, including cultures related to those of the ELLs in their classroom.

Print Resources for Further Study

In this section, we provide a list of print resources, with annotations, that may be of benefit to those interested in further study related to meeting the mathematics education needs of ELL students. There are certainly many excellent resources in print and on the internet related to teaching mathematics. There are also many resources that speak to the needs of ELL students in general across all content disciplines. Rather than attempt to provide a long list of generic resources, we have chosen to focus on a limited number of resources that we believe have potential to be of particular benefit in meeting the needs of mathematics teachers as they strive to provide rich, comprehensible instruction for their ELL students.

Teaching Ideas

Anstrom, K. (1999). *Preparing secondary education teachers to work with English language learners: Mathematics*. Washington, DC: Center for the Study of Language and Education, Graduate School of Education and Human Development. (Also available at www.ncela.gwu.edu/pubs/resource/ells/math.pdf.)

In this resource, strategies are discussed that specifically relate to helping ELLs in the mathematics classroom, and mathematics examples are provided to illustrate use of the approaches. Of particular interest is discussion of issues related to language, creating a supportive classroom environment, building on students' prior background knowledge, and appropriate assessment.

Bay-Williams, J. M., and Herrera, S. (2007). Is "just good teaching" enough to support the learning of English language learners? Insights from sociocultural learning theory. In W. G. Martin, M. E. Strutchens, and P. C. Elliott (eds.), *The learning of mathematics*. Reston, VA: National Council of Teachers of Mathematics, pp. 43–63.

The authors of this chapter focus on learning theory as it relates to helping ELLs move from where they are in mathematics and language learning to the next level in order to facilitate growth. With specific focus on mathematics, the authors provide insights into strategies that teachers can use to make instruction comprehensible to students, including appropriate modifications that do not lessen the mathematical challenge of the instruction.

Beilenberg, B., and Fillmore, L. W. (Dec. 2004/Jan. 2005). The English they need for the test. *Educational Leadership*, 62: 45–49.

As high-stakes assessments increasingly include more problems set in context rather than simply skill problems, ELLs need to understand language that may appear on such assessments. This article describes a project in which ELLs used a challenging curriculum supported with scaffolding instruction. The use of revoicing in supporting students' language development is described.

Bouchard, M. (2005). *Comprehension strategies for English language learners.* New York: Scholastic.

This book provides 30 reading strategies to help English language learners deal with textbook materials with examples. The author identifies the potential benefits of each strategy for ELL students. Templates for use with various strategies are provided as blackline masters. Although not specifically geared to mathematics, many of the strategies will resonate with mathematics teachers of ELLs and provide added support for the use of these strategies in teaching ELLs.

Civil, M., Bratton, J., and Quintos, B. (2005). Parents and mathematics education in a Latino community: Redefining parental participation. *Multicultural Education,* 13 (2): 60–64.

Readers of this article will find strategies that can be used with parents to help them become learners and teachers of mathematics with their children. The strategies are useful to help parents become partners with teachers in order to enhance the mathematics learning of ELLs.

Coggins, D., Kravin, D., Coates, G. D., and Carroll, M. D. (2007). *English language learners in the mathematics classroom.* Thousand Oaks, CA: Corwin Press.

This book provides specific strategies for helping ELL students in mathematics, including building conversational language and academic language. Emphasis is placed on the use of materials, visual learning, and the role of questioning strategies. Vignettes are provided throughout to illustrate how the suggestions are enacted in the classroom. The focus of the book is at the elementary grades, but middle school and high school teachers can gain insights into potential approaches to use with their students.

Edwards, C. (Ed.) (1999). *Changing the faces of mathematics: Perspectives on Asian Americans and Pacific Islanders.* Reston, VA: National Council of Teachers of Mathematics.

Hankes, J. E., and Fast, G. R. (2002). *Changing the faces of mathematics: Perspectives on indigenous people of North America.* Reston, VA: National Council of Teachers of Mathematics.

Ortiz-Franco, L., Hernandez, N. G., and de la Cruz, Y. (Eds.) (1999). *Changing the faces of mathematics: Perspectives on Latinos.* Reston, VA: National Council of Teachers of Mathematics.

These three books are part of the NCTM series *Changing the Faces of Mathematics,* which was designed to provide perspectives on how educators can meet the needs of students of various ethnic backgrounds. Each of the books contains a series of articles written by a range of scholars. Some articles deal with theoretical perspectives to provide the reader with background knowledge about cultural issues or language issues related to the groups covered by the specific volume. Other articles provide resources for designing lessons with a multicultural focus. The various grade bands are represented across the range of articles in each book.

Eschevarria, J., and Graves, A. (2007). *Sheltered content instruction: Teaching English language learners with diverse abilities.* (3rd edn.) Boston: Pearson.

Written by two leaders in sheltered instruction, this resource offers a number of examples from various disciplines to explain the concept of sheltered instruction and its enactment in classrooms. Some historical perspectives on education for English language learners duplicate that provided in Part 1 of this book. Chapters focus on affective issues that influence learning, different learning strategies and styles, and adjusting discourse.

Herrell, A. L., and Jordan, M. (2008). *50 Strategies for teaching English language learners.* (3rd Edn.). Upper Saddle River, NJ: Pearson.

Although not specifically designed for mathematics teachers, this book contains 50 specific teaching strategies along with examples and vignettes. Strategies are classified in terms of strategies for planning, for student involvement, for developing vocabulary and fluency, and for building comprehension. Not all of the strategies are necessarily applicable to the mathematics classroom, but the range of examples will provide additional suggestions for approaches that can meet the needs of ELL students.

Hill, J. D., and Flynn, K. M. (2006). *Classroom instruction that works with English language learners*. Alexandria, VA: Association for Supervision and Curriculum Development.

Although written to cover the range of disciplines, the suggestions offered in the book are written in a teacher-friendly style with classroom examples throughout, a few of which are mathematics-based. Each chapter focuses on a particular set of recommendations, including setting objectives, using advance organizers, and taking notes. Readers can use the information in this resource to supplement the ideas and information gained from this book.

Jarrett, D. (1999). *The inclusive classroom: Teaching mathematics and science to English-language learners. It's just good teaching.* Portland, OR: Northwest Regional Education Laboratory. (Also available at www.nrwel.org/msec.just_good/8.)

This print publication, also available online at the NWREL website, provides perspectives on second language learning strategies that can be beneficial in teaching and learning mathematics and science. Issues related to vocabulary development, discourse, assessment, inquiry, and affective influences are included, as are ways to involve the families of ELLs.

Kauffman, D. and Apple, G. (2000). *Oxford picture dictionary for the content areas.* New York: Oxford University Press.

Kopriva, R., and Saez, S. (1997). *Guide to scoring LEP student responses to open-ended mathematics items*. Washington, DC: Council of Chief State School Officers. (ERIC ED452704)

Assessment of ELLs often poses special challenges for teachers who desire to assess their students' mathematics knowledge without language proficiency being a barrier. This publication provides insights into scoring of open-ended items and provides examples of errors that are common among ELLs at different levels of language proficiency, including code-switching, phonetic spelling, word transposition, and stylistic preferences in responses as a function of culture.

Lee, H.-J., and Jung, W. S. (2004). Limited-English-Proficient (LEP) students: mathematical understanding. *Mathematics Teaching in the Middle School*, 9: 269–272.

The authors discuss instructional strategies useful in the mathematics classroom when working with ELL students. They begin by helping teachers become aware of issues that may impact their interactions with ELLs.

Perkins, I., and Flores, A. (2002). Mathematical notations and procedures of recent immigrant students. *Mathematics Teaching in the Middle School*, 7: 346–351.

ELLs who have had mathematics education in other cultures or countries often document their use of algorithms and other mathematics procedures in ways that differ from the notation used in most U.S. classrooms. This article provides insights to teachers about procedures that may be used by students from Mexico.

Pilar, R. (1998). My family taught me this way. In L. J. Morrow and M. J. Kenney (Eds.), *The teaching and learning of algorithms in school mathematics*. Reston, VA: National Council of Teachers of Mathematics, pp. 115–119.

Many ELL students have learned computation using algorithms commonly taught in other countries. This article compares the U.S. standard algorithms for arithmetic computations to algorithms from other countries and highlights errors that students make when the algorithms become confused. Although the focus is on elementary mathematics, it can be a helpful resource for middle or high school teachers whose students are making computational errors.

Reed, B., and Railsback, J. (2003). *Strategies and resources for mainstream teachers of English language learners*. Portland, OR: Northwest Regional Educational Laboratory. (Also available at www.nwrel.org/request/2003may.)

A set of broad principles for instruction of ELLs is provided. Although not specifically related to mathematics, the strategies embedded within the principles apply to the mathematics classroom and readers can use these ideas to support the changes encouraged in this book.

Short, D. J., and Eschevarria, J. (1999). *The sheltered instruction observation protocol: A tool for teacher–research collaboration and professional development* (Educational Practice Report 3.) Santa Cruz, CA: Center for Research on Education, Diversity and Excellence. (ERIC ED434533)

This report describes work with a group of teachers who spent an extended professional development period designing instruction for their classroom using the Sheltered Instruction Observation Protocol (SIOP). The report describes implementing language objectives in content lessons and assessing students' comprehension. In addition, it summarizes what was learned about supporting teacher change for appropriate instruction of ELLs.

Thompson, D. R., Kersaint, G., Richards, J. C., Hunsader, P. D., and Rubenstein, R. N. (2008). *Mathematical literacy: Helping students make meaning in the middle grades*. Portsmouth, NH: Heinemann.

This book provides strategies that mathematics educators can use to help students build mathematical literacy across the entire literacy spectrum (reading, writing, listening, and speaking). Specific strategies are illustrated with numerous examples and classroom vignettes.

Trentacosta, J., and Kenney, M. J. (Eds.) (1997). *Multicultural and gender equity in the mathematics classroom: The gift of diversity*. Reston, VA: National Council of Teachers of Mathematics.

The focus of this 1997 NCTM yearbook is on encouraging teachers to consider their classrooms from a multicultural perspective in order to promote equity for all students of mathematics. Among the chapters are some that focus on theoretical perspectives in teaching ELLs while others focus on specific teaching approaches. In addition, some of the chapters provide insights on integrating culture into the mathematics classroom. All are written in a teacher-friendly style.

Zaslavsky, C. (1994). *Multicultural math: Hands-on math activities from around the world*. New York: Scholastic Professional Books, 1994.

This earlier resource by a mathematics educator long known for her multicultural work consists of blackline masters with multicultural activities ready-made for the mathematics classroom.

Zaslavsky, C. (1996). *The multicultural math classroom: Bringing in the world*. Portsmouth, NH: Heinemann, 1996.

Although not specifically focused on ELLs, this book presents a myriad of approaches and ideas for integrating culture into the mathematics classroom. Thus, it is a valuable resource for teachers who are interested in tying mathematics instruction to the cultural backgrounds of their students when possible.

(no authors listed). (2005). *Tips for English language learners in mathematics: Grades 7, 8, 9, Applied, and 10 Applied*. Ontario, Canada: Queen's Printer for Ontario.

This resource, developed by the Ministry of Education of Ontario, provides a series of strategies useful for teaching mathematics to ELLs, including oral, visual, instructional, scaffolding, and assessment strategies.

Research Issues

Chamot, A. U. (1995). Implementing the cognitive academic language learning approach: CALLA in Arlington, Virginia. *Bilingual Research Journal*, 19 (3–4): 379–394.

CALLA is a recognized approach used to aid ELLs as they learn academic language for content courses. This article discusses the implementation and success of CALLA in the Arlington, Virginia, school district.

Cocking, R. R., and Mestre, J. P. (Eds.) (1988). *Linguistic and cultural influences on learning mathematics*. Hillsdale, NJ: Lawrence Erlbaum.

Although an older resource, the various chapters in this edited book provide research insights about language issues and how they interact with achievement for language-minority students. These chapters provide a basis for understanding strategies developed to increase the opportunities for comprehension by ELLs.

Gorgorió, N. and Planas, N. (2001). Teaching mathematics in multilingual classrooms. *Educational Studies in Mathematics*, 47: 7–33.

The research in this article, set in Catalonia in Spain, highlights the fact that issues related to language-minority students face educators throughout the world. The research, based on extensive work in classrooms, brings to the fore the role of cultural expectations and norms in learning mathematics, as well as the role of language. As such, it emphasizes the need to consider culture as well as language in designing instruction that will move ELLs' mathematical knowledge forward.

Gutstein, E., Lipman, P., Hernandez, P., and de los Reyes, R. (1997). Culturally relevant mathematics teaching in a Mexican American context. *Journal for Research in Mathematics Education*, 28: 709–737.

Research in this article provides further evidence of the need to incorporate cultural experiences into mathematics instruction for language-minority students, in this case students from a Mexican-American background. The importance of focusing on critical thinking is highlighted to enhance mathematical growth.

Khisty, L. L. (1995). Making inequality: Issues of language and meanings in mathematics teaching with Hispanic students. In W. G. Secada, E. Fennema, and L. B. Adajian (Eds.), *New directions for equity in mathematics education*. Cambridge, UK: Cambridge University Press, pp. 279–297.

This chapter focuses on research related to teaching, particularly discourse, in classrooms with large numbers of students whose mother tongue is not English and attempts to consider how instruction interacts with achievement. In particular, the author considers how discourse can engage or disengage students in the mathematics classroom and highlights the importance of considering students' first language and cultural experiences in designing instruction. The research suggests that "just good teaching" is not sufficient to facilitate high achievement among language minority students.

Khisty, L. L. (2002). Mathematics learning and the Latino student: Suggestions from research for classroom practice. *Teaching Children Mathematics*, 9: 32–35.

This article suggests methods of enhancing mathematics instruction for ELLs based on current research findings. The suggestions support the strategies recommended in this book.

Roberson, S., and Summerlin, J. (2005). *Mathematics and English language learners: A review of the literature*. Available at www.tsusmell.org/images/MELL_P2_Lit_Rvw.pdf.)

A set of recommendations for instruction of ELLs is provided, supported by research findings.

Wang, J., and Goldschmidt, P. (1999). Opportunity to learn, language proficiency, and immigrant status effects on mathematics achievement. *Journal of Educational Research*, 93 (2): 101–111.

The research reported by these authors highlights the connection between achievement and opportunity to learn. Language-minority students are often relegated to less demanding mathematics courses, which has a negative influence on their ability to learn challenging mathematics and to perform at a high level.

Glossary

Additive bilingualism: Theory that the acquisition of a second language does not interfere in the learning of the native language; second language can be acquired either simultaneously or after native language development.

Basic Interpersonal Communication Skills (BICS): In effect, language skills needed for everyday personal and social communication.

Bilingual education: Although most instruction is in English, concepts are explained in students' primary language and a Sheltered English approach is used for academic subjects.

Cognitive/Academic Language Proficiency (CALP): Language skills needed for cognitive/academic tasks in the mainstream classroom.

Comprehensible input: Language presented at the student's level of comprehension. Input is made comprehensible through the use of visuals, context, and other cues.

Developmental bilingual education: Instruction is provided in the student's native language for an extended time period while simultaneously learning English resulting in bilingualism; often used synonymously with "late exit bilingual education."

Dual-language programs: Instruction occurs in both the native language and in English to develop strong skills and proficiency in both. Also known as **two-way immersion**.

Early-exit bilingual education: Transition to English as quickly as possible, often using sheltered instructional strategies; some content instruction in the native language is provided; transition to mainstream in 2–3 years.

English language learner (ELL): Student whose limited proficiency in English affects his or her academic achievement in school. Also known as Limited English Proficient (LEP) student.

English as a New Language (ENL): Used by the National Board for Professional Teaching Standards.

English as a Second Language (ESL): The learning of English by speakers of other languages; often used synonymously with ESOL.

English for Speakers of Other Languages (ESOL): The learning of English by speakers of other languages; often used synonymously with ESL.

Heritage learner: Student who is exposed to a language other than English at home. Heritage learners usually have varying degrees of knowledge of the home language.

Immersion: Instructional approach wherein 100 percent of the instructional time is spent communicating through the target language; in contrast to **submersion**, the class is composed mostly of speakers of the target language with only a few non-native speakers.

Language-minority student: A student whose primary home language is not English. Language-minority students may have limited English proficiency or may be fluent in English.

Late-exit bilingual education: In contrast to early-exit bilingual education, the transition to mainstream occurs in 4–6 years; a significant amount of instruction occurs in the native language while instruction in English gradually increases.

Limited English Proficiency (LEP) student: Student whose limited proficiency in English affects his or her academic achievement in school. Also known as English language learner (ELL).

Mainstreaming: Practice of integrating ELLs into regular classrooms.

Maintenance bilingual education: Instruction is delivered in both the native language and the target language; often used synonymously with late-exit bilingual education.

Pull-out: Removal of students from their regular, English-only classrooms for special instruction to develop English language skills.

Self-contained classes: ELL classrooms located in "regular" schools but separate from regular education classrooms; ELLs are provided special instruction apart from their peers.

Sheltered English instruction: Use of comprehensible content and strategies to teach grade-level subject matter in English while simultaneously developing English language skills. Also known as Specially Designed Academic Instruction in English (SDAIE).

Sheltered immersion: Instructional approach that promotes English language development while providing comprehensible grade-level content.

Silent period: Common, varying period of time during which a new language learner listens to, but does not speak in, the new language.

Specially Designed Academic Instruction in English (SDAIE): Use of comprehensible content and strategies to teach grade-level subject matter in English while simultaneously also developing English language skills. Also known as Sheltered English instruction.

Structured immersion: Immersion-based instructional approach in which students' proficiency levels in English are taken into account so that subject matter is made comprehensible.

Submersion: Instructional approach wherein the class is composed entirely of students learning a target language; 100 percent of the instructional time is spent communicating through the target language.

Subtractive bilingualism: Result when the acquisition of a second language interferes with the maintenance of the native language, and effectively replaces the first language.

Total Physical Response: Instructional approach integrating both verbal and physical communication (and often movement) so that students can internalize and eventually "code-break" a new language; especially effective with beginning language students and for vocabulary instruction, and with students who are primarily kinesthetic learners.

Transitional bilingual education: Language acquisition theory emphasizing acquisition of fluency in the learner's native language first, before acquiring fluency in a second language.

Two-way immersion: Instruction occurs in both the native language and in English so that strong skills and proficiency are developed in both. Also known as **dual-language programs**.

Notes

1.1 Orientation

1 Proposition 227 was part of a referendum in California to abolish bilingual education for ELLs in favor of more instruction in English. The *No Child Left Behind* legislation is a federal initiative to oversee teacher performance and student improvement in literacy and numeracy through such accountability measures as standardized testing in schools.

1.7 Not All Parents are the Same: Home–School Communication

1 Two research studies from the Center for Research on Education, Diversity & Excellence (CREDE) have recently been published through the Center for Applied Linguistics. The two books, arising out of a four-year and a three-year study, respectively, center on the solidification of home–school ELL communication. The first, entitled *Creating Access: Language and Academic Programs for Secondary School Newcomers*, describes the ins and outs of an effective education model—newcomer programs for immigrant students—and is designed to help district personnel create a newcomer program or enhance an existing program. The second book, called *Family Literacy Nights: Building the Circle of Supporters within and beyond School for Middle School English Language Learners*, discusses a project to improve students' education through a home–school collaboration called "Family Literacy Nights." The program brought parents of linguistically and culturally diverse students together with teachers and students, resulting in greater parental involvement and improved student learning. This report offers practitioners strategies for implementing similar programs.

3.6 Teaching Mathematics in Ways that are Culturally Responsive

1 Videotapes of students are available at the Teaching English Language Learners website, available at www.celt.sunysb.edu/ell/default.php.

References

Series Introduction

Ladson-Billings, G. (2001). *Crossing over to Canaan: The journey of new teachers in diverse classrooms*. San Francisco: Jossey-Bass.

Part 1

Baca, L. and Cervantes, H. (2004). *The bilingual special education interface*. Columbus, OH: Merrill.

Bailey, A. L., Butler, F. A., Borrego, M., LaFramenta, C., and Ong, C. (2002). Towards a characterization of academic language. *Language Testing Update*, 31: 45–52.

Baker, C. (2001). *Foundations of bilingual education and bilingualism*, 3rd edn. Clevedon: Multilingual Matters.

Bassoff, T. C. (2004) Three steps toward a strong home–school connection. *Essential Teacher*, 1 (4). Retrieved July 17, 2007, from www.tesol.org/s_tesol/sec_document.asp?CID=659&DID=2586.

Brinton, D. (2003). Content-based instruction. In D. Nunan (Ed.), *Practical English language teaching*. New York: McGraw-Hill, pp. 199–224.

Boscolo, P. and Mason, L. (2001). Writing to learn, writing to transfer. In P. Tynjälä, L. Mason, and K. Lonka (Eds.), *Writing as a learning tool: Integrating theory and practice*. Dordrecht, the Netherlands: Kluwer Academic Publishers, pp. 83–104.

Carrasquillo, A. L. and Rodriguez, V. (2002). *Language minority students in the mainstream classroom*, 2nd edn. Boston: Multilingual Matters.

Clark, D. (1999). *Learning domains or Bloom's taxonomy*. Retrieved August 3, 2007, from www.nwlink. com/~donclark/hrd/bloom.html.

Coady, M., Hamann, E. T., Harrington, M., Pacheco, M., Pho, S., and Yedlin, J. (2003). *Claiming opportunities: A handbook for improving education for English language learners through comprehensive school reform*. Providence, RI: Education Alliance at Brown University.

Collier, V. P. (1995). Acquiring a second language for school. *Directions in Language and Education*, 1 (4). Washington, DC: National Clearinghouse for Bilingual Education.

Collier, V. and Thomas, W. (1997). *School effectiveness for language minority students*. Washington, DC: National Clearinghouse for Bilingual Education. Retrieved December 2, 2006, from www.ncela.gwu/pubs/resource/effectiveness/index.htm.

Consent Decree (1990) Retrieved January 17, 2007, from www.firn.edu/doe/aala/lulac.htm.

Crawford, J. (2004). *Educating English learners: Language diversity in the classroom*, 5th edn. Los Angeles: Bilingual Educational Services.

Cummins, J. (1979). Cognitive/academic language proficiency, linguistic interdependence, the optimum age question and some other matters. *Working Papers on Bilingualism*, 19: 121–129.

Cummins, J. (1980). The cross-lingual dimensions of language proficiency: Implications for bilingual education and the optimal age issue. *TESOL Quarterly*, 14 (2): 175–187.

Cummins, J. (1986). Empowering minority students: A framework for intervention. *Harvard Educational Review*, 56 (1): 18–36.

Cummins, J. (1992). Bilingual education and English immersion: The Ramírez report in theoretical perspective. *Bilingual Research Journal*, 16: 91–104.

Cummins, J. (2001). *Negotiating identities: Education for empowerment in a diverse society*. Los Angeles: California Association for Bilingual Education.

Dalton, J. and Smith, D. (1986). *Extending children's special abilities – strategies for primary classrooms*. Retrieved February 19, 2007, from www.teachers.ash.org.au/researchskills/dalton.htm.

Diaz-Rico, L. and Weed, K.Z. (2006). *The crosscultural, language and academic development handbook*, 3rd edn. Boston: Pearson Education.

Echeverria, J. and McDonough, R. (1993). *Instructional conversations in special education settings: Issues and accommodations*. Educational Practice Report 7. National Center for Research on Cultural Diversity and Second Language Learning. Retrieved May 10, 2007, from www.ncela.gwu.edu/pubs/ncrcdsll/epr7.htm.

Ellis, R. (2005). *Instructed second language acquisition: A literature review*. Report to the Ministry of Education, New Zealand. Retrieved January 18, 2007, from www.educationcounts.edcentre.govt.nz/publications/downloads/instructed-second-language.pdf.

Gay, G. (2000). *Culturally responsive teaching: Theory, research, and practice*. New York: Teachers College Press.

Genesee, F. (Ed.) (1999). *Program alternatives for linguistically diverse students*. Santa Cruz, CA: Center for Research on Education, Diversity and Excellence. Retrieved January 8, 2007, from www.cal.org/crede/pubs/edpractice/Epr1.pdf.

Gold, N. (2006). *Successful bilingual schools: Six effective programs in California*. San Diego: San Diego County Office of Education.

Gollnick, D. M. and Chinn, P. C. (2002). *Multicultural education in a pluralistic society*, 6th edn. New York: Merrill.

Hakuta, K., Butler, Y. G., and Witt, D. (2000). *How long does it take English learners to attain proficiency?* Santa Barbara: University of California Linguistic Research Institute Policy Report (2000–2001).

Hoover, J. J. and Collier, C. (1989). Methods and materials for bilingual education. In M. Baca and H. T. Cervantes (Eds.), *The bilingual special interface*. Columbus, OH: Merrill, pp. 231–255.

Kern, R. (2000). *Literacy and language teaching*. Oxford: Oxford University Press.

Kindler, A. (2002). *Survey of the states' limited English proficient students and available educational programs and services: 2000–2001 summary report*. Washington, DC: National Clearinghouse for English Language Acquisition.

Krashen, S. (1981). *Principles and practice in second language acquisition*. English Language Teaching series. London: Prentice-Hall International.

Long, M. (1996). The role of the linguistic environment in second language acquisition. In W. Ritchie and T. Bhatia (Eds.), *Handbook of second language acquisition*. San Diego: Academic Press, pp. 413–468.

Long, M. H. (2006). *Problems in SLA*. Mahwah, NJ: Lawrence Erlbaum Associates.

Lyster, R. (1998). Recasts, repetition and ambiguity in L2 classroom discourse. *Studies in Second Language Acquisition*, 20: 51–81.

Lyster, R. (2001). Negotiation of form, recasts, and explicit correction in relation to error types and learner repair in immersion classrooms. *Language Learning*, 51 (Suppl. 1): 265–301.

Lyster, R. (2004). Differential effects of prompts and recasts in form-focused instruction. *Studies in Second Language Acquisition*, 26: 399–432.

Lyster, R. (2007). *Learning and teaching languages through content: A counterbalanced approach*. Amsterdam: John Benjamins.

Lyster, R. and Ranta, L. (1997). Corrective feedback and learner uptake: Negotiation of form in communicative classrooms. *Studies in Second Language Acquisition*, 19: 37–66.

Lyster, R., and Mori, H. (2006). Interactional feedback and instructional counterbalance. *Studies in Second Language Acquisition*, 28: 321–341.

Meltzer, J. (2001). *The adolescent literacy support framework*. Providence, RI: Northeast and Islands Regional Educational Laboratory at Brown University. Retrieved on August 11, 2004, from http://knowledgeloom.org/adlit.

Meltzer, J. and Hamann, E. T. (2005). *Meeting the literacy development needs of adolescent English language learners through content-area learning. Part Two: Focus on classroom teaching strategies*. Providence, RI: Education Alliance at Brown University.

Oberg, K. (1954). *The social economy of the Tlingit Indians of Alaska*. Unpublished doctoral dissertation. University of Chicago.

Ortiz, A. (1984). Language and curriculum development for exceptional bilingual children. In Chinn, C. P. (Ed.), *Education of culturally and linguistically different exceptional children*. Reston, VA: Council for Exceptional Children–ERIC Clearinghouse on Handicapped and Gifted Children, pp. 77–100.

Ovando, C. and Collier, V. (1998). *Bilingual and ESL classrooms: Teaching in multicultural contexts*. Boston: McGraw-Hill.

Pienemann, M. (1988). Determining the influence of instruction on L2 speech processing. *AILA Review*, 5: 40–72.

Pienemann, M. (1989). Is language teachable? Psycholinguistic experiments and hypotheses. *Applied Linguistics*, 10 (1): 52–79.

Pienemann, M. (2007). Processability theory. In B. van Patten and J. Williams (Eds.), *Theories in second language acquisition: An introduction*. Mahwah, NJ: Lawrence Erlbaum Associates, pp. 137–154.

Ragan, A. (2005). Teaching the academic language of textbooks: a preliminary framework for performing a textual analysis. *The ELL Outlook*. Retrieved on 13 August, 2007, from www.coursecrafters.com/ELL-Outlook/2005/nov_dec/ELLOutlookITIArticle1.htm.

Richards, H. V., Brown, A. F., and Forde, T. B. (2004). *Addressing diversity in schools: Culturally responsive pedagogy*. Tempe, AZ: National Center for Culturally Responsive Educational Systems. Retrieved 27 July, 2007, from www.nccrest.org/Briefs/Diversity_Brief.pdf.

Ruiz, N. T. (1989). An optimal learning environment for Rosemary. *Exceptional Children*, 56 (2): 130–144.

Ruiz, N. T. (1995a). The social construction of ability and disability: I. Profile types of Latino children identified as language learning disabled. *Journal of Learning Disabilities*, 28 (8), 476–490.

Ruiz, N. T. (1995b). The social construction of ability and disability: II. Optimal and at-risk lessons in a bilingual special education classroom. *Journal of Learning Disabilities*, 28 (8), 491–502.

Scarcella, R. (2003). *Academic English: A conceptual framework*. Technical Report 2003-1. Irvine, CA: University of California Linguistic Minority Research Institute. Retrieved July 2, 2007, from www.ncela.gwu.edu/res-about/literacy/2_academic.htm.

Skehan, P. (1998). *A cognitive approach to language learning*. Oxford: Oxford University Press.

Swain, M. (1995). Three functions of output in second language learning. In G. Cook and B. Seidlhofer (Eds.), *Principle and practice in applied linguistics*. Oxford: Oxford University Press, pp. 125–144.

U.S. Census Bureau (2005). *Statistical abstract of the United States*. Retrieved February 24, 2008, from www.census.gov/prod/www/statistical-absract.html.

Valdez, G. (2000) Nonnative English speakers: Language bigotry in English mainstream classes. *Associations of Departments of English Bulletin*, 124 (Winter): 12–17.

de Valenzuela, J. S. and Niccolai, S. L. (2004). Language development in culturally and linguistically diverse students with special education needs. In L. Baca and H. Cervantes (Eds.), *The bilingual special education interface*, 4th edn. Upper Saddle River, NJ: Merrill, pp. 125–161.

Zamel, V. and Spack, R. (1998). *Negotiating academic literacies: Teaching and learning across language and cultures*. Mahwah, NJ: Lawrence Erlbaum.

Zehler, A. (1994). *Working with English language learners: Strategies for elementary and middle school teachers.* NCBE Program Information Guide, No. 19. Retrieved May 25, 2007, from www.ncela.gwu.edu/pubs/pigs/pig19.htm.

Part 2

Abedi, J. (1995). Language backgrounds as a variable in NAEP mathematics performance. (ERIC Document Reproduction Service No. ED404176)

Abedi, J. (2004). The No Child Left Behind Act and English language learners: Assessment and accountability issues. *Educational Researcher*, 33 (1): 4–14.

Abedi, J., Courtney, M., and Leon, S. (2003). Research supported accommodations for English language learners in NAEP. Los Angeles, CA: National Center for Research on Evaluation, Standards, and Student Testing. (ERIC Reproduction Services No. ED474868)

Abedi, J. and Hejri, F. (2004). Accommodations for students with limited English proficiency in the National Assessment of Educational Progress. *Applied Measurement in Education*, 17 (4): 371–392.

Abedi, J., Hofstetter, C. H., and Lord, C. (2004). Assessment accommodations for English Language Learners: Implications for policy-based empirical research. *Review of Educational Research*, 74 (1): 1–28.

Abedi, J., Leon, S., and Mirocha, J. (2003). Impact of student language background on content-based performance: Analyses of extant data. (CSE Tech. Rep. No. 603.) Los Angeles: University of California, National Center for Research on Evaluation, Standards, and Student Testing.

Abedi, J. and Lord, C. (2001). The language factor in mathematics tests. *Applied Measurement in Education*, 14 (3): 219–234.

Abedi, J., Lord, C., Hofstetter, C., and Baker, E. (2000). Impact of accommodation strategies on English language learners' test performance. *Educational Measurement: Issues and Practice*, 19 (3): 16–26.

Abedi, J., Lord, C., and Plummer, J. (1997). Final report of language background as a variable in NAEP mathematics performance. (CSE Tech. Rep. No. 429.) Los Angeles: University of California, National Center for Research on Evaluation, Standards, and Student Testing.

Aiken, L. R. (1971). Verbal factors and mathematics learning: A review of the literature. *Journal for Research in Mathematics Education*, 2 (4): 304–313.

Aiken, L. R. (1972). Language factors and learning mathematics. *Review of Educational Research*, 42: 359–385.

Anstrom, K. (1999). *Preparing secondary education teachers to work with English language learners: Mathematics.* NCBE Resource Collection Series, No. 14 (P. DiCerbo, editor). Washington, DC: National Clearinghouse for Bilingual Education. (ERIC Document Reproduction Service No. ED439618)

Bellman, A. R., Bragg, S. C., Charles, R. I., Handlin, W. G., and Kennedy, D. (2004). *Algebra 1*, Florida edition. Needham, MA: Pearson Prentice Hall.

Bernardo, A. B. (2002). Language and mathematical problem solving among bilinguals. *Journal of Psychology*, 136 (3): 283–297.

Boyd, C. J., Cummins, J., Malloy, C., Carter, J., and Flores, A. (2004). *Geometry*, Florida edition. Columbus, OH: McGraw-Hill.

Bradby, D. (1992). *Language characteristics and academic achievement: A look at Asian and Hispanic eighth graders in NELS: 88.* Washington, DC: U.S. Department of Education.

Brenner, M. (1998). Development of mathematical communication in problem solving groups by language minority students. *Bilingual Research Journal*, 22 (2–4): 149–174.

Brown, C. L. (2005) Equity of literacy-based math performance assessments for English language learners. *Bilingual Research Journal*, 29 (2): 337–363.

Cahnmann, M. S. and Hornberger, N. H. (2000). Understanding what counts: Issues of language, culture, and power in mathematics instruction and assessment. *Educator for Urban Minorities*, 1 (2): 39–52.

Cahnmann, M. S. and Remillard, J. T. (2002). What counts and how: Mathematics teaching in culturally, linguistically, and socioeconomically diverse urban settings. *Urban Review*, 34 (3): 179–204.

Cleghorn, A., Mtetwa, D., Dube, R., and Munetsi, C. (1998). Classroom language use in multilingual settings: Mathematics lessons from Quebec and Zimbabwe. *Qualitative Studies in Education*, 11 (7): 463–477.

Clement, J., Lochhead, J., and Monk, G. (1981). Translation difficulties in learning mathematics. *American Mathematical Monthly*, 88: 282–290.

Cocking, R. R., and Chipman, S. (1988). Conceptual issues related to mathematics achievement of language minority children. In R. R. Cocking and J. P. Mestre (Eds.), *Linguistic and cultural influences on learning mathematics*. Hillsdale, NJ: Lawrence Erlbaum Associates Publishers, pp. 17–46.

Crandall, J., Dale, T., Rhodes, N., and Spanos, G. (1985). The language of mathematics: The English barrier. In A. Labarca and L. Bailey (Eds.), *Issues in L2: Theory as practice, practice as theory*. Norwood, NJ: Ablex Publishing, pp. 129–150.

Dale, T. C. and Cuevas, G. J. (1992). Integrating mathematics and language learning. In P. A. Richard-Amato and M. A. Snow (Eds.), *The multicultural classroom: Reading for content area teachers*. White Plains, NY: Longman, pp. 330–349.

De Corte, E., Verschaffel, L., and DeWin, L. (1985). Influence of rewording verbal problems on children's problem representation and solutions. *Journal of Educational Psychology*, 77: 460–470.

Diaz-Rico, L., and Weed, K. (1995). *The crosscultural, language, and academic development handbook: A complete K–12 reference guide*. Boston: Allyn and Bacon.

Echevarria, J., Vogt, M., and Short, D. (2004). *Making content comprehensible for English language learners: The SIOP model*. Boston: Allyn and Bacon. (Also available at www.lessonlab.com/professional-development/english-language-learners/overview.cfm.)

Ezeife, A. (2002). Mathematics and culture nexus: The interactions of culture and mathematics in an aboriginal classroom. *International Education Journal*, 3: 176–187.

Gandara, P., Maxwell-Jolly, J., and Driscoll, A. (2005). *Listening to teachers of English language learners: A survey of California teacher challenges, experiences, and professional development needs*. Santa Cruz, CA: Center for the Future of Teaching and Learning.

Gay, G. (2000). *Culturally responsive teaching: Theory, research, and practice*. New York: Teachers College Press.

Gonzales, P., Guzmán, J. C., Partelow, L., Pahlke, E., Jocelyn, L., Kastberg, D., and Williams, T. (2004). *Highlights from the Trends in International Mathematics and Science Study (TIMSS) 2003* (NCES 2005–005). U.S. Department of Education, National Center for Education Statistics. Washington, DC: U.S. Government Printing Office.

Gorgorió, N., and Planas, N. (2001). Teaching mathematics in multilingual classrooms. *Educational Studies in Mathematics*, 47 (1): 7–33.

Gronna, S., Chin-Chance, S., and Abedi, J. (2000). *Differences between the performance of limited English proficient students and students who are labeled proficient in English on different content areas: Reading and mathematics*. New Orleans: American Educational Research Association. (ERIC Document Reproduction Service No. ED440551)

Gustein, E., Lipman, P., Hernandez, P., and de los Reyes, R. (1997). Culturally relevant mathematics teaching in a Mexican American context. *Journal for Research in Mathematics Education*, 28 (6): 709–737.

Henningsen, M., and Stein, M. K. (1997). Mathematical tasks and student cognition: Classroom-based factors that support and inhibit high-level mathematical thinking and reasoning. *Journal for Research in Mathematics Education*, 28: 524–549.

Hiebert, J., Gallimore, R., Garnier, H., Givvin, K.-B., Hollingsworth, H., Jacobs, J., Chiu, A. M.-Y., Wearne, D., Smith, M., Kersting, N., Manaster, A., Tseng, E., Etterbeek, W., Manaster, C., Gonzales, P., and Stigler, J. (2003). *Teaching mathematics in seven countries: Results from the TIMSS 1999 video study* (NCES 2003-013). Washington, DC: National Center for Education Statistics.

Jacobson, C., and Lehrer, R. (2000). Teacher appropriation and student learning of geometry through design. *Journal of Research in Mathematics Education*, 31: 71–88.

Kaput, J. J., and Sims-Knight, J. E. (1983). Errors in translation to algebraic equations: Roots and implications. *Focus on Learning Problems in Mathematics*, 5: 63–76.

Kersaint, G. (2007). The learning environment: Its influence on what is learned. In W. G. Martin and M. E. Struchens (Eds.), *The learning of mathematics*. Reston, VA: National Council of Teachers of Mathematics, pp. 83–96.

Kessler, C., Quinn, M., and Hayes, C. (1985). Processing mathematics in a second language: Problems for LEP students. In A. Labarca and L. Bailey (Eds.), *Issues in L2: Theory as practice, practice as theory*. Norwood, NJ: Ablex Publishing, pp. 151–163.

Kimball, M. H. (1990). How can we best help ESL students? *Mathematics Teacher*, 83: 604–605.

Kiplinger, V. L., Haug, C. A., and Abedi, J. (2000). Measuring math—not reading—on a math assessment: A language accommodation study of English language learners and other special populations. Paper presented at the annual meeting of the American Educational Research Association, New Orleans, April.

Kloosterman, P. and Lester, F. K., Jr. (Eds.) (2007). *Results and interpretation of the 2003 mathematics assessment of the National Assessment of Educational Progress.* Reston, VA: National Council of Teachers of Mathematics.

Kopriva, R. and Saez, S. (1997). *Guide to scoring LEP student responses to open-ended mathematics items.* Washington, DC: Council of Chief State School Officers.

Krashen, S., and Brown, C. L. (2005). The ameliorating effects of high socioeconomic status: A secondary analysis. *Bilingual Research Journal,* 29 (1): 185–196.

Lampert, M. and Blunk, M. L. (1998). *Talking mathematics in school: Studies of teaching and learning.* New York: Cambridge University Press.

Lane, S., Silver, E. A., and Wang, N. (1995). *An examination of the performance gains of culturally and linguistically diverse students on a mathematics performance assessment within the QUASAR Project.* (Eric Document Reproduction Service No. ED390927)

Leap, W. H. (1988). Assumptions and strategies guiding mathematics problem solving by Ute Indian students. In R. R. Cocking and J. P. Mestre (Eds.), *Linguistic and cultural influences on learning mathematics.* Hillsdale, NJ: Lawrence Erlbaum Associates Publishers, pp. 161–186.

Leon, R. (1994). The effects of the presence of extraneous information in the mathematical word problems on the performance of Hispanic learning disabled students. *New York State Association for Bilingual Education Journal,* 9: 15–26.

Liu, K., Anderson, M., and Thurlow, M. (2000). *Report on the participation and performance of limited English proficient students on Minnesota's basic standards tests, 1999.* St. Paul: Minnesota State Department of Children, Families, and Learning. (ERIC Document Reproduction Service No. ED447718)

Lovett, C. J. (1980). Bilingual education: What role for mathematics teaching? *Arithmetic Teacher,* 27: 14–17.

MacCorquodale, P. (1988). Mexican-American women and mathematics: Participation, aspirations, and achievement. In R. R. Cocking and J. P. Mestre (Eds.), *Linguistic and cultural influences on learning mathematics.* Hillsdale, NJ: Lawrence Erlbaum Associates, pp. 137–160.

McNair, R. E. (2000). Working in the mathematics frame: Maximizing the potential to learn from students' classroom discussions. *Educational Studies in Mathematics,* 42: 197–209.

Martin, T. F. (Ed.). (2007). *Mathematics teaching today: Improving practice, improving student learning* (2nd edn.). Reston, VA: National Council of Teachers of Mathematics.

Meskill, C. (2005). Infusing English language learner issues throughout professional educator curricula: The Training All Teachers project. *Teacher College Record,* 107 (4): 739–756.

Moschkovich, J. N. (1999). Supporting the participation of English language learners in mathematics discussions. *For the Learning of Mathematics,* 19 (1): 11–19.

Moschkovich, J. (2002). A situated and sociocultural perspective on bilingual mathematics learners. *Mathematical Thinking and Learning,* 4 (2–3): 189–212.

Moya, S., and O'Malley, J. M. (1994). A portfolio assessment model for ESL. *Journal of Educational Issues of Language Minority Students,* 73: 13–36.

National Council of Teachers of Mathematics (1989). *Curriculum and evaluation standards for school mathematics.* Reston, VA: Author.

National Council of Teachers of Mathematics (1991). *Professional standards for teaching mathematics.* Reston, VA: Author.

National Council of Teachers of Mathematics (1995). *Assessment standards for teaching mathematics.* Reston, VA: Author.

National Council of Teachers of Mathematics (2000). *Principles and standards for school mathematics.* Reston, VA: Author.

National Council of Teachers of Mathematics (2007). *Mathematics teaching today: Improving practice, improving student learning.* Reston, VA: Author.

Olivares, R. A. (1996) Communication in mathematics for students with limited English proficiency. In P. C. Elliot and M. J. Kenney (Eds.), *Communication in mathematics, K–12 and beyond.* Reston, VA: National Council of Teachers of Mathematics, pp. 219–230.

Park, C. C. (1997a). Learning style preferences of Asian American (Chinese, Filipino, Korean, and Vietnamese) students in secondary schools. *Equity and Excellence in Education*, 30 (2): 68–77.

Park, C. C. (1997b). Learning style preferences of Korean, Mexican, Armenian-American and Anglo students in secondary schools. *NASSP Bulletin*, 81 (585): 103–111.

Park, C. C. (2002). Cross cultural differences in learning styles of secondary English language learners. *Bilingual Research Journal*, 26 (2): 213–229.

Philipp, R. A. (1992). A study of algebraic variables: Beyond the student–professor problem. *Journal of Mathematical Behavior*, 11: 161–176.

Reeves, J. R. (2006). Secondary teacher attitudes toward including English language learners in mainstream classrooms. *Journal of Education Research*, 99 (3): 131–142.

Reid, J. M. (1987). The learning style preferences of ESL students. *TESOL Quarterly*, 21 (1): 87–110.

Reyhner, J., Lee, H., and Gabbard, D. (1993). A specialized knowledge base for teaching American Indian and Alaska Native students. *Tribal College: The Journal of American Indian Higher Education*, 4 (4): 26–32.

Rhine, S. (1995a). Students' language proficiency effects upon teachers' assessment of students' mathematical understanding. Paper presented at the annual meeting of the American Educational Research Association, San Francisco.

Rhine, S. (1995b). The challenge of effectively preparing teachers of limited-English-proficient students. *Journal of Teacher Education*, 46 (5): 381–389.

Rhine, S. (1999). *Mathematics reform, language proficiency, and teachers' assessment of students' understanding.* Salem, OR: Willamette University. (ERIC Document Reproduction Services No. ED429121)

Rhodes, R. W. (1990). Measurement of Navajo and Hopi brain dominance and learning styles. *Journal of American Indian Education*, 29 (3): 29–40.

Rubenstein, R. N. and Thompson, D. R. (2001). Learning mathematical symbolism: Challenges and instructional strategies. *Mathematics Teacher*, 94 (4): 265–271.

Schmidt, W., McKnight, C., and Raizen, A. (1997). *A splintered vision: An investigation of U.S. science and mathematics education.* Dordrecht, Netherlands: Kluwer.

Secada, W. G. (1983). *The educational background of limited English proficient students: Implications for the arithmetic classroom.* Washington, DC: Office of Bilingual Education and Minority Languages Affairs. (ERIC Document Reproduction Service No. ED237318)

Secada, W. G. and Carey, D. A. (1990). *Teaching mathematics with understanding to limited English proficient students.* New York: ERIC Clearinghouse on Urban Education.

Secada, W. G. and de la Cruz, Y. (1996). *Teaching mathematics for understanding to bilingual students.* (ERIC Document Reproduction Service No. ED393646.)

Solano-Flores, G. and Trumbull, E. (2003). Examining language in context: The need for new research and practice paradigms in the testing of English language learners. *Educational Researcher*, 32 (2): 3–13.

Spanos, G., Rhodes, N. C., Dale, T. C., and Crandall, J. (1988). Linguistic features of mathematical problem solving: Insights and applications. In R. R. Cocking and J. P. Mestre (Eds.), *Linguistic and cultural influences on learning mathematics.* Hillsdale, NJ: Erlbaum, pp. 221–240.

Stanley, C., and Spafford, C. (2002). Cultural perspectives in mathematics planning efforts. *Multicultural Education*, 10 (1): 40–42.

Stathopoulou, C., and Kalabasis, R. (2006). Language and culture in mathematics education: Reflections and observing in Romany class in a Greek school. *Educational Studies in Mathematics*, 64: 231–238

Stein, M. K., Grover, B. W., and Henningsen, M. (1996). Building student capacity for mathematical thinking and reasoning: An analysis of mathematical tasks used in reform classrooms. *American Educational Research Journal*, 33: 455–488.

Stigler, J. W. and Hiebert, J. (1999). *The teaching gap: Best ideas from the world's teachers for improving education in the classroom.* New York: Free Press.

Strizek, G. A., Pittsonberger, J. L., Riordan, K. E., Lyter, D. M., and Orlofsky, G .F. (2006). Characteristics of schools, districts, teachers, principals, and school libraries in the United States: 2003–04 schools and staffing survey (NCES 2006-313 Revised.) U.S. Department of Education, National Center for Education Statistics. Washington, DC: U.S. Government Printing Office.

Swisher, K. and Dehle, D. (1987). Styles of learning and learning of styles: Educational conflicts for American Indian/Alaskan Native Youth. *Journal of Multilingual and Multicultural Development*, 8 (4): 345–360.

Thompson, D. R., Kersaint, G., Richards, J. C., Hunsader, P. D., and Rubenstein, R. N. (2008). *Mathematical literacy: Helping students make meaning in the middle grades.* Portsmouth, NH: Heinemann.

Thompson, D. R., and Rubenstein, R. N. (2000). Learning mathematics vocabulary: Potential pitfalls and instructional strategies. *Mathematics Teacher*, 93 (7): 568–574.

Tsang, S. (1988). The mathematics achievement characteristics of Asian American students. In R. R. Cocking, and J. P. Mestre (Eds.), *Linguistic and cultural influences on learning mathematics*. Hillsdale, NJ: Lawrence Erlbaum Associates, pp. 123–136.

Usiskin, Z. (1996). Mathematics as a language. In P. C. Elliott and M. J. Kenney (Eds.), *Communication in mathematics, K–12 and beyond*. Reston, VA: National Council of Teachers of Mathematics, pp. 231–243.

Vygotsky, L. S. (1978). *Mind in society*. Cambridge, MA: Harvard University Press.

Watson, S., Miller, T. L., Driver, J., Rutledge, V., and McAllister, D. (2005). English language learner representation in teacher education textbooks: A null curriculum? *Education*, 126 (1): 148–157.

Wauters, J. K., Bruce, J. M., Black, D. R., and Hocker, P. N. (1989). Learning styles: A study of Alaskan native and non-native students. *Journal of American Indian Education* (Special Issue): 53–62.

Part 3

Abedi, J., Hofstetter, C., Baker, E. and Lord, C. (1998). *NAEP math performance and test accommodations: Interactions with student language background*, draft report. Los Angeles: University of California, Los Angeles, National Center for Research on Evaluation, Standards, and Student Testing.

Abedi, J. and Lord, C. (2001). The language factor in mathematics tests. *Applied Measurement in Education*, 14 (3): 219–234.

August, D. and Pease-Alvarez, L. (1996). *Attributes of effective programs and classrooms serving English language learners*. Santa Cruz, CA: National Center for Research on Cultural Diversity and Second Language Learning.

Barber, R. (2003). *Report to the National Education Association on Trends in Foreign Teacher Recruitment*. Center for Economic Organizing. Retrieved on June 17, 2007 from www.nea.org.

Bouchard, M. (2005). *Comprehension strategies for English language learners*. New York: Scholastic.

Chamot, A. U. and O'Malley, J. M. (1994). *The CALLA handbook: Implementing the Cognitive Academic Language Learning Approach*. Reading, MA: Addison-Wesley.

Coggins, D., Kravin, D., Coates, G. D., and Carroll, M. D. (2007). *English language learners in the mathematics classroom*. Thousand Oaks, CA: Corwin Press.

Crandall, J., Dale, T., Rhodes, N., and Spanos, G. (1985). The language of mathematics: The English barrier. In A. Labarca and L. Bailey (Eds.), *Issues in L2: Theory as practice, practice as theory*. Delaware Symposium on Language Studies. Norwood, NJ: Ablex Publishing, pp. 129–150.

Cummins, J. (1992). Bilingual education and English immersion: The Ramírez report in theoretical perspective. *Bilingual Research Journal*, 16: 91–104.

D'Ambrosio, U. (1995). Multiculturalism and mathematics education. *International Journal of Mathematics Education in Science and Technology*, 26 (3): 337–346.

Davidson, N. (1990). *Cooperative learning in mathematics: A handbook for teachers*. Menlo Park, CA: Addison-Wesley.

Davis, B. (1994). Mathematics teaching: Moving from telling to listening. *Journal of Curriculum and Supervision*, 93: 267–283.

Davis, B. (1996). *Teaching mathematics: Towards a sound alternative*. New York: Garland Publishing.

Garrison, L. and Mora, J. K. (1999). Adapting mathematics instruction for English-language learners: The language–concept connection. In L. Ortiz-Franco, N. G. Hernandez, and Y. de la Cruz (Eds.), *Changing the faces of mathematics: Perspectives on Latinos*. Reston, VA: National Council of Teachers of Mathematics, pp. 35–48.

Goldenberg, C. (1991). *Instructional conversations and their classroom application* (Educational Practice Report 2). Los Angeles: National Center for Research on Cultural Diversity and Second Language Acquisition, University of California.

Gutierrez, R. (2002). Beyond essentialism: The complexity of language in teaching mathematics to Latina/o students. *American Educational Research Journal*, 39 (4): 1047–1088.

Gutstein, E. (2000). *When what you see is not what you get: Urban Latino students read the world with mathematics*. Paper presented at the annual meeting of the National Council of Teachers of Mathematics, Chicago, April.

Gutstein, E., Lipman, P., Hernandez, P., and de los Reyes, R. (1997). Culturally revelant mathematics teaching in a Mexican American context. *Journal for Research in Mathematics Education*, 28 (6): 709–737.

Herber, H. (1978). *Teaching reading in content areas*, 2nd edn. Englewood Cliffs, NJ: Prentice Hall.

Herrell, A. L., and Jordan, M. (2008). *50 strategies for teaching English language learners*. Upper Saddle River, NJ: Merrill/Prentice Hall.

Hill, J. D. and Flynn, K. M. (2006). *Classroom instruction that works with English language learners*. Alexandria, VA: Association for Supervision and Curriculum Development.

Howard, T. C. (2003). Culturally relevant pedagogy: Ingredient for critical teacher reflection. *Theory into Practice*, 42 (3): 195–202.

Jarrett, D. (1999). *The inclusive classroom: Teaching mathematics and science to English language learners. It's just good teaching*. Portland, OR: Northwest Regional Educational Laboratory.

Kagan, S. (1994). *Cooperative learning*. San Clemente, CA: Kagan Cooperative Learning.

Khisty, L. L. (1995). Making inequality: Issues of language meanings in mathematics teaching with Hispanic students. In W. G. Secada, E. Fennema, and L. B. Adajian (Eds.), *New directions for equity in mathematics education*. Reston, VA: National Council of Teachers of Mathematics, pp. 279–297.

Krashen, S. (1985). *The input hypothesis: Issues and implications*. London: Longman.

Ladson-Billings, G. (1995). But that's just good teaching! The case for culturally relevant pedagogy. *Theory into Practice*, 34 (3): 159–165.

McTighe, J. and Lyman, F. T., Jr. (1988). Cueing thinking in the classroom: The promise of theory-embedded tools. *Educational Leadership*, 45: 18–24.

Moschkovich, J. (1999) Understanding the needs of Latino students in reform-oriented mathematics classrooms. In L. Ortiz-Franco, N. G. Hernandez, and Y. de la Cruz (Eds.), *Changing the faces of mathematics: Perspectives on Latinos*. Reston, VA: National Council of Teachers of Mathematics, pp. 5–12.

Moschkovich, J. (2000). Learning mathematics in two languages: Moving from obstacles to resources. In W. G. Secada (Ed.), *Changing the faces of mathematics: Perspectives on multiculturalism and gender equity*. Reston, VA: National Council of Teachers of Mathematics, pp. 85–93.

Murray, M. (2004). *Teaching mathematics vocabulary in context*. Portsmouth, NH: Heinemann.

National Council of Teachers of Mathematics (2000). *Principles and standards for school mathematics*. Reston, VA: Author.

Nelson, D., Joseph, G. G., and Williams, J. (1993). *Multicultural mathematics: Teaching mathematics from a global perspective*: New York: Oxford University Press.

Perkins, I., and Flores, A. (2002). Mathematical notations and procedures of recent immigrant students. *Mathematics Teaching in the Middle School*, 7: 346–351.

Polya, G. (1957). *How to solve it*, 2nd edn. Princeton, NJ: Princeton University Press.

Remillard, J. T. and Cahnmann, M. (2005) Researching mathematics teaching in bilingual–bicultural classrooms. In T. L. McCarty (Ed.), *Language, literacy, and power in schooling*. Mahwah, NJ: Lawrence Erlbaum Associates, pp. 169–187.

Richard-Amato, P. A. and Snow, M. A. (1992). Strategies for content-area teachers. In P. A. Richard-Amato and M. A. Snow (Eds.), *The multicultural classroom: Reading for content area teachers*. White Plains, NY: Longman Publishing Group.

Robinson, F. P. (1970). *Effective study*, 4th edn. New York: Harper and Row.

Ron, P. (1999). Spanish–English language issues in the mathematics classroom. In L. Ortiz-Franco, N. G. Hernandez, and Y. de la Cruz (Eds.), *Changing the faces of mathematics: Perspectives on Latinos*. Reston, VA: National Council of Teachers of Mathematics, pp. 23–34.

Rubenstein, R. N. (1997). Communication strategies to support preservice mathematics teachers from diverse backgrounds. In J. Trentacosta and M. J. Kenney (Eds.), *Multicultural and gender equity in the mathematics classroom: The gift of diversity*. Reston, VA: National Council of Teachers of Mathematics, pp. 214–221.

Rubenstein, R. N. and Thompson, D. R. (2001). Learning mathematical symbolism: Challenges and instructional strategies. *Mathematics Teacher*, 94: 265–271.

Shield, M. and Swinson, K. (1996). The link sheet: A communication aid for clarifying and developing mathematical ideas and processes. In P. C. Elliott and M. J. Kenney (Eds.), *Communication in mathematics, K–12 and beyond*. Reston, VA: National Council of Teachers of Mathematics, pp. 35–39.

Siegel, M., Borasi, R., Fonzi, J. M., Sanridge, L. G., and Smith, C. (1996). Using reading to construct mathematical meaning. In P. C. Elliott and M. J. Kenney (Eds.), *Communication in mathematics, K–12 and beyond*. Reston, VA: National Council of Teachers of Mathematics, pp. 66–75.

Solano-Flores, G. and Trumbull, E. (2003). Examining language in context: The need for new research and practice paradigms in the testing of English language learners. *Educational Researcher*, 32 (2): 3–13.

Stanley, C. A. and Spafford, C. S. (2002). Cultural perspective in mathematics planning efforts. *Multicultural Education*, 10 (1): 40–42.

Thompson, D. R., Kersaint, G., Richards, J. C., Hunsader, P. D., and Rubenstein, R. N. (2008). *Mathematical literacy: Helping students make meaning in the middle grades*. Portsmouth, NH: Heinemann.

Usiskin, Z. (1996). Mathematics as a language. In P. C. Elliott and M. J. Kenney (Eds.), *Communication in mathematics, K–12 and beyond*. Reston, VA: National Council of Teachers of Mathematics, pp. 231–243.

Valdez-Pierce, L. (2003). *Assessing English language learners*. Washington, DC: National Education Association.

Waxman, H. C. and Tellez, K. (2002). *Research synthesis on effective teaching practices for English language learners*. Philadelphia: Mid-Atlantic Lab for Student Success. (Eric Document Reproduction Services ED 474 821)

Williams, L. (2007). *Bringing students' culture and experiences into the mathematics classroom*. Unpublished action research paper as part of a Master of Arts in Teaching program. University of South Florida.

Zaslavsky, C. (1996). *The multicultural math classroom: Bringing in the world*. Portsmouth, NH: Heinemann.

Index

Note: Italic numerals refer to figures or tables.